Praise for *Fire Hall Cooking wit*

This cookbook would be great for anyone— The recipes are tasty, hearty, they use readily av... easy to follow. Filled with anecdotes, *Fire Hall Cooking* is a peek at real life at the station.

—*Winnipeg Free Press*

I'm a probationary firefighter, and before I started my first shift my mom gave me your book as a present. Soon the time came when I had to step up to the plate and cook for the guys. I have to admit I was a little nervous because my cooking skills were . . . well, okay, I had no cooking skills. I remembered the book my mom gave me and took that to work. The first recipe I attempted was the Tequila Lime Chicken. I madly toiled away in the kitchen, clanging pots and pans, sweating profusely and covering the pages of your book in sauce, but I got it done . . . and it turned out awesome. The guys were blown away. To make a long story short, your book has become the most important training manual I have in the hall. I have made many recipes out of it and every time the guys are left satisfied and raving about the meal. Thanks again, and I hope you make another cookbook.

—Cameron, Vancouver, BC

I run a busy B&B in Sparwood, B.C., and because there are few restaurants here, I often cook dinner for hungry guests. I've used every one of your excellent recipes, and not one has failed me. The ironic part of all this is that I'm a vegetarian— have been for 20 years or more—and so I don't taste any of your meat recipes, I just rely totally on you for how much seasoning to add. How's that for faith? And one of my dear guests has labelled me "The David Copperfield of Culinary Cuisine." I didn't tell him it's all because of *Fire Hall Cooking*. Apologies for that. (By the way, your Peaches 'n' Cream Pie is so wonderful I've started serving it for breakfast.) I love this cookbook! When are you writing a sequel?

—Bobby Hutchinson, proprietor, and author of
Blue Collar B&B, Adventures in Hospitality

So here's what we can understand about this author: he knows from feeding hungry guys, he is concerned about health, he likes variety. And, additionally, he's funny and he can write.

—*January Magazine*

First of all I want to thank you! Your book has made my probation with Vancouver Fire and Rescue so much less painful. My (your) oatmeal blueberry muffin recipe has made me a star in my class.

—Scott Turner, Vancouver firefighter

WHERE THERE'S FOOD, THERE'S FIREFIGHTERS

MORE Surefire Recipes to Feed Your Crew

Jeff Derraugh

TouchWood
Editions

TouchWood Editions
www.touchwoodeditions.com

Library and Archives Canada Cataloguing in Publication
Derraugh, Jeff, 1959–
Where there's food, there's firefighters / Jeff Derraugh.

ISBN 978-1-894898-94-2

1. Cookery. 2. Fire stations—Anecdotes. 3. Fire fighters—Anecdotes.

I. Title.
TX714.D465 2009   641.502'4   C2009-902907-3

Edited by Marial Shea
Proofread by Anne Brennan
Book cover by Tobyn Manthorpe
Illustrations by Tobyn Manthorpe
Book design by Jacqui Thomas
Cover photographs by Lee Harrison

 BRITISH COLUMBIA ARTS COUNCIL   Canada Council Conseil des Arts
for the Arts   du Canada

We gratefully acknowledge the financial support for our publishing activities from the
Government of Canada through the Book Publishing Industry Development Program
(BPIDP), Canada Council for the Arts, and the Province of British Columbia through the
British Columbia Arts Council and the Book Publishing Tax Credit.

 Mixed Sources
Product group from well-managed
forests, controlled sources and
recycled wood or fibre
www.fsc.org Cert no. SW-COC-000952
© 1996 Forest Stewardship Council
FSC

 85%

The interior pages of this book have been printed on 100% post-consumer recycled paper,
processed chlorine free, and printed with vegetable-based inks.

1 2 3 4 5 12 11 10 09

PRINTED IN CANADA

This book is dedicated to the fallen—firefighters who made the ultimate sacrifice. This tribute recognizes brothers and sisters taken while on duty, and those who succumbed to the silent firefighter killers of heart disease and occupational cancers. We will never forget you and will never quit. We fight on in your memory.

INITIAL SIZE-UP

INTRODUCTION

NOTHING TO SEE HERE, MOVE ALONG!

I said there's nothing to see here, move along! Excuse me, but this is a no-rubbernecking zone, so just keep your eyes on the road. We don't need another accident here to clean up; we're busy enough with this one as it is . . . Oh, it's *you!* Sorry, I didn't recognize you at first. *Hey, Cap, would you mind if I chatted with my friend here for a second?*

That's my captain. We've been so busy today that we haven't had a chance to eat at the fire hall yet, so he's cutting me a little slack here. Once the food's safely in his stomach, however, it may be a different story.

So how have you been? As you may have heard, we're back, and I say "we" because it's thanks to you that I got the chance to write a second book. When my debut, *Fire Hall Cooking with Jeff the Chef*, hit the shelves, I was often asked, "So, how do you think the book will do?" I'd reply, "I hope to sell three copies worldwide." I figured it was best to be realistic and keep my expectations low to avoid disappointment. I have to admit, though, that my dream was to sell enough copies that the publisher would ask me to write another one.

Six months after the release of *Fire Hall Cooking*, I got a call from Ruth Linka at TouchWood Editions with the news that they had ordered a second printing. "When do you think you'll have a second book ready?" she asked me. I was completely humbled. You should be, too, because we're a team here, you know. I'll tell you, words alone can't express how much I appreciate you recommending *Fire Hall Cooking* to others. I'm convinced that's how the book sold—by word of mouth, *your* word of mouth. Thank you. You've certainly inspired me, and just like the goofy kid back in school, "don't encourage the boy or he'll just keep doing it!" So, while I'm thanking you, others may in fact be cursing you.

I remember you saying that you like how the fire hall recipes are based on everyday ingredients—stuff you usually have on hand. Well, this new book continues with that tradition, with a few minor exceptions that you'll find listed in Fire Hall Essentials. Stock up your pantry with this small list of items—available at a reasonable price in the Asian foods section of your local grocer—and you'll be ready to fire up your kitchen . . . in a good way, of course.

When people tell me they've picked up *Fire Hall Cooking*, I'll ask if they've tried any recipes. The answer I often get is, "Not yet, I'm just enjoying reading the book." I know, an odd reply for a cookbook. So, due to popular demand, I've dug up another batch of fire house stories for you. Yes, we're going behind the big overhead doors for another fun-filled look at fire hall life.

A misconception some people had about *Fire Hall Cooking* was that the recipes were designed to feed large groups of people. Well, the truth is that since some fire halls have as few as four firefighters on duty, the majority of the recipes were designed for groups of four to six, four being hungry diners (as in famished firefighters getting back to the hall late at night after fighting a fire) and six being mere mortals with more reasonable appetites. The recipes in this book follow the same trend.

Like *Fire Hall Cooking*, this book will help you prepare food for any time of day and any kind of food hankering. Yes, we've combed the globe for another collection of diverse dishes that make sitting down for a meal together great. And I say "we" here because the recipes again come from various sources— mainly firefighters and friends who have either contributed recipes or inspired their development. Hmm, considering all these similarities to my first book, do you think I've fallen into the formula trap?

Well, not exactly. I realize that since *Fire Hall Cooking* came out you've grown as a chef, so I've included several . . . well, call them more advanced recipes, with the hope that they'll enable you to dazzle others with your culinary brilliance.

Don't let that intimidate you, however. My goal, as always, is to make the gourmet easy. In a fire hall time can be tight, just like when you get home from work and have to feed your family with activities beckoning. So, as a means of survival—and believe me, fire hall chefs feel more heat under their collars from ravenous crewmates than they do battling a basement fire—we've learned to adapt and create shortcuts, to break down recipes and simplify them. Yes, the smoke-eater fraternity sympathizes with dinner dilemmas.

By the way, nothing makes me happier than hearing that a recipe I shared worked for you. It's what this whole wacky cookbook-writing dealybob is all about. Given that we firefighters are all about helping others, it certainly is rewarding to know that the recipes shared are helping you make good food and good times for friends, family or for your second family at work.

Having said that, I also must confess to reports of recipes that went awry. Despite rumours to the contrary, firefighters aren't hired for their cooking skills. Becoming a good fire cook takes time and tutelage from senior fire chefs. Firefighters learn by watching others, by trial and error and by experiencing the thrill of victory and the agony of defeat—as judged by the "critics" in the hall. That's how I learned, and to be honest, I still feel that I have much to learn—perhaps even about the art of being *very* specific in writing recipes.

For example, *Fire Hall Cooking* featured a recipe for Coconut Curried Rice. The rookie at No. 13 station was given the task of interpreting this recipe while the meal's head chef left the hall to drive the district chief on his rounds.

When the crew dug into their meal, a panicked call for "water, *water!*" went out. No, it wasn't the heat from the curry. "Oh man, what's with the rice?"

"Well, I followed Jeff's recipe word for word," the rookie replied in defence.

Initially, I took the heat. However, a forensic audit and inquiry launched by the chief's driver revealed that instead of one cup of chicken broth (being liquid) the rookie had used one cup of straight-up chicken bouillon powder. For the poor dining firefighters it was like trying to swallow a salt stick.

As it turns out, the chef at No. 11 also made this flub, so I should share the blame, since I am the common denominator here. As per my firefighter job description, I'm with you in good times and bad.

Well, traffic is backing up here and the tow truck is just pulling in, so I should get back to work. Hey, did you happen to receive that "Instructions-for-Life Mantra" chain e-mail the Dalai Lama is said to have penned? As a parting thought I'll leave you with this, Hello Dalai's key to life: "Approach love and cooking with reckless abandon!"

So get out there into that big bad kitchen world of ours, recipes in hand, and cook, love and smile like there's no tomorrow. Yes, once again it's time for food, folks and fire house fun!

FIRE HALL ESSENTIALS

If you're planning to use this handy cooking guide on a regular basis—*and that's certainly the best way to get your money's worth*—then I say it's time for you to stock up your pantry. There are a few spice mixes and marinades from my debut, *Fire Hall Cooking with Jeff the Chef*, that I just can't live without, so I've included them here as an easy reference for you.

I try to use everyday ingredients in my recipes as much as possible, but there are a few exceptions to this rule, so I thought I'd take a moment to familiarize you with them. These ingredients may not be considered everyday here in North America, but they are increasingly popular, readily available and deliciously different. Chances are, if you check out the Asian foods section of your local supermarket, you'll have no trouble finding this small group of funky condiments. Not to worry, in most cases the price of these items is very reasonable. Here's your grocery list.

Hoisin Sauce—Made from fermented soybeans with chilies, vinegar, sweet potato and garlic, this actually tastes way better than it sounds. It works great in stir-fry sauces and is also great as a stand-alone barbecue or dipping sauce.

Oyster Sauce—This adds a nice funkiness to stir-fry sauces. I often use it as a substitute for fish sauce when I just can't stand the thought of cracking open the fish sauce bottle. Oh, and I always buy the premium variety of oyster sauce, because I'm scared to try the cheap one.

Fish Sauce—Use this in Thai dishes for authenticity, or use it for practical jokes around the fire hall. It's super cheap, and I certainly know why. It *stinks!*

Sweet Soy Sauce—Once you try the sweet variation of soy sauce, a.k.a. *kecap manis* or Indonesian soy sauce, you'll be hooked and it will surely become a staple in your kitchen. It's great on its own as a condiment over rice, or as a base for stir-fry sauces and marinades.

Chili-Garlic Sauce—Don't confuse this with Vietnamese and Indonesian chili pastes, such as *sambal oelek*, which don't have garlic. Be forewarned, the heat quotient of this sauce can vary from brand to brand. I like to use a mild Chinese chili-garlic sauce. Believe me, some brands could set asbestos on fire.

Sweet Chili Sauce—Here's a sauce that I see in fire hall fridges with increasing regularity. As with chili-garlic sauce, the intensity of this sauce can vary from brand to brand. I like the sweet chili sauce for chicken, the one that comes in the big red bottle. It's excellent as a chicken topping, as a barbecue sauce for chicken or ribs, as a base for salad dressings and stir-fry sauces or on its own as a dip for wings and spring rolls.

FIRE AND SPICE

There are four spice mixes I call for with great regularity. The first two are Italian and Greek seasonings, which you can buy off the spice rack. The other two are personal blends you can make up yourself with a few easy-to-find spices. Bringing them together may make for a messy counter—at least, it does when I make them up—but the results you get from these spices are well worth the cleanup.

FIRED-UP SPICE

- 3 tablespoons kosher salt
- 2 tablespoons paprika—sweet, if possible
- 2 tablespoons granulated garlic—I like the roasted variety
- 1 tablespoon freshly ground or restaurant-style black pepper
- 1 tablespoon onion powder
- 1 tablespoon dried basil—use the leaf form, not the powdered
- 1 tablespoon dried oregano—ditto the leaf form
- 1 tablespoon cayenne

FIRED-UP SANTA FE SPICE

- 2 tablespoons paprika—sweet, if possible
- 2 tablespoons chili powder
- 2 tablespoons kosher salt
- 1 tablespoon granulated garlic—roasted, if you have it
- 1 tablespoon cayenne
- 1 tablespoon ground coriander
- 1 tablespoon dried (leaf) oregano
- 2 teaspoons ground cumin
- 2 teaspoons freshly ground or restaurant-style black pepper
- 2 teaspoons onion powder

I'VE PULLED OUT ALL THE SPICES, NOW WHAT DO I DO WITH THEM, JEFF?

For either the Fired-Up Spice mix or the Fired-Up Santa Fe Spice, simply combine the ingredients in a bowl and spoon them into a tight-sealing container. (I use empty spice bottles, but then, I'm your typical cheap firefighter.) Be sure to stow the containers in a cupboard away from sun and heat. I've been told that dried herbs and spices lose their flavour after about six months. But if you're like me, you won't have to worry, as your spice mixes won't last that long anyway, so moot point to that!

SOAKIN' IT UP!

There are several new marinades in this book for you to try, but I've resigned myself to the fact that a couple of classics from *Fire Hall Cooking* refuse to give up and go away. Resistance is futile and they're here to stay. I must admit, they do make great house guests. Why, they'll fill your lives with such joy that soon you'll be asking them to take up permanent residence in *your* kitchen as well.

I like to use zip-top freezer bags, as they make marinating easy. Simply cram the meat in with the marinade, squeeze the air from the bag, zip it up, massage the marinade into the meat and turn it every once in a while, for even marinating. The longer it sits, the more pronounced the flavour. I find that four hours in the fridge usually works well, but sometimes overnight works best.

LEMON-GARLIC MARINADE

I primarily use firefighter Glen Godri's infamous mix as a poultry marinade. For a flavour gauge, think chicken souvlaki. Definitely a big Greek/Italian influence here.

FOR EVERY 2 POUNDS OF MEAT, USE

- 1 cup lemon juice—go fresh or go . . . bottled
- ⅓ cup olive oil—I like extra-virgin, but regular or even canola will work
- 8 garlic cloves, run through the press first, please
- 1½ tablespoons Greek seasoning
- ½ tablespoon dried oregano—2 tablespoons if you aren't using the Greek seasoning
- 2 teaspoons kosher or 1 teaspoon sea salt
- ½ teaspoon cayenne

Simply get all of the ingredients together in a bowl and whisk away!

CUBAN LIME MARINADE

I originally used this as a pork marinade, but I soon discovered that it rocks with chicken as well. Cuba isn't exactly located in the southwest, but the flavour of this marinade sure screams New-Mex, Tex-Mex!

FOR EVERY 2 POUNDS OF MEAT, USE

- 10 garlic cloves, pressed
- 1½ teaspoons kosher salt
- 2 tablespoons dried oregano
- 1 tablespoon ground cumin
- ½ teaspoon cayenne
- 1 cup lime juice—fresh is best, but I'll accept the bottled stuff
- ⅓ cup extra-virgin olive oil

Mash the garlic with the salt and add the oregano, cumin and cayenne. Whisk in the lime juice and olive oil. Marinate away!

ON THE DAY SHIFT

THE BRUNCH BRIGADE

Blazing Steak and Eggs Benedict 12
Decadence is batting leadoff!

Brunchiladas 13
Another great Tex-Mex twist for the brunch table

Breakfast Lasagna 14
A.k.a. Brek-Mex-Agna

Fruit Cocktail for Breakfast 15
Off the tree and into the bowl it goes!

Huevos Rancheros a.k.a. Mexican Eggs 16
Poached eggs with a tasty bit of salsa-fication

Pesto-Packed Scrambled Eggs 17
Our goal is scrambled egg perfection

Smoked Salmon Omelette 18
Smoke 'em if you got 'em!

Sleep 'n' Bake Stuffed French Toast 19
So simple it almost makes itself

Sweet Apple Dutch Baby Pancake 20
Call Godzilla! It's a monster pancake invasion!

THE LUNCH BUNCH

Chicken Fajitas Go Cuban 23
Is that a fajita you're rolling, or a cigar?

Donairraughs 24
The Maritime fire halls wanted in on lunch, too

Fire Hall Heroes 26
We're pitching spicy, saucy, Fireballs onto a stacked sub

Korean Beef Wraps 27
How can it be Korean if it's wrapped in a tortilla?

Kutzy's Chicken Salad Sandwiches 28
These chicks are so cookbook worthy!

New-Mex-Fire Steak Sandwiches 29
With that steak-and-cheese Philly feel

Not Your Frozen Chicken Fingers 30
With honey-dill sauce

Thai Chicken Wraps 32
Are tortillas Thai cuisine?

Veal Parmesan Bunwiches 33
A gourmet lunch for when time is tight

Wacky Teriyaki Burgers 34
Grilled pineapple on a chicken burger? Really?

What Came First, the Turkey or the Egg Salad Sandwich? 35
Hmmm????

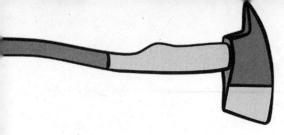

THE BRUNCH BRIGADE

GETTING THE GROCERIES

If you see firefighters shopping on duty for groceries, rest assured that we are in our response district and will drop everything to attend an alarm. We've abandoned shopping carts full of groceries in aisles and checkouts many times. In fact, we once returned to a store three times before we finally got away "call free."

By the way, we really don't want special treatment, or even to cut in line, unless you happen to insist on paying by cheque without having it certified first or you love to rummage around in your purse or pockets for loose change that you *know* you have. Ever grow cobwebs waiting for the "chronologically challenged" to dig into the deep recesses of their 10-gallon purses? "Just a minute, I know I have the exact change here somewhere." AHHHHHHH! I'm losing my will to live! Did we just miss shift change?

Speaking of on-duty shopping, a firefighter from No. 13 was grabbing groceries when the woman behind him in line asked the oft-heard question, "So, what's cooking today? I hear you guys eat pretty well there at the fire hall."

"We're having BLTs," Jim replied.

"Oh, I love BLTs. What time are you eating?"

"We're shooting for about 11:30."

"Ohhhhh, sounds good. I'll be there."

Jim had experienced many similar chats in line while shopping, so he didn't give her a second thought—until she showed up at the hall. As Jim had shopped alone, his crewmates had no idea who the woman was, and Jim wasn't about to clue them in. The firefighters just figured she must be someone's spouse in for a visit. "So, are all you guys married?" she asked a firefighter as she happily helped out by flipping the bacon.

"Yeah, all except for Randy I think."

When Jim entered the kitchen moments later he complimented his guest. "Hey, you're sure doing a great job there on the bacon."

"Little good it'll do me," she shot back. "You're married."

And so it goes. Whether it's a weekend brunch or a weekday lunch, one thing's for sure: we're setting the table on day shift and dining at the fire hall. Best of all, we've got a place set right here for you.

BLAZING
STEAK AND EGGS BENEDICT

We were working at the fire hall on Christmas Day '06, and being that it was a special day we decided to throw the budget to the wind and go for all-out brunch decadence. How's this for a treat? Sourdough garlic toast topped with salsa, barbecued marinated rib-eye steaks, poached eggs and hollandaise sauce. Did King Henry VIII ever have it this good?

$$$$$$$$ . . . OH, DON'T WORRY, BE HAPPY!

- Southwest Chipotle 'n' Lime Marinade (page 123)
- 4 rib-eye steaks—we're talking 1 steak each
- Packaged hollandaise sauce
- 8 large eggs
- Garlic butter—as in butter with minced garlic and a little Italian seasoning
- Sourdough bread—a little fatter in diameter than baguette style
- Your favourite salsa
- Cayenne, to taste

LET'S GET THE SUPER BRUNCH $$STACK GOING HERE

Get the marinade together and toss the flavour-laden liquid and steaks together in a zip-top freezer bag. Toss 'em in the fridge overnight. (Alternately, you can rub a 50/50 ratio of brown sugar and Fired-Up Santa Fe Spice over the steaks and let stand for about one hour.)

Get 'em on the Q or under the broiler and grill until medium rare. A trusty barbecue buddy would be ideal to free you up to cook the rest.

Meanwhile—yes, that's you, the indoor chef—in a small saucepan, bring the hollandaise sauce together

as directed on the package. Don't abandon the sauce until it has thickened, as it sticks and burns quite easily.

When the steaks are happily done, let them stand out on the counter for 5 minutes before cutting each of them in half. Meanwhile . . .

The eggs need poaching, so bring a large frying pan of water to a boil with a couple tablespoons of vinegar to keep the eggs together. Turn the water down to barely a boil, break each egg individually into a bowl and pour it into the hot tub. Poached eggs should take about 4 to 5 minutes. If you have an egg poacher (perhaps you got one for Christmas), well, la-de-dah, aren't you the pampered chef!

Spread garlic butter on sourdough slices and broil 'em to toast.

Let's do it! Place 2 slices of garlic toast on each plate. Top each slice with about 2 or 3 tablespoons of salsa, half a steak, a poached egg, hollandaise and a light sprinkle of cayenne to fire it up.

You've stared decadence straight in the eye and embraced it. Way to go! Now, can anyone manage to get up from the table to do the dishes?

BRUNCHILADAS

Here's a great south-of-the-border brunch or breakfast treat. One tortilla will satisfy most—unless of course they're firefighters, in which case you'd better make two each, otherwise a ravaged crew will be gnawing on your leg.

DID BRUNCH ORIGINATE IN MEXICO?

- 1 pound hot Italian or chorizo sausage
- 1 bunch green onions, sliced
- 1 medium-sized red, orange or yellow pepper, diced
- 2 jalapeno peppers, diced fine
- 10 large tortillas—try the flavourful Roma tomato or pesto flavour
- 3 cups nacho, Monterey Jack or marble cheese, grated
- ½ bunch cilantro, chopped fine
- 10 eggs, beaten
- 2 cups buttermilk (or half-and-half cream, if you prefer)
- 1 teaspoon each kosher salt and freshly ground black pepper
- A few shots of Louisiana hot sauce (or enough to suit your taste)
- Bottled salsa—just pick your fave and force everyone else to enjoy it!
- Sour cream, as a garnish

JUST FILL 'EM UP AND ROLL 'EM OUT, SEÑOR!

Take the sausage out of its casing and place in a frying pan over medium heat, breaking up the meat as you go. Cook through and drain. Set aside to cool.

Now get those green onions, peppers and jalapenos ready. When the meat is cool, combine it in a bowl with the veggies.

Place each tortilla flat on the counter. Place about ⅓ cup of the meat-and-veggie mix along with 3 tablespoons of the cheese and a bit of cilantro in the middle of each tortilla. Resist the innate firefighter temptation to overfill the tortilla.

Roll up each tortilla tightly—this is a key point—and place seam-side down in a large lasagna dish, at least 9 x 13 inches with high sides. Line up the tortillas in the pan. It's a tight fit, but you'll make it.

Meanwhile, get the eggs, milk, salt, pepper and hot sauce together in a bowl, and whisk to combine.

Pour the egg mixture evenly over the tortillas. You'll find that it'll seep into the corners and crannies and will all miraculously fit in, albeit barely.

Cover the pan with aluminum foil and either refrigerate to cook it the next morning, or get it into a 350°F oven for 50 to 60 minutes or until the egg mix is set up.

Remove the foil and top with a 2-inch-wide swatch of salsa and the remaining cheese and bake till melted.

Let stand for 10 minutes, then serve with sour cream and additional salsa.

BREAKFAST LASAGNA

In Fire Hall Cooking with Jeff the Chef *we explored the magic of Breakfast Pizza. With that expedition now considered a success, it's time to bring lasagna to the breakfast nook with a spicy Mexican twist. This is a great brunch meal for home or the fire hall, as all the work is done the day before. In the morning, just drag your lazy butt out of bed, bake the lasagna and serve. How easy is that, my friends?*

A GOOD-MORNING MEXICAN TRADITION

- 2 pounds hot Italian or chorizo sausage
- 2 tablespoons butter or vegetable oil
- 1 medium yellow or white onion, diced
- 2 bell peppers, diced—go for red, orange and/or yellow, for colour
- About ½ pound mushrooms, cut into Ts
- 2 teaspoons Fired-Up Santa Fe Spice (page 5), divided
- 2 teaspoons chili powder
- 1 teaspoon dried cumin
- 1 teaspoon oregano
- 1 bunch green onions, chopped
- ⅓ cup finely chopped cilantro
- 1-pound bag shredded nacho, Tex-Mex or Monterey Jack cheese
- 5 or 6 10-inch corn or flour tortillas, cut into eighths
- 12 large eggs
- 2½ cups buttermilk (or milk, if you prefer)
- Freshly ground black pepper
- Salsa—pick your favourite brand
- Sour cream

SINCE COLUMBUS BROUGHT THE IDEA OVER FROM ITALY

Let's start by unwrapping the rap. Get those sausages out of their casings. I just run a knife along the inside of the sausage skin and peel it off.

Let's move the sausages to a frying pan and break them up with a spatula as you fry. You want a ground-beef-like consistency. Drain when browned. Set aside.

In a separate pan, get the butter or vegetable oil going over medium heat and toss in the onion first, fry for a couple of minutes, then follow up with the peppers and mushrooms.

Dust the lot with 1 teaspoon each of Santa Fe Spice, chili powder, cumin and oregano (hang onto the other teaspoon of Santa Fe and chili for a minute). We're in the Southwestern zone now, my siesta-loving friends.

Bring the cooked sausages and veggies together with the green onions.

In a separate bowl, combine the cilantro and nacho cheese.

In bowl 3—oh, how I love to make a mess in the kitchen—whisk the eggs and buttermilk together with the remaining Fired-Up Santa Fe Spice and chili powder.

Looks like we're all staged and ready to rock, so let's lay it out!

Spray a deep-sided 9 x 13-inch lasagna dish or an enamel roaster with cooking spray and lay down ⅓ of the meat-meets-veggie mixture (see the note at the end of the recipe).

Top with 33% of the cilantro/cheese, followed by a single layer of tortillas.

Repeat the layers once more... *Hang on, doesn't 33 + 33 = 66%? I know, but there's a reason I didn't say repeat the layers twice.* You see, for layer 3, the final instalment, lay the remaining meat/veg down and follow up with the tortillas. Then lay a nice bit of salsa on top, a decorative layer, so to speak, and finish with what's left of the cheese.

Here comes the big finish! Pour the egg/milk mix over top. This casserole needs to sit for at least a couple hours, but better yet overnight. So cover it with aluminum foil and send it to the fridge for the resting phase.

In the morning, just move it on over, cover and all, to a 350°F oven for about an hour and 15 minutes. Pull off the foil and bake another 15 minutes or till our puffed-up lasagna is set in the middle and lightly browned on top.

Allow the Brek-Mex-Agna to sit out for 10 to 15 minutes before slicing.

Serve garnished with salsa and sour cream.

Note: If your lasagna dish is fairly shallow, you may want to eliminate the second layer of tortillas, to create a little extra room for the other players.

FRUIT COCKTAIL

I know, this ranks as one of those "duh!" recipes because it's so blatantly simple, one you can likely create without a recipe, so let's just call this a little friendly reminder. In our department it's standard practice to serve orange juice with brunch, but I like to break with tradition on occasion and serve a batch of fruit cocktail instead. Like any salad, when it comes to ingredients, simply use your imagination. If it's in season, on hand or just one of those must haves, by all means, get it in there.

CONSIDER THIS A GUIDE, NOT AN ORDER

- 28-ounce can peaches and mandarins, with juice
- 14-ounce can pineapple tidbits, with juice
- 2–3 apples, sliced (toss with the fruit juice to keep from browning)
- 1 big bunch grapes (or sliced strawberries)
- 2–3 kiwis, sliced and diced
- 2 bananas, sliced thin

IN THIS DRILL SESSION, FREELANCING IS ENCOURAGED

Get the canned fruit into the bowl first and add the fresh ingredients as you prepare them. Don't add the bananas, though, until just before serving.

This is also terrific served in a bowl with vanilla yogurt or as a dessert over a bowl of ice cream.

HUEVOS RANCHEROS
A.K.A. MEXICAN EGGS

There are a million versions of this recipe out there . . . and now here's mine, version 1,000,001. It may sound a little odd, poaching eggs in salsa, but the result is unique and tangy Tex-Mex-style eggs. They go great with barbecued chorizo sausages and hash browns, so don't delay, make them today!

EGGS IN SALSA TOPPED WITH CHEESE? SOUNDS GOOD TO ME!

- Tex-Mex cheese mix (marble, cheddar or Monterey Jack will also work)
- 3 tablespoons salsa combined with 3 tablespoons salsa/ranch (or regular ranch) dressing-or, try ⅓ cup salsa, straight up
- 4 eggs
- Chopped cilantro
- Sour cream or refried beans (optional)

HEY, THIS IS GREAT! I ONLY NEED TO DIRTY ONE PAN!

Grate the cheese, and try to leave your knuckles out of the mix.

Bring a medium-sized nonstick frying pan up to medium heat. Get the salsa/ranch in there, and stir it up a bit until it starts to simmer.

Break the eggs into the salsa. Bring the salsa back to a light boil and cover the pan. You may need to turn the heat down if the salsa becomes too frantic. Cook for about 3 minutes to set up the eggs.

Spread a light layer of cheese over the eggs and cook, uncovered, for 2 to 3 more minutes, or until the eggs are as runny (or solid) as you like them.

Scoop the eggs out of the pan with a solid spatula or spoon. Garnish with cilantro, and perhaps even a little sour cream or refried beans.

If you're using a larger pan in order to feed a bigger group—say, a hall full of firefighters—simply adjust the salsa/ranch, egg and cheese mix.

The huevos and garnish can also be served in a tortilla as a wrap.

BUT WHAT IF I HAPPEN TO BE ITALIAN, NOT MEXICAN?

Simply sub in spaghetti sauce for salsa, mozzarella cheese for Tex-Mex, fresh basil leaves for cilantro and Italian bread for tortillas. Leftover spaghetti sauce—I love it with sautéed vegetables and even hot Italian sausage slices—is perfect for this. Why should eggs be bland, when we have such advanced technology at our fingertips?

AND WHAT IF I'M GREEK, NOT ITALIAN, IRISH, OXYGENARIAN OR MEXICAN?

Oh, man! I guess you're going to have to go the marinara sauce/ feta cheese route. Try fresh oregano for the herb, and garlic toast for dipping. Olives, anyone?

PESTO-PACKED
SCRAMBLED EGGS

District Chief Terry Gardiner raved to me about a favourite restaurant of his that serves the fluffiest scrambled eggs around, adding, "I just don't know how they do it." Well, it got me to thinking, and led me to search for a way to recreate that light texture at home. While I was in the lab, I enlisted the help of my old pal pesto to fire up the flavour quotient. The result? You may want to tell your crew to hold the ketchup and salsa, 'cause you've got a new way to serve tasty-on-their-own, light-as-a-feather super-scrambled eggs.

A PESTO-BACON-VEGGIE FLAVOUR INFUSION, YOU SAY?

- 8 slices bacon
- About half a red onion, diced
- About half a red pepper, diced up too
- Say about a dozen mushrooms—T them up (optional)
- 12 eggs (mandatory—it is an egg dish)
- ¼ cup milk—1 tablespoon for every 3 eggs
- ½ teaspoon seasoning salt
- ¼ cup pesto—about a tablespoon for every
- 3 eggs

EGGXACTLY, ALL YOKING ASIDE

Let's get the bacon fried up until fairly crisp. Drain off all but a couple tablespoons of the bacon grease, and toss in the red onion, followed up by the red pepper and the mushrooms. Sauté to soften the veggies.

Drain the bacon and cut it into small pieces.

Meanwhile, let's get those eggs crackin' in a blender with the milk, and hit "Blend." Let it run for 20 seconds. This will add air to the eggs, giving them that fluffy texture. As a bonus— depending on where you live—air adds zero calories! Alternately, get the eggs into a bowl, tilt the bowl a bit to the side and, using your trusty whisk, beat the eggs for about 2 minutes.

Toss in the seasoning salt and pesto and blend briefly.

Pour the eggs into a bowl and combine them with the bacon and veggies.

Bring a frying pan to medium heat, and add your choice of a wee bit more of the reserved bacon drippings or a couple of tablespoons of butter, canola oil or, even better, olive oil. We need a little bit of egg lube here!

Once the lube has taken on some of that heat, pour in the eggs and let them set up for a bit on the bottom of the pan. Use a spatula to move the set chunks (a.k.a. curds) to the centre of the pan, and tilt the pan so the runny stuff gets a turn on the heat.

Flip the eggs over to cook them evenly, but try not to over-handle them or break them up into bits with the spatula. Let's keep them light!

By the way, Pesto-Packed Scrambled Eggs go great with **Sweet Apple Dutch Baby Pancakes** (page 20) or **Sleep 'n' Bake Stuffed French Toast** (page 19).

OMELETTE

Want to turn a plain lifeless omelette into a mighty flavour explosion? Well, all you have to do is round up a few groceries and get out the pesto!

GET OUT THE CALCULATOR . . . FOR 4 OMELETTES YOU'LL NEED

- 12 large eggs
- Milk
- Seasoning salt
- 4 tablespoons Everybody Goes Pesto (page 144)
- Butter
- 12–16 stalks fresh asparagus
- About ¼ pound mushrooms (optional)
- 1 package hollandaise sauce—it's easy
- Olive oil (canola oil will also work)
- About ¾ pound smoked salmon, cut into thin slices

I LOVE IT WHEN A PLAN COMES TOGETHER!

For each omelette, combine 3 eggs with a dash each of milk and seasoning salt and 1 tablespoon pesto. Give it the tried-and-true whisk treatment.

Melt a couple tablespoons of butter in a frying pan over medium heat. Introduce the asparagus to the butter and follow up with a dusting of kosher salt and freshly ground black pepper. Fry until just tender-crisp. Set aside.

Do the same routine to the 'shrooms. Make up the hollandaise as per the handy, yet tiny font instructions on the package. Are you squinting? If you're like me, you'll be reaching for the reading glasses.

Bring a large nonstick frying pan to temperature over medium-low heat. If it's too hot, the eggs are going to scorch when you add them, so stay low. Pour in a tablespoon or so of olive oil, and carefully lift the pan to swish the oil around so it coats the entire surface.

Get the eggs in there, making sure they spread out to the pan's edges. Cover the pan and cook until the eggs are just set.

Place slices of smoked salmon and 3 to 4 stalks of asparagus down the middle of the omelette and drizzle with the hollandaise. With a spatula, bring each side of the omelette over the filling, one side at a time, holding the omelette side in place for a moment until it stays put without any encouragement or idle threats. Or if you just can't be bothered, put the ingredients on one half and fold the other half over top.

Serve the omelette topped with mushrooms plus another light drizzle of that wonderfully rich hollandaise. Ah, but life is surely good!

You can also use leftover cooked salmon if you like, or whatever seafood you have on hand—cooked shrimp, for example, works amazingly well.

You know, the only thing missing is the caviar! In a fire hall? Yeah, right!

FRENCH TOAST

The problem with serving brunch is having everyone's meal ready at the same time. Well, how about instead of trying in vain to keep batches of pancakes, waffles or, in this case, French toast, warm, we simply cook the whole lot all at once? Bake 'em together and we can all dine together.

BAKED APPLES, BROWN SUGAR AND CINNAMON

- 5 or 6 large Macintosh, Spartan or Granny Smith apples, peeled, cored and sliced
- 2 tablespoons butter
- 3 tablespoons brown sugar, plus more for later
- Cinnamon
- 12 slices oatmeal raisin bread (or other fave bread)
- 8 eggs
- 1½ cups buttermilk (or give eggnog a try during the holiday season)
- 1 teaspoon vanilla

A LITTLE WORK AT NIGHT MAKES FOR LITTLE WORK IN THE MORNING

Let's get our apples sliced up, and bring a large frying pan to medium heat. Melt the butter in the pan, and combine it with the brown sugar. Let it bubble for a minute or so, then get the apples in there before that bully oxygen tells them to turn brown, and cook until they start to soften. Sprinkle the apples with a bit of cinnamon as you go.

Remove the apples from the heat with a slotted spatula and allow them to cool. Make sure you drain off any excess liquid.

Let's pull out that 9 x 13-inch lasagna dish and lay down 6 slices of the raisin bread. Depending on the size of the bread loaf, this should all just make it in. You're looking for a pretty tight fit in the pan here.

Top the bread with the apple slices— the so-called apple stuffing—and in sandwich-artist style, put a lid on it with another layer of bread slices.

It's time to draw the bath, Jeeves. So let's get the eggs, buttermilk and vanilla whisked together and pour them evenly over the bread.

Cover your creation with cling wrap and send it off to the fridge for a nap. Nighty night, see you in the morning, you big sweetie!

When the rooster crows, pull the dish from the fridge and pour yourself a cup of coffee. Let it rest for a bit, to acclimatize itself. Oh, and before you sit down, fire up your trusty oven to 400°F.

Uncover the dish and place it in the middle of the oven for 20 minutes.

Sprinkle the top layer of bread with another hit of brown sugar and cinnamon, and return it to the oven until it's toasty on top and a toothpick driven into the centre of the dish comes out clean.

SWEET APPLE DUTCH
BABY PANCAKE

Look, on that plate! It's an apple pie, it's a Yorkshire pudding, it's a giant pancake—no, it's a Sweet Apple Dutch Baby! Oh, and the great part is that it's such a snap to make! There are no wooden shoes to build and no dikes to plug!

LET'S GET THIS BABY TOGETHER

- 4 tablespoons butter—2 for round 1, and 2 for round 2
- 6 eggs—farm fresh, of course
- 1½ cups buttermilk
- 2 teaspoons vanilla—that's total; we have 2 jobs for it, too
- ¼ cup white sugar
- ½ teaspoon salt
- ¾ cup each all-purpose and whole-wheat flour
- 4 large Mac, Granny Smith or Spartan apples, peeled, cored and sliced
- Cinnamon
- ¼ cup brown sugar
- Pancake syrup (optional)
- Icing sugar (optional as well)

AND THEN GET THIS BABY INTO THE OVEN

Fire up your oven to 425°F (400 for convection ovens). When it's up to speed, place 2 tablespoons of the butter in a large casserole, ovenproof frying pan, or 9 x 13-inch glass lasagna dish. Place the pan in the oven to heat and melt the butter. Ah, yes, the Yorkshire pudding connection!

Okay, let's get to work here, move it, Double Dutch! Pull out the blender and toss in the eggs and let it run for a minute on full throttle. While it's running, add the buttermilk slowly, and follow up with 1 teaspoon of the vanilla and the sugar, salt and flour. Watch in wonder as your batter thickens.

Let your blender do its thing for a good 30 seconds, to smooth it out.

Wondering where the baking powder or baking soda is? No worries, there isn't any.

Pull the pan from the oven ... *ouuucchh!!!* Did you forget the oven mitts? Carefully swish the butter around the bottom and sides of the pan, to coat it. Pour in the batter, place the pan on the middle oven rack and let it go for 20 to 25 minutes—that's when it'll be time to do a visual.

While our baby's in the oven, let's get the topping going. Sprinkle the apple slices with cinnamon. Melt the remaining 2 tablespoons butter in a frying pan over medium heat. Add the brown sugar and combine. Toss in the last teaspoon of vanilla, then bring the apples in and cook them up until softened. Remove the pan from the heat. If desired, add pancake syrup to the mix.

Once Dutchy has crawled up the sides of the pan and is puffed up in places—as it tends to do—and happily browned on top, remove it from the oven . . . *ouccchhh!!!!* So, your short-term memory isn't what it used to be?

Slice our baby into portions and top with the sautéed apples and a nice dusting of icing sugar. Serves 4 to 6, depending on diner demographics.

Note: As an alternate method, try adding the sautéed apples to the bottom of the pan just before adding the batter. Then simply bake this baby and watch the apples puff up with the batter.

THE GUY'S GOT FINGERS LIKE SAUSAGES!

A crewmate showed up at the hall for our first day shift with a big band-aid on his thumb. This, of course, piqued everyone's curiosity. "Murray, what did you do to your thumb?"

"I had a blood blister, and I popped it," he replied. "Now I've developed some sort of growth that I have to get surgically removed on Monday."

Of course, being the medically trained professionals that we first responders are, we all just *had* to have a look, and it wasn't pretty.

A while later Angela came into the kitchen with the sausages she had expertly barbecued for brunch, including one that had rolled off the Q and got semi-mulched. "Hey, that one looks like that thing on Murray's thumb," Romeo said, laughing. "Wait a second, I have an idea."

Romeo cut off a half-inch sausage chunk and Scotch-taped it to his thumb. Then our captain and a couple of other firefighters followed suit and I taped one to my forehead. "Murray, that growth of yours is contagious!" the cap exclaimed as we, the mutants, paraded by Murray in the front floor watch area, where he was seated.

Soon after, the fire truck Murray piloted got a call. When he pulled the machine into the parking lot he finally took notice of the sausage slices taped at random intervals around the circumference of the steering wheel. With no time to remove them, he drove to the emergency call with greasy sausage bits for added grip and manoeuvrability.

Hmmmm, I wonder how those got there?

THE LUNCH BUNCH

SO, WHAT'S FOR LUNCH?

I get a kick out of Captain Al Gray's food terminology. "I got so discouraged when I was bouncing around as an acting captain from hall to hall," he said. "When the guys discussed possible lunch items, I couldn't believe how often I heard, 'Let's just have cold cuts and a tin of soup.' I never complained, but I did say to myself, 'Come on, guys, we can do *so* much better.' I mean, wet meat and factory soup?"

Now, thanks to Al (a.k.a. Elwood), every time I look at luncheon meat I think "wet meat"—especially that cheap, soggy cooked ham. Nitrites, nitrates, pillars of sodium and hitters of polysorbate 80—mm-mmm, not so good for you, especially given some of the recent health scares.

Granted, wet meat and factory soup is a quick-and-easy lunch fix, but as Elwood says, we can do better. At home I often make lots for dinner so we can have leftovers for lunch the next day. At the fire hall, however, leftovers are a rarity, so during the winter months, more often than not, we prepare a hearty soup, and in the summer we'll likely have a salad plus a barbecued meat such as marinated chicken or steaks for the carnivores.

But since variety is the spice of lunch, the season doesn't always dictate what we have, and an assortment of other lunch dishes makes its way to the fire house table as well. Just take a look at the menu here, and you'll find all sorts of great lunch meals that won't cost a lot of time or money to make. **Kutzy's Chicken Salad Sandwiches** (page 28), **Veal Parmesan Bunwiches** (page 33) and **Korean Beef Wraps** (page 27) come to mind as quick-and-easy noon-hour solutions. Hey, and if you plan ahead and get the meat in the fridge to marinate the night before, recipes such as **Wacky Teriyaki Burgers** (page 34), **Chicken Fajitas Go Cuban** (page 23) and **Thai Chicken Wraps** (page 32) will come together in a flash, as well.

Oh, and don't forget some of the main-course meals in this book as possible lunches. **Boot-Shaped Burgers** (page 116), **Thai Fish Cakes** (page 105), **Sizzlin' Salisbury Steaks with Mushroom Gravy** (page 86) and **Greek-Style Turkey Burgers** (page 118), to name but a few, will all serve to satisfy those cruel midday hunger pangs.

So, there you go, I've given you some ideas. Now there's no excuse for the wet-meat, factory-soup default. Come on, crew, live a little. Be brave and creative. Let's try something new for lunch today.

GO CUBAN

Fajitas are a surefire lunch or dinner winner. You can go low-fat by using skinny sour cream and holding off on the cheese, and low-carb depending on the wraps you use. You can even make them with beef or pork. Come on, let's fire up a batch!

DON'T MAKE ME HUNGRY

- Cuban Lime Marinade (page 6)
- 4–6 boneless, skinless chicken breasts (depending on size) or 12 thighs
- Red onion—I know, it looks more purple than red
- 2 large coloured peppers—be adventurous; mix up the colours
- 8 large flour or corn tortillas (or try those low-carb wraps, Mr. Atkins)
- Sour cream—I tend to use the nonfat, but that's just me
- Salsa—whatever your fave brand happens to be
- Lettuce, thinly sliced
- Chopped cilantro
- Marble or Monterey Jack cheese (optional)

YOU WON'T LIKE ME WHEN I'M HUNGRY!

As my wife, Lori, often says when I come home from work or a workout and make a beeline for the fridge, "I'd sure hate to be with you if there was ever a famine." Ditto for my brethren and sistren at the fire hall.

Speaking of hunger, enough chit-chat. Let's get that funky Cuban Lime Marinade together. Be sure to set aside about ¼ cup of the jungle juice so you can share that Cuban-essence with the vegetables, as well.

Place the chicken in a zip-top freezer bag and pour in the marinade. Seal it up and pass it along to the fridge for at least 4 hours, or overnight.

When lunchtime approaches, cut the red onion and peppers into thin strips and toss them in a bowl with a light coating of the reserved Cuban Lime Marinade. If you let this sit for 30 minutes to an hour, I'd say you're good to go.

Get the chicken on the barbecue over medium heat. Grill until cooked through—that's 165°F on the meat thermometer. Allow the chicken to cool on the counter for 5 to 10 minutes so it can set up before you cut it into thin strips.

While the chicken cools, stir-fry the marinated onions and peppers in a frying pan over medium heat and soften them until they're tender-crisp.

Warm up the tortillas briefly in the microwave. Serve the fajitas by laying the chicken and veggies down the centres of the tortillas and garnishing them with your choice of sour cream, salsa, lettuce, cilantro and even cheese.

Then roll 'em up and eat 'em. *Whoa!* Nice overstuff! You're not the only one eating here, you know. You can always come back for more.

DONAIRRAUGHS

Here's a request from one of our department's world travelers, Dwayne "Army" Huot. According to our boy, Donairs are a regional delicacy prevalent on just about every street corner in Nova Scotia. If you like meatloaf sandwiches and gyros, then give these Atlantic taste treats a go. The combination of spicy meat and a sweet, creamy sauce served with raw onions and tomatoes in a pita pocket is so good! This recipe serves four ravenous firefighters or six regulation eaters.

FOR THE SPICY MEAT

- 2 teaspoons salt
- 2 teaspoons all-purpose flour
- 1 teaspoon freshly ground black pepper
- 1 teaspoon Italian seasoning
- 1 teaspoon granulated garlic
- 1 teaspoon onion powder
- ¾ teaspoon cayenne
- 2 pounds medium ground beef

AND FOR THE SWEET, SUPER-THICK DONAIR SAUCE

- 1⅓ cups sweetened condensed milk
- ⅔ cup vinegar
- ¾ teaspoon garlic powder

AND

- 8 pita pockets
- 1 red onion, cut into thin slices
- 4 medium tomatoes, diced

LET'S BRING ALL THE COMBATANTS TOGETHER

Fire up the oven to 350°F.

Combine the spices in a small bowl. In a larger, metal bowl, work the spices into the ground meat. Unlike for a hamburger, where you avoid over-handling the meat because you want to keep it light, here you want *density*, so you're going to knead the meat lots. Toss it hard into the bowl—we're talking at least 20 times, to pack that burger tightly together.

Pack the burger into a meatloaf or bread pan and bake for about 1 hour.

Meanwhile, whisk the sweetened condensed milk, vinegar and garlic powder together in a medium-sized steel bowl. Get the sauce into the fridge to set up for an hour or so.

Remove the meat from the pan and refrigerate for at least 1 hour, longer if possible, even overnight if you want. This makes the meat so much easier to slice. Of course, this requires foresight and patience, so if you didn't bother to preread the recipe and you're motivated by the thunderous roar from your stomach, don't come running to me, pally, if the hot loaf falls apart when you go to cut into it!

With a sharp carving knife—remember, a sharp knife is a safe knife—slice the meat into very thin pieces. Reheat the slices briefly in a large frying pan or, better yet, on one of those breakfast grill deals.

Moisten the pita breads slightly by spreading a dab of water over the shell of each. Heat the pitas briefly in either a frying pan or the microwave. Your goal is to make the pitas pliable.

Well, the choice is yours. You can either cut a hole in the side of one end of the pita, so you can stuff the whole pita pocket with ingredients, or slice the pita in half, so you can stuff the pockets with the goodies—being slices of beef, onions, tomatoes and of course *lots* of donair sauce.

Take a bite. Here's the ultimate test for accuracy. If you don't have sauce *oozing* and *dripping* all over the place, then you need to open up the pita pocket and take another big hit of sauce. Squirt, drip, splosh! There, that's much better!

CHECK THIS OUT

For the second year running, my mom gave me a gift certificate to a cookware store for a birthday present. Now, don't get me wrong. I'm very appreciative. The gift enabled me to pick up some cool kitchen tools that I would never buy with my own money. But I do have issue with the gist of the gift here. I mean, really, Mom used to *hate* when we bought her appliances and cookware for her birthday. I remember her freaking out when we bought her a blender for Mother's Day so my brothers and I could mix ourselves protein drinks. "Is that all you think of me, the slave in the kitchen?"

Fast-forward to today, and the shoe is clearly on the other foot. How sexist can you be, Mom? Is this payback, or have you blocked those past gift experiences from your memory?

How about the card that accompanied the gift? On the front it said, "Must be great to know that even at your age women still check you out."

Open the card and there's a picture of a supermarket cashier behind the till: "That'll be $36.95, please."

FIRE HALL HEROES

Do you suffer from Hero Envy? When you spot big sub buns loaded sky high with ingredients, do you wish your sub could somehow measure up? You've come to the right place, my friend, as we have the technology to help you make your sub big, bold and, above all, the envy of others!

WHEN HUNGER CALLS, WE START ROLLIN'

- 2 pounds Fireballs (page 149)
- 2 cups prepared spaghetti sauce
- 1 cup salsa—mild, medium or hot, whatever you prefer
- 1½ teaspoons Fired-Up Spice (page 4)
- 2 tablespoons butter
- 1 red onion, sliced
- About ½ pound mushrooms, sliced
- Kosher salt and freshly ground black pepper
- 1 teaspoon Italian seasoning
- 4–6 8-inch or 12-inch sub buns—go big or go home!
- Great Garlic Cheese Toast (found way up ahead on page 189)

THIS OUGHT TO EXTINGUISH THOSE HUNGER PANGS

Make up a batch of those funky Fireballs. I'll let you decide how big you want them, but I'm happy with a medium-sized Fireball. Fry 'em, bake 'em or barbecue 'em, the choice is yours.

Meanwhile, combine the spaghetti sauce, salsa and Fired-Up Spice. Although not known for culinary theatrics, my dad did have one or two tricks up his sleeve, including adding salsa to pasta sauce. It really lends a nice kick to the standard spag sauce routine. Let's bring the combo to a light simmer.

While you're at home there on the range, get a frying pan going over medium heat and add a couple of tablespoons of butter. Get the onions in there and fry until they're caramelized (a little browned on the edges).

Follow up with the mushrooms and a light shot of kosher salt, freshly ground black pepper and Italian seasoning. Let's bring out the flavour, folks!

Get those sub buns cut and opened up. I like to apply the method from the Great Garlic Cheese Toast recipe, but you can lightly toast the buns under the broiler if you like.

Toss the Fireballs with the sauce to coat and heat through.

Are all the combatants ready to rumble here? Then go to it, you fire-hall-hero sandwich artist, you. Top that Great Garlic Cheese bun with the onions, mushrooms and Fireballs. Don't be shy, feel free to exceed the load limit!

If you simply toasted the bun, then you can choose to top Fireball Mountain with mozzarella cheese and finish it under the broiler.

These go great with a Caesar salad on the side or over top. Bacon, tomatoes, peppers—top it with your wildest ideas!

KOREAN BEEF WRAPS

If you're cooking for firefighters, you must keep in mind the three golden rules of fire hall cooking: it better be good, it better be cheap and there better be lots! Well, here's a great lunch or dinner meal that covers all the bases, plus these wraps are a snap to prepare. Oh, and in the ancient Korean-martial-art tae-kwon-do tradition, they pack a nice kick, to boot!

BOW TO THE BLACK BELT AND KINDLY REQUEST . . .

- 2 pounds lean ground beef
- 5 garlic cloves, pressed
- 1 tablespoon ginger, minced
- 1 red and 1 yellow pepper, diced
- Kosher or sea salt plus freshly ground black pepper, to taste
- ½ cup sweet soy sauce (available in your grocer's Asian food section)
- 2 tablespoons chili-garlic sauce (also in the Asian food section)
- 2 teaspoons toasted sesame oil
- 8 tortillas for wraps (or large leaves of lettuce, for the traditional touch)
- Lime juice
- Chopped green onions
- Grated carrot
- Chopped cilantro
- Bottled hoisin sauce

AND SOON YOUR TASTE BUDS WILL BE HUMBLY HONOURED

Let's get a frying pan—or a wok, if you insist on doing this the traditional way—going over medium heat, and brown up that burger along with the garlic, ginger and peppers. Oh, and toss in a little salt and pepper, boss, because as the Grand Master so often says, "Meat and veggies don't come preseasoned."

Drain off the heart-attack-helper fat, and mix up the sweet soy sauce, chili-garlic sauce and sesame oil. All right, let's bring that sweet-and-spicy sauce to the beef and warm it through for a few minutes, for a kickin' flavour assault on the taste buds. Give the mix the old taste test and consider adding more salt and pepper.

Move the meat mix into a bowl and place it on the table. Give everyone a wrap or, if you're a traditionalist or one of those Atkins or South Beach diet freaks, a large leaf of lettuce.

Spoon the filling into the wrapper, and top that spicy meat mix with your choice of toppings. Personally, I like to go with the works—a little squirt of lime juice, some green onion, grated carrot, chopped cilantro and a drizzle of hoisin sauce.

Roll 'em up, and this wrap is ready to spar with your taste buds!

KUTZY'S CHICKEN SALAD
SANDWICHES

Captain John Webster invited me back to my old hall, No. 18, to fill in for a vacationing crew member. It was John's final four-day tour before retirement, and being the food fanatic he is, he'd preplanned a wish list of favourite dishes. He had three requests for me to fill, adding, "On the second day shift, Justin [Kutzak] has a great chicken recipe he's going to make." This is just the dish, an amazingly tasty chicken salad fired up with a wee bite of curry.

AND IN THIS CORNER, WEIGHING . . .

- About 2½ pounds boneless, skinless chicken thighs or breasts
- Fired-Up Santa Fe Spice (page 5)
- 1+ cup red grapes, cut in half (diced apple could substitute)
- 1+ cup finely diced red onion
- 1+ cup finely diced celery
- ⅓ cup finely chopped pecans or walnuts
- ½ cup mayonnaise
- ½ cup mango chutney (in the Indian food section of your favourite supermarket)
- 2 tablespoons white or red wine vinegar
- 1½ tablespoons mild curry paste—you can adjust to suit your taste
- Lettuce and tomatoes, for serving
- Buns, pita pockets or wraps

LLLEEEEEEEEETTT'SSSSSSS GET READY TO RUMBLE!

And rumble we did. On the first tour I worked with John as my captain, we paired up and were first in to fight a raging trailer home fire. Three years later, on this his final tour, a trailer home across the street from the one we battled was burning. Talk about déjà vu—we were the first in to fight that fire, as well! What are the chances?

Talk about going out in a blaze of glory! The flames were licking at our . . . What am I doing? This is a cookbook, not a memoir. Sorry about that. Anyway, let's season both sides of the chicken with the Fired-Up Santa Fe Spice.

Your best bet's the barbecue—speaking as we were about flames—but you can broil or roast the chicks. Or if you have leftover chicken, use it.

Cut up your fruit, veggies and nuts and set them aside. The amount of each that you add is up to you—that's why I've listed them as "1+ cup." I like to sauté the red onions in a tablespoon or so of butter to soften and sweeten them up a bit, but you can leave them in the raw, if you prefer.

Let's get that sauce happening. In a bowl bring the mayo, mango chutney, wine vinegar and curry paste together with a whisk. At this point you can either trust my curry measure or add the funky paste to taste.

Dice up the chicken and toss it in the sauce to coat. Bring on the fruit/veggie/nut mix and toss, rumble and tumble them together to combine.

Serve the chicks with lettuce and tomatoes on buns, pitas or wraps.

NEW-MEX-FIRE
STEAK SANDWICHES

I know, we discussed steak sandwiches in Fire Hall Cooking. *This time, though, we're really firing them up with a little kick, and, yes, that secret little ingredient, garlic. If you like a Philly steak sandwich, then you've got to try this "on-the-border" version on for size.*

GET DOWN TO THE NEW-MEX RANCH FOR . . .

- Brown sugar
- Fired-Up Santa Fe Spice (page 5)
- Red chili pepper flakes (optional)
- About a ½-pound sirloin steak per person
- Red onion, sliced
- Butter
- Sliced Texas toast bread, or French bread thick-sliced by you!
- Great Garlic Cheese Toast butter (page 189)
- Jalapeno or green peppers, sliced
- Tomatoes, sliced (as if you'd use them whole!)
- Lettuce

OH MAN, HOW'S THIS FOR A SIZZLING SANDWICH?

Combine the brown sugar and Fired-Up Santa Fe Spice. Go for a ratio of 1 to 1. If you want to up the ante a bit—put in a second alarm, so to speak—then toss in a shot of red chili pepper flakes.

Get the rub combo on the meat. Be generous, now. If you're in a rush you can go straight to the Q, but if you have the time . . .

Place the rubbed steak in a nonreactive dish, like a CorningWare or glass lasagna dish, and cover with plastic wrap. Allow the rub to penetrate the meat in the fridge for at least an hour, or even better, 3 hours.

As an option, try marinating the steaks in the **Southwest Chipotle 'n' Lime Marinade** (page 123) instead of the brown sugar and Fired-Up Santa Fe Spice.

Bring the steak out onto the counter to come to room temperature. About a half hour should be good.

Fire up the Q to high. When it's up to operating temperature, get the steaks on there. Do a quick sear of each side, and turn the barbecue down to medium. Cook the steaks to medium-rare.

Meanwhile, sauté the onions in a little butter to soften and sweeten them.

Lightly toast the bread slices. Spread the Great Garlic Cheese Toast butter over each slice and place it on a baking pan. Place under the broiler until lightly browned. Keep an eye on them, now, this is no time for distractions!

Place the steak on a plate and allow it to cool for 5 to 10 minutes.

Slice the steak against the grain; this will get the tenderness happening. Place steak slices on Garlic Cheese Toast and top with onions, peppers, tomatoes and lettuce. Top your New-Mex Carnivore Dagwood with another slice of Garlic Cheese Toast, and you're ready to rock!

CHICKEN FINGERS

The rookie meal is part of a probationary firefighter's rite of passage. A few weeks after arriving at No. 18 station, Marco asked our rookie, Dean, "Hey, when are you going to step up to the plate and give Jeff a break by cooking us a meal? It's your duty as a rookie, you know . . . So, what are you going to make us?"

"Oh, man. Ahhhhh . . . I don't know," Dean replied.

"Well, what's your specialty?" Marco continued. "Come on, everyone has at least one good meal that he makes as his specialty."

After a pregnant pause, the light bulb went off in Super-Rook's head. "Oh, I know!" he exclaimed with a beaming smile. "How about chicken finger sandwiches?"

"Sure, sounds good," I said. "I'm curious. Do you have your own special batter? Do you deep-fry them, pan-fry or bake? Have you got a homemade sauce to go with them, maybe?"

"No, no," Dean replied, shaking his head and waving his arms. "You buy them frozen, the generic brand. Then you bake them in the oven and put them on white bread. They're awesome!"

"What?" our size XXXXL captain Jo fired off. "Have you not been paying attention here in the kitchen the last few weeks? We're not eating that *☞##! Sorry, Jeff, you're back on the hook. He won't be cooking a rookie meal as long as we're both here."

Well, that's one way out of cooking. Truth be known, Dean proved to be an awesome barbecue go-to guy, and every fire hall needs a ringer to barbecue while the head chef prepares the rest of the meal inside. Dean made me look good on countless occasions during our years together at both No. 18 and No. 1.

Here's what I was expecting Dean to say when I asked how he would prepare chicken fingers: "Fresh, juicy chicken coated in a tasty batter. Oh, and don't forget the honey-dill dipping sauce!"

FRESH, NOT FROZEN—IT'S THE FIRE HALL COOKING PROMISE

- Your daily bread
- Chicken tenders or chicken breasts, cut into strips
- Fired-Up Spice (back on page 4)
- All-purpose flour
- 1 egg, beaten with 1 tablespoon water
- Canola or peanut oil

THEY'RE EASY TO MAKE AND SOOOOOOOO MUCH BETTER

Take your favourite bread—I prefer homemade whole-grain—and toss it in the food processor. (Those mini-food processors work great, too.) As an alternative, you can use seasoned Italian or *panko* bread crumbs. Spread the bread shavings on a plate.

Season both sides of the chicken slices with a nice crop dusting of Fired-Up Spice, then dip it through a light coating of flour.

Take the chick strip through the egg wash station and on to the bread crumbs. Set the fingers aside. Not yours, the chicken fingers, man!

Get a large, nonstick frying pan going over medium heat and pour in a light layer of oil. When the oil has reached temperature, carefully get the chicken fingers in there. Fry until nicely browned. Flip and do likewise to the other side.

If you're making a megabatch of fingers and you want to keep them warm, place them on a rack set on a baking pan so any accumulated oil can drip free. Stash in a 200°F oven till you've fried them all up.

Serve à la Dean on bread with lettuce, onion, tomatoes, even crispy bacon slices, with a nice dollop of . . .

NOT YOUR STORE-BOUGHT HONEY-DILL SAUCE, EITHER

- 3 tablespoons whipped salad dressing (¾ cup for a megabatch)
- 1 tablespoon honey (¼ cup for the masses)
- Dill (fresh or dried) to taste

Simply mix the above together in a bowl. If you have any sauce left over, cover and refrigerate.

WHAT'S THE R FACTOR, KENNETH?

Those wonderful cans of expanding foam insulation have not only been used to fill up and seal a firefighter's locker, but one clever co-worker even inserted the nozzle into a firefighter's shaving bag and let 'er rip. The shaving cream, razor, toothpaste, toothbrush, hairbrush and deodorant were all rendered inaccessible by the lock of insulation that bonded the kit bag together.

NUMBING THE AREA

Anbesol is another versatile product. It wasn't designed simply to relieve pain and enable people to eat despite toothaches and canker sores. No, in the hands of a firefighter it's also a treasured gag tool. Anbesol shows up at the fire hall on toothbrushes, coffee cup rims and water-bottle tops. It's always a treat to watch a first-time Anbesol victim in action. He'll lick his lips and examine them by prodding and poking with his tongue and fingers. Rarely will he admit that something is wrong despite the fact that his mouth is contorting to the form of Jean Chrétien's as he speaks in the mushmouth voice of Fat Albert. "Heyba youba guysba . . ."

THAI CHICKEN WRAPS

Firefighter buddy Gale Osterman and I dissected this lunch item in a local restaurant, aided by the server, who whispered the secret ingredient: "Bottled Szechuan peanut sauce." Not to worry, the secret's safe with me! Who would I tell, anyway? So, wrap the taste of Thailand into a funky, rolled-up, Far Eastern flavour treat today. It's easy and deliciously different. You have no choice—you've gotta go for it!

A CHICK, HER BATH AND HER FUNKY FRIENDS

- ¼ cup each soy sauce, peanut oil, brown sugar and fish sauce
- 2 tablespoons chopped fresh ginger
- 1 tablespoon chili-garlic sauce
- 4 good-sized chicken breasts
- 2 coloured sweet peppers—try a mix of red, orange and yellow
- 1 bunch green onions—chop up the greens
- Bean sprouts—definitely give these a wash first
- Bottled Szechuan or Thai peanut sauce—I know, Szechuan is Chinese, not Thai, but geographically and flavourfully speaking, it's close enough
- 8 whole-wheat flour tortillas or wraps

YOU DON'T NEED TO KNOW ORIGAMI TO WRAP THIS ONE UP

Combine the marinade ingredients—being the soy sauce, peanut oil, sugar, fish sauce, ginger and chili-garlic sauce—in a bowl.

Line the chicken breasts up in a Pyrex dish or zip-top freezer bag, and pour on the marinade. Allow the concoction to marinate for 2 hours plus.

Wash and cut up your veggies (as if you wouldn't, anyway).

Barbecue the chicken until happily done. That's 165°F on the meat thermometer.

Allow the chicken to cool for about 5 minutes, then slice into strips.

As an alternate, Gale-inspired method, rather than marinating and Q'ing the chicken, simply cut it into strips and pan-fry, adding the bottled peanut sauce to the chicken to create a ready-to-rock chick-'n'-sauce combination.

Lay your tortillas down and place the chicken, peppers, onions, sprouts and that spicy bottled peanut sauce over top.

Bring up the base—that's the southern tip—of the tortilla (what does "tortilla" translate to in Thai?) about a quarter of the way up, being north, to cover. Now, bring the 2 sides over top and . . . what the???? *Oh, for crying out loud*, you did it again. You loaded your wrap *so full* of ingredients that you can't even close the stupid thing! How many times do I have to tell you? You can always come back for seconds, you know; that's why there are 2 wraps each. Another fine example of firefighters trying to get their money's worth. I've definitely seen this movie before.

VEAL PARMESAN
BUNWICHES

These are so simple and easy, and one of my favourite sandwiches of all time. Oh, sure, if we were to make this from scratch it would be a little time consuming, but we aren't going to go there because I just don't feel like it today. I say let's you and I buy a box of those frozen breaded veal cutlets and leave that messy flour, egg, bread-crumb, pan-frying stuff up to their makers. Give yourself permission to go lazy.

ALL YOU REALLY NEED ARE . . .

- Frozen breaded veal cutlets—preferably Italian style
- Spaghetti sauce—go lazy again; go bottled
- Mozzarella cheese
- Garlic butter—just add minced garlic to soft butter or margarine
- Italian panini buns
- Tomato slices (optional)
- Romaine lettuce (also optional)
- Caesar salad dressing

YOU CAN MAKE THEM SIMPLE SIMON OR DELUXE CAESAR

Read the veal's packaging for cooking instructions. Women, please proceed to the next paragraph. Men, I know following directions is difficult for us to accept, but brands of frozen veal patties vary in their cooking times, so we need to know what the deal is here before we proceed any further. So boys, suck it up and read the directions first!

At half-time (men only: we're not talking about the game, we're talking the I-just-flipped-the-veal-over mark), top each tasty cutlet with a couple of tablespoons of spaghetti sauce and 2 thick slices of mozzarella. Finish baking until the cheese is melted and the veal is cooked through.

Meanwhile, garlic-butter the panini buns, and place them under the broiler.

Locate a veal cutlet on each halved garlic bun. If you want to go the deluxe route, top the veal with tomato slices and romaine lettuce, and put it right over the top by laying down a little creamy Caesar dressing. Viva la decadence!

Still insist on doing this from scratch? Simply follow the **Turkey Scallopini Schnizel** recipe (page 177) and sub in veal cutlets for turkey.

By the way, veal Parmesan is also a great quick dinner served over spaghetti and sauce.

Try these Tex-Mex style. For the sauce, use equal parts salsa and ranch dressing and top with Tex-Mex or Monterey Jack cheese.

I know what you're thinking. What's with Mr. Contradiction here? He gets after the rookie for even mentioning chicken finger sandwiches made from frozen chicken fingers, then he tells us to make veal sandwiches with frozen veal patties. Well, the choice is yours. You can do as I do, or do as I say.

TERIYAKI BURGERS

There's something about that wonderful combination of teriyaki sauce and pineapples that just works, even on a burger. Thinking about a barbecue for friends and looking for something easy, yet fancy? Give this a shot.

GET STARTED WITH . . .

- 4 good-sized chicken breasts

FLAVOUR THE CHICKEN WITH THE TERIYAKI MARINADE

- ¾ cup soya or teriyaki sauce
- ¼ cup vegetable oil
- 1 teaspoon garlic powder
- 1 teaspoon ginger powder
- 3 green onions, chopped small
- 3 tablespoons liquid honey—heat in the microwave if it's crystallized
- Wasabi paste (optional)

BUILD A BETTER, HEALTHIER BURGER WITH . . .

- Pineapple slices (canned sliced pineapple will work)
- Mozzarella or Swiss cheese (consider this optional)
- Whole-wheat burger buns
- Whipped salad dressing or mayo
- Red onions, sautéed in a frying pan with a little butter
- Sliced tomatoes and butter lettuce

AND CUE THE Q

Flatten the breasts slightly with a cast iron frying pan or between the duals on the fire truck. If the breasts are large enough, cut them in half. You're looking for a size that will fit nicely on a bun.

Mix up the marinade and toss it in a zip-top freezer bag. Add the breasts and let them soak up the wacky flavours for 1 to 4 hours to overnight. Give the bag a turn every so often, to be fair to the chicken.

Let's get the barbecue fired up. Grill the breasts over medium heat. When the breasts are ready to flip over to side B, toss the pineapple slices on the grill, as they won't take nearly as long. Cook the breasts until just cooked through. Don't dry them out, now!

You knew to grill the pineapples on both sides, right? I say that rhetorically, of course. You can take the Hawaiians off the Q too.

Top the breasts with cheese slices, close the lid and cook long enough to melt the cheese.

Broil or Q the buns to crisp them up and brown slightly.

Let's build that wacky teriyaki burger beast! Toss a little whipped salad dressing on the bun, followed by the cheesy chicken breast, a barbecued pineapple slice, the fried onions, a slice of tomato and a hit of lettuce.

Feel free to fire this burger up by combining ½ cup mayonnaise with 1 teaspoon or more of wasabi paste and use as a substitute for the dressing.

EGG SALAD SANDWICH?

Alarms are coming into the hall in rapid succession and you haven't had a chance to pick up groceries for lunch yet? If time is tight and your crew is starting to circle the kitchen like vultures, I've got just the solution: a deluxe egg salad sandwich. Deluxe egg salad, you say, old boy? Eggs-actamundo, my friend!

OFF WE GO TO THE HENHOUSE

- 2 healthy tablespoons butter
- 1 cup diced red onion
- 8 large eggs
- Vegetable oil
- 8 strips turkey bacon (yes, you can use pork, if you insist)
- 4 good dollops mayo or whipped salad dressing
- 2 teaspoons prepared mustard
- Kosher salt and freshly ground black pepper to taste
- Homemade multigrain bread, buns, pita bread, or how about focaccia bread sliced through the middle like a pita pocket—oh, yeah!
- Your favourite lettuce—Boston sure is nice

SO, WHAT PART OF THE TURKEY DOES BACON COME FROM, ANYWAY?

Get the "healthy tablespoons" of butter—which may be an oxymoron, depending on who you ask—going in a frying pan. Sauté the red onions until they are nicely caramelized, as in a little browned on the edges.

Get the eggs into a pot of cold water and turn up the heat. Once it reaches a boil, turn down to a simmer and count

10 minutes: 1 one thousand, 2 one thousand, 3 one thousand, 4 one thousand . . . *ready or not, here I come!*

Meanwhile, add a healthy touch of vegetable oil to a nonstick frying pan and bring it up to medium-low heat. Get the turkey bacon in there and flip it often until nicely browned. Yes, the turkey bacon is so lean that it needs a little veggie oil to fry. Dice up the bacon when it's browned and cooled.

Remove the eggs and cool with running cold water. Peel the eggs. They seem to co-operate best if you start peeling them at the top, but there are days when they conspire to frustrate you and resist peeling. Consider a host of conspiracy theories as a reasonable explanation.

Get the peeled eggs into a bowl and mash them up, then add the mayo, mustard and salt and pepper. Bring on the fakin' bacon and onions, and stir 'em through.

Get some toast happening. Lay down a "healthy whack"—yes, it's another oxymoron—of the egg salad and top it off with the lettuce. If you want to BELT up your creation, simply add sliced tomatoes to the mix.

OUT OF THE FIRE AND INTO THE FRYING PAN

Your mission, should you accept it: to make lunch for a crew of 40, including delegates in town to scout out Winnipeg as a possible site for the 2015 World Police and Fire Games. Your goal: to impress them with a menu that reflects local flavour and fire hall cuisine. You'll have four and a half hours. Oh, and one more thing: you'll be on duty at the city's busiest fire hall, and fire and police department brass will be in attendance. Sounds like an episode of Food TV's *Dinner Impossible*, doesn't it? That was the challenge I accepted.

Luckily, I had an ace up my sleeve in crewmate/fire hall chef Lieutenant Al Dawydiuk, an old pro at serving meals to the masses. Al and I decided on the menu. At No. 1 truly anything can happen, so to ease our burden, I roasted and shredded 25 pounds of pork a day ahead.

Game day, 7:30 AM No sooner had I unloaded the groceries than we got a call. Luckily, it was a false alarm. But before we could get out of our gear, we picked up another run, this time for a well-involved house fire. "Just my luck," I thought as we pulled the hose off the truck. Tick, tick, tick . . .

Two hours later, after much shooting of water and swinging of axes, we were back at the hall, tired and stinky. With our time slashed in half, showering was not an option. We split our crew: half worked to get our trucks back on duty, while the rest helped chop veggies. I whipped up dressings for the salads and sauces for the baked beans and pulled pork bunwiches, while Al focussed on his famous perogies. "Don't worry, we're good, we'll make it," Al reassured me.

At 11:15, lunch prep screeched to a halt as the hall emptied with a rapid succession of calls. We didn't get back till noon. We alerted the organizers, and they took a scenic detour as we madly finished prepping.

"Did you get the buns while you were out, Al?"

"I thought *you* were getting the buns, Jeff."

Doh! Panicked, we sent a squad truck for 80 fresh buns, praying they didn't pick up a call.

The delegation arrived and, bunless, we started with the salads. Just as our guests cleaned their plates, the buns arrived. We did it! Sure, we were a tad late, but everyone left with bulging bellies and happy faces. *"The cake, Al, we forgot to serve the cake!"* With that, Al scooped up the "Welcome to Winnipeg" cake and ran it out to the parking lot as the group boarded the bus.

FIRE UP THE SOUP POT!

SOUP STARTERS—A FEW HANDY TIPS FOR THE ASPIRING SOUP NAZI

When you look at a soup recipe, view it as a guide. Sure, you can make it verbatim, but you might not like some of the spice, veggy or meat choices the author made, and you may have some additions to make the soup even better. Have a look in the fridge. There are very few illegal substitutions, unless there's less than two minutes on the clock, you're behind and the substitution will take longer than that to cook. Believe me, I throw in whatever I have lying around, and I've rarely said, "Whooooop, that doesn't go." Develop your own soup sensation.

You'll notice that when it comes to soups, I rarely leave out the big three. *GM, Ford and Chrysler?* No, I mean onions, celery and carrots. This holy trinity truly works together to give soup flavour. The big three are as essential as stock or broth, combining to make the rock-solid foundation of a great soup.

Purées are a great way to naturally thicken soup without resorting to heavy creams, calories and coronaries. It's an absolutely amazing way of blending flavours into one fired-up, knock-your-socks-off soup sensation. Potatoes, squash, root veggies, peppers, onions, garlic—simply roast till soft and add to a soup broth. Cook the veggies for a bit with the liquid, then toss into the blender in batches. Whirl together and *kaboom*, fabulous soup!

The longer soup simmers, the better the flavour. Even better, get the soup on the stove the day before, let it cool in the fridge overnight, and you'll have an incredible flavour meld. As an added bonus, the fat from the meat will rise to the top and congeal. To keep your heart pumping along merrily, simply scoop off the layer of artery clogger.

Not all bouillons are created equal. Some beef bouillons, for example, have an odour akin to the monkey house at the zoo. In fact, at No. 1 station I once spent about an hour combing the cupboards to find what surely must have died. It turned out to be the highly offensive beef bouillon powder. If your stock is missing a little something, try adding some *quality* bouillon. Just keep in mind that when you add bouillon, you're also adding salt. Sure, bouillon or canned broth is a bit of a cheat, but it works, it saves time and it's really all about the end product anyway, so who cares if you take a shortcut on the journey to succulent soup? As I'm currently stationed at a large fire hall with a big crew and lots of calls, we don't have the time to do the boil-soup-bones-for-hours trick, unless we do it a day in advance. Therefore the soups I've been making lately—as you'll soon see—depend on ready-made broths or other foundations to create reasonably quick yet flavourful soups.

So, have you digested all that? Great, then we'll proceed. Level-one stage (a.k.a. ready) your ingredients on the kitchen counter—it's time to fire up the soup pot!

BEEF AND BARLEY SOUP

Here's a tasty beef soup that doesn't require boiling soup bones for hours on end. Instead, we're going to take a shortcut. Not to worry, it won't rob the soup of any flavour. Yes, there's still a time commitment, but it's a reasonable one.

BRING ON THE BEEF

- 2 pounds stewing beef
- 4 tablespoons butter or margarine, divided
- 1 cup red wine (or sherry)
- 4 cups beef broth or consommé
- 1 cup water
- 1 package onion/roasted garlic (or just onion) soup mix
- 28-ounce can diced tomatoes, with juice
- ⅓ cup pearl barley
- 1 large yellow or white onion, diced
- 4 carrots, sliced
- 4 stalks celery, diced
- About ½ pound mushrooms, sliced
- 1 teaspoon kosher salt
- 1 teaspoon Italian seasoning
- Freshly ground black pepper

AND BRING ON THE HEAT

Cut the beef into 1-inch squares, or whatever you consider to be bite sized. Be sure to dry the beef off with paper towels, so it will brown.

Heat 2 tablespoons of the butter or margarine over medium-high heat, and toss in half of the beef. When it's browned, remove, and cook up another batch.

Toss the first batch of beef back in and introduce the wine, broth, water, onion soup mix and tomatoes. Simmer the lot for about 1½ hours, adding the barley to the mix after an hour.

So, what does a firefighter look like after gorging at the fire hall, you ask? Hmmmmmm . . . Well, have you ever seen a picture of a Burmese python after it's swallowed a pig? Huge belly, bloated, can't move . . .

Meanwhile, cut up your veggies. Get a frying pan going over medium heat, toss in the remaining 2 tablespoons butter or margarine, plus the kosher salt and Italian seasoning and a few grinds from the old pepper mill.

Bring on the onion, carrots and celery, and finish up with the mushrooms.

When the veggies are tender-crisp, add them to the soup, and continue to simmer until the veggies are softened, the barley is cooked and the beef is tender. We're talking another half hour, but why stop there? As with most soups or stoups, the longer it stews, the better it gets.

Taste-test your masterpiece, and add salt and pepper, if required.

If you want to create more of a stew than a stoup, then toss the beef in flour before browning. The flour will thicken and therefore super-stoupify the soup!

FIREBALL SOUP

You may know this as Italian Wedding Soup. You know, the odd wedding has taken place at a Winnipeg fire hall, usually at old No. 2, where I started my career, which now serves as our historical society's museum. Wait a second. I used to work in a hall that's now a museum? Man, oh man, it must be time to retire. Anyway, this is a great, flavourful soup that's quick and really quite easy to make.

A MEATBALL FLOAT, YOU SAY?

- 2-pound batch of Fireballs (page 149)
- 3 tablespoons extra-virgin olive oil
- 2 cups diced onions
- 1 cup each diced celery and carrots
- 1 cup sliced zucchini
- 1 teaspoon kosher salt
- 1+ teaspoon Italian seasoning
- Freshly ground black pepper—grind away, my friend
- 8 cups chicken broth
- 4 garlic cloves, run through the press
- ½ small bag baby spinach or bunch of kale, coarsely chopped
- ⅓ cup chopped fresh parsley
- 2 large eggs
- 2 tablespoons Parmesan cheese

GET THE WET STUFF ON THE RED STUFF!

Mix up a batch of Fireballs. The idea here is to make wee little meatballs, no bigger than an inch in diameter, as in bite-sized. If you and your crew have big traps that constantly flap, then size them accordingly.

You can fry the Fireballs in a pan or place them on a greased baking sheet in a 400°F oven for 15 to 20 minutes, until nicely browned and just cooked through. I know, traditional wedding soups cook the meatballs in the soup, but I'm not into grease drippings in our soup.

Meanwhile, let's get a Dutch oven or soup pot going over medium heat. Swirl in a little of that ever-loving extra-virgin olive oil, followed up by the onions, celery, carrots and zucchini. Season the veggies with kosher salt, the Italian seasoning and lots of that freshly ground pepper.

Pour in the chicken broth and add the garlic. Bring our soup to a light boil.

Carefully add the cooked Fireballs and the chopped spinach or kale.

Let the soup simmer for at least 15 minutes, or even longer to bring all of the diverse flavours together. Toss in the chopped parsley.

Here's the big finish. Whisk the eggs together with the Parmesan cheese, and stir the soup in a circular motion while slowly adding the egg mix.

Give it a taste. Add more kosher salt, pepper and Italian seasoning, as needed.

Serve with garlic bread and a Caesar salad, for the full-meal deal.

SQUASH AND PEAR SOUP

This recipe is an example of a soup that came together accidentally from the ingredients I happened to have in the fridge. You see, I'd searched the net for butternut squash soup recipes, and found six to draw ideas from. The problem was that I didn't have enough squash on hand, so I decided to substitute carrots and orange peppers in an attempt to maintain the sweetness of the squash and the colour of the soup. The result? In a word, eureka!

SEE WHAT'S IN YOUR FRIDGE—DON'T BE SHY, TOSS IT IN!

- 2 cups diced carrots
- Orange or red pepper, seeded and cut into quarters (about 2 cups)
- Extra-virgin olive oil
- Kosher salt and freshly ground black pepper
- 1 medium butternut squash, cut in half lengthwise
- 1 head garlic—don't worry, it's going to mellow as we roast it
- ¼ cup butter
- 1 jumbo onion, diced fine
- 2 large celery stalks, diced fine
- 2 large ripe pears (or how about mangos, diced?)
- 2 teaspoons curry powder
- 1 teaspoon dried tarragon
- 4 cups chicken broth
- ½ cup cream—the heavier the better, but 'arf and 'arf is acceptable
- What do ya say, a little cilantro for garnish, perhaps?

ROAST 'EM, FRY 'EM, BOIL 'EM, AND FINALLY PURÉE 'EM!

Fire up the oven to 400°F.

Get the carrots and peppers together in a mixing bowl. Drizzle a light lube of olive oil over top and toss through. Sprinkle in a teaspoon of kosher salt and lots of freshly ground black pepper. Oh, and lube, salt 'n' pepper the cut side of the squash, while you're at it.

Spread the veggies out on a greased baking sheet, with the squash cut-side down. Snip the tips of the garlic head with a knife, toss a little olive oil in among the cloves, and enclose tightly with foil.

Place the garlic packet on the baking sheet as well, and bake the lot for 20 to 30 minutes, or until all of the veggies are soft.

Meanwhile, melt the butter in a large saucepan over medium heat. Get the onion in there with 1 teaspoon kosher salt, and fry until they caramelize (you'll notice a little brown forming around the edges).

Bring the celery in with the onions and cook until soft. The pears are to follow, but not to worry, they won't take long to cook.

Spice it up! Sprinkle in the curry powder and tarragon and . . . *wait a second!* Why, it looks like those arms of yours could use a workout. Don't hold back—go nuts working that pepper mill, my friend!

Stir the spices through the veggies for a couple of minutes to bring on the flavours, and follow up with the chicken broth. Yes, you can use vegetable broth if you're such a die-hard vegetarian that you can't even handle a little chicken broth! Not to worry, we're still friends.

Are the oven-roasted veggies softened yet? If so, plunge the peppers into cold water; this will make it easy for you to peel off their sunburned skins. As for the squash, simply peel the skins or scoop out the goodies.

Introduce the roasted veggies to the rest of the diverse cultures in the melting pot, and bring to a very light boil for about 15 minutes.

If I had any gray matter in my cranium at all, I'd let the soup cool a bit before I go to town with the blender, but I don't, and therefore I likely won't, but you really should. Get the blender out, and fill it up about halfway with ladles full of that rich soup. Cover tightly, place a dishcloth over top and *carefully* pulse the blender to minimize volcanic explosions. I really don't want to come to your house in the fire truck, lights and siren blaring, to help patch you up. So let's pulse it to start, then give 'er until the soup is puréed.

Repeat in batches until—*wait for it*—the final batch. That's when I want you to purée the soup and, while the blender's running slowly, add the cream.

Bring all them batches together in a large saucepan, and stir until your creation is completely combined.

It's taste-test time! If you like your soup fired up, try a dash of cayenne. Or go for another hit of kosher salt, or maybe even a bit of brown sugar if you'd like it a touch sweeter.

For a nice finishing touch, garnish each bowl with a little swirl of cream (say ½ tablespoon) and a sprinkle of chopped cilantro.

Want to make this soup a meal? Why not add some cooked shrimp? How about grilling them on the barbecue first, for a little extra flavour?

TOO MANY COOKS

At No. 1, years back, firefighter Al was making chicken soup. On day one he boiled the bones for hours to make a tasty stock. On day two—game day—he added the vegetables, reserved chicken meat and spices with the care and precision of a master craftsman. Oh, this soup was going to be so good.

What he hadn't factored into the mix was the firefighter's friend, garlic. So firefighter Dan kindly stepped in and dumped a whack of the pungent veggie into the soup. When Al found out his soup had been tampered with, he was enraged. "If I can't have the soup the way I prepared it, then no one can!"

He dumped the huge pot of soup—enough to feed 20 guys—into the floor grate sewer on the apparatus floor. That'll learn ya!

LEMON CHICKEN SOUP

One of my all-time favourite foods has to be barbecued lemon-garlic chicken. Now here's a soup that takes that awesome chicken and fires it up with veggies in a velvety broth. Not velvety like the tacky Elvis painting for sale in the strip mall parking lot— we're talking velvety as in smooth and creamy. It's thick, hearty, tangy and not at all tacky! Go Greek or go home!

CHICKEN WITH RICE REALLY IS NICE

- Lemon-Garlic Marinade (page 6)
- 8 boneless, skinless chicken thighs
- ¼ cup margarine or butter
- 1 cup diced red onion
- 1 cup diced celery
- 1 cup diced carrots
- 1 teaspoon kosher salt
- 1 teaspoon dried oregano
- ½ teaspoon pepper—or use lemon pepper
- 10 cups chicken broth
- 1 large lemon—zest it first, then squeeze the daylights out of it, keeping the juice
- ⅔ cup basmati rice (cut back to ½ cup if using long grain)
- 4 eggs

ESPECIALLY WITH THAT FUNKY TWIST OF LEMON

Pull out the old standby Lemon-Garlic Marinade recipe and make a batch. Place the chicken thighs in a zip-top bag and bring on the bath water. Let 'em soak in the fridge for about 2 to 6 hours.

It's time to show that chick the heat. So either pull out the barbecue or place the chicken on a pan with a rack, and broil until just cooked through.

Meanwhile, fire up a frying pan over medium heat, toss in the butter followed up by the onion, celery, carrots, kosher salt, oregano and lemon pepper. Sauté the veggies until slightly softened.

Meanwhile, meanwhile—yes, we're multi-tasking here in the kitchen—get the broth, lemon zest and lemon juice into a soup pot and bring to a boil.

Toss in the rice and cover the pot. Turn down the heat on the range and simmer our developing soup broth for, say, about 15 minutes.

Now, let's uncover that pot and add the veggies and chicken to the mix. Simmer the chick-'n'-vegified soup for half an hour, to combine the flavours.

Whisk the eggs together. Into a larger bowl, pour a couple of cups of the hot soup. Get that soup circling the bowl with a serious whisking, and let's temper those eggs by adding them to the small soup extraction. Now, whisk the 2 cups of eggified soup back into the big pot and heat through.

Great optional additions to this soup are sautéed asparagus and chopped parsley.

HEART ATTACK SOUP

Well, that's what we kiddingly call it at the fire hall. Oh, I've seen firefighters clutch their chests as they gasp, "That soup is sooo gooooooodddd!" I'm happy to report that Captain/Soupologist Mike Dowhayko has tuned this recipe to save us on stress tests, stents and cardiograms. Why, this soup is so skinny now that it's lobbying to be renamed "The Soup Formerly Known as Heart Attack Soup."

PULL OUT THE PADDLES

- 6 Yukon gold or red potatoes, cut into bite-sized pieces (about 6 cups)
- 2 teaspoons salt
- 8 cups chicken broth
- 3 pounds hot Italian sausage—turkey's your lean sausage choice
- 3 tablespoons butter or margarine
- 1 jumbo onion, diced
- 3 celery stalks, diced as well
- 3 carrots, sliced fairly thin
- Kosher salt and freshly ground black pepper to taste
- 1 tablespoon Italian seasoning
- 4 cups half-and-half cream (or lower-fat milk, if desired)
- 1 large or 2 small bunches kale (or spinach, as a pinch hitter)

EVERYONE CLEAR!

If you have 3 range burners ready to roll, then it's time to multi-task. Let's pull out the big soup pot, toss in the taters and pour in just enough water to cover. Better add a couple of teaspoons of salt, as well.

Bring the spuds to a boil. Of course, you'll have to find someone with a boil to bring them to. Ahh, better make that turn the heat on that pot and boil the spuds 'n' water until the potatoes just start to become tender. To keep them from overcooking, add the chicken broth to the spuds 'n' water when they're done—no draining of water required.

Meanwhile, get the sausage meat into a frying pan; break it up into small bits, and brown it. Drain off all the fat and watch that calorie count plummet.

In a separate frying pan—or the same pan, if you've finished the sausages and time isn't an issue, but range space is—add the butter and sauté the onion, celery and carrots until tender. A little salt and pepper plus a hit of that mandatory kitchen-issue Italian seasoning will help the flavour cause.

When the 3 separate range issues are settled, intro the sausage meat and veggies into the tater broth, add the cream—*does that make it Cream of Coronary Soup now, Jeff?*—and bring our soup to a light boil.

Pull the kale off its stems, tear it into small pieces, and toss the greenery into the mix. The soup sensation's ready when the kale is tender.

What are you doing? There's no need to pull out the defibrillator. A little salt, pepper and fresh bread is all you're going to need now.

Got a hungry crew? This is a big batch of soup that will easily feed 8.

MEGASTRONI
SOUPASAURUS

If it were brothy, it would be minestrone, but this soup's so thick it has to be Megastroni Soupasaurus. This is an easy, delicious soup with a nice, spicy twist.

YOUR SHOPPING LIST

- 28-ounce can tomato sauce—I like something zesty like Hunt's
- 28-ounce can diced tomatoes
- 4 cups chicken broth—be health conscious; insist on sodium-reduced broth, and then simply add tons of salt . . . just kidding!
- 1 teaspoon Worcestershire sauce
- 6 cups water
- 3 tablespoons butter
- 4 garlic cloves—or more! Make it mega-garlic-stroni!
- 1 jumbo onion, diced
- 5 each carrots and celery stalks, diced
- 1 sweet red, orange or yellow pepper, diced
- About ¼ pound mushrooms, cut into Ts
- 1 small zucchini, sliced
- 2 teaspoons kosher salt
- Freshly ground black pepper to taste
- 3 teaspoons Italian seasoning (or about 3 tablespoons fresh chopped basil or oregano)
- 2 pounds Italian sausages—hot or mild
- 2 19-ounce cans romano, navy or kidney beans, or a combination
- 1 cup chopped fresh parsley
- Approximately ¾ pound cheese tortellini

AND YOUR TO-DO LIST

Get the tomato sauce, diced tomatoes, chicken broth, Worcestershire sauce and water into a mighty soup pot and bring it to a light boil.

Meanwhile, toss the butter into a large frying pan over medium-high heat and stir-fry the garlic, onion, carrots, celery, peppers, mushrooms and zucchini until tender-crisp. Dust the lot with kosher salt, lots of pepper and the Italian seasoning. The veggies are set to take a bath, so toss them into the soup.

Prick the sausages and boil them in a separate pot of water until fat accumulates on the surface. Remove, rinse and cut the sausages into bite-sized pieces.

Stir-fry the sausage bites in a frying pan until well browned. Drain off any fat. Add the tasty sausage nuggets to the soup, along with the beans and parsley. Reduce the soup to a simmer and cook until all of the veggies are tender.

In yet another separate pot, this time featuring boiling water, cook the tortellini till done. If you think all the soup will go in a sitting—as in the fire hall—then add the pasta to the soup just before serving. If this is a multi-day soup, however, place the tortellini in each serving bowl and place the soup over top. Failure to do so will result in swollen tortellini the size of orbiting satellites and soup devoid of liquid. Oh, well, you could always add water or serve it as an entrée.

Give the soup a final seasoning check. Oh, yeah, that's got a little zip!

RED-HOT-AND-SOUR
SOUP

It's been my experience that about half the adult and about 100 percent of the child population hates this concoction. I, on the other hand, am in the 50 percentile that absolutely loves hot-and-sour soup, and order it often—or at least I used to. Now I simply make it myself at home. Here's how.

SOME REQUIRE A STRAY FROM THE BEATEN PATH

- 6 cups chicken broth—I'll even go 4 cups chicken and 2 cups beef broth
- 2 tablespoons soy sauce
- 2 tablespoons chili-garlic sauce—wimpy starts at 1; try 3+ for fire!
- ½ pound lean pork or chicken breast, cooked, cut in small strips
- About ¼ pound shiitake mushrooms, stems removed
- 14-ounce can straw mushrooms (in your grocer's Asian food section)
- 1 tablespoon peanut oil
- 1 yellow, orange or red (but, please, not green) pepper, cut into strips
- 1 tablespoon ginger paste (or finely chopped fresh ginger)
- ¼ cup + 2 tablespoons seasoned rice vinegar
- ½ cup bamboo shoots in strips (canned, also in the Asian section)
- 3 tablespoons cornstarch combined with 3 tablespoons water
- 6 ounces firm plain tofu, sliced in strips (or cooked shrimp, whole)
- 2 eggs, lightly beaten
- 1 teaspoon toasted sesame oil
- Kosher salt and freshly ground black pepper, to taste
- 1 bunch green onions, sliced
- Fresh (never dried) cilantro, chopped up

BUT IT WON'T TAKE LONG TO GET THIS FUNKY SOUP ROLLIN'

Place the broth in a big old stockpot and bring it to a simmer. Introduce the soy sauce and chili-garlic sauce. Mix it around and toss in the pork or chicken and the mushrooms, and simmer for 10 minutes.

Meanwhile, get a frying pan going over medium heat, add the peanut oil and stir-fry the pepper strips for a minute to slightly soften them.

Get the ginger paste, rice vinegar, bamboo shoots and pepper strips into the funky broth and simmer the tangy blend for, say, about 5 minutes.

Fire the soup up so it's just starting to boil, and stir in the cornstarch and water blend, to thicken and give your soup some body.

Return the soup to a simmer and toss in the tofu and/or shrimp, and carefully pour the eggs in a steady stream over the surface of the soup.

Allow the eggs a few seconds to set up and then stir in the sesame oil.

As per standard soup-making operations, salt and pepper to taste.

Serve each bowl garnished with sliced green onions and cilantro.

Serves 8 . . . but that's only because half the people won't touch it.

ROASTED BROCCOLI AND
CHEESE SOUP

Don't you just love broccoli with cheese sauce? What a surefire combination! So, logic and food chemistry dictate that this combo should work in a soup. Let me see here, carry the 3, add the broth plus the spices . . . hey, the equation works! This is an easy soup you can make in about 45 minutes.

THIS BROC IS READY TO ROCK

- 8 cups broccoli florets—about 2 large heads, broken up
- Extra-virgin olive oil
- Kosher salt and freshly ground black pepper
- 4 tablespoons butter, divided by 2
- 1 cup finely diced yellow onion
- 1 cup finely diced celery
- 4 garlic cloves, minced
- 2 tablespoons all-purpose flour
- 2 cups milk
- Cayenne to taste
- 1½ cups grated cheddar cheese—I like that Tex-Mex blend, myself
- 3 cups chicken broth

ROAST THOSE LITTLE TREES AND TAKE THEM TO THE MULCHER

Fire up that oven to 425°F.

Place the broccoli florets in a mixing bowl. Toss with just enough olive oil to lightly coat. A teaspoon of kosher salt and a few grinds from the pepper mill should be added to the mix, as well.

Get the broc laid out on a baking sheet and roast it until tender, tossing once or twice along the way. This could take 15 to 20 minutes.

While that's roasting, bring a Dutch oven or soup pot to medium heat on the range. Toss in 2 tablespoons of the butter and follow up with the onion, celery and garlic. Add a dash of salt and pepper and cook until very soft. Remove the lot from the pot and set aside.

Turn the soup pot down a bit and add the remaining 2 tablespoons of butter. Once the butter is melted, add the flour and whisk it in. Slowly pour in the milk, whisking as you go, to combine it all. A little salt couldn't hurt, and, hey, I like to add a dash of cayenne to fire it up. Get the cheese in there, melt, whisk and presto! There's our cheese sauce!

Bring the broccoli to the blender. Toss half the broccoli in with half the onion mixture plus 1½ cups of the chicken broth. Purée and repeat with the broccoli, onion mix and chicken broth you've got left.

Let's bring it all together. Pour the 2 batches of puréed veggies into the Dutch oven with the cheese sauce. Stir it all together and heat through.

Perform the obligatory final seasoning of salt and pepper, and soup up!

Since the fire hall is known as Carnivore's Corner, you can save face by adding 1 pound diced ham or boiled or pan-fried sliced Italian sausages. Yes, we've got all the food groups in attendance now!

ROCKIN' REUBEN'S
A SOUP?

The first time I made this at the fire hall, the crew were highly skeptical. "He must mean Reuben sandwiches with soup, not Reuben soup," they thought. As much as I pleaded for their patience and trust, they just couldn't imagine this soup working. But once the initial big slurp of soup hit their palates, they were sold. Rockin' Reuben, the fire hall staple, isn't simply a sandwich anymore.

REUB'S HEADIN' FOR THE HOT TUB

- ¼ cup butter
- 1 cup finely chopped yellow or white onion
- 1 cup each finely chopped celery and carrot
- Kosher salt and its sidekick, freshly ground black pepper
- 2 tablespoons flour—more if you're going the skinny route
- 4 cups beef broth
- ¾ pound, or more, corned beef, chopped
- 1 cup sauerkraut, drained completely, please
- 2 cups half-and-half cream (you can go as thin as 2%, if need be)
- 2 tablespoons Dijon mustard
- 1 cup grated Swiss cheese to start, plus more for topping the . . .
- Pumpernickel bread
- Russian dressing—for a tasty toast-topping treat

BEFORE BASKING UNDER THE HOT, HOT BROILER . . .

Get a large saucepan, like a Dutch oven, going over medium heat and toss in the butter, followed up by the onion, celery and carrot.

Add a teaspoon or so of kosher salt and some freshly ground black pepper to wake up the veggies' taste buds. Fry God's good earthly produce until tender.

Dust the veggies with the flour. If you're using 2% milk, boost the flour to about 3 tablespoons to make up for the skinny cow. Slowly add the beef broth to the veggies, giving it a stir as you go, so the flour gets a chance to work its thickening magic.

Let's get the corned beef, sauerkraut, cream, Dijon mustard and Swiss cheese in there, and reduce the soup to a simmer. The longer it simmers, the more pronounced the flavour, but this one is edible early, say about ½ hour in. Great for a busy day at the fire hall.

Toast the pumpernickel and top it with a healthy dose of Russian dressing and a nice layer of grated Swiss cheese as a grand finale mountaintop. Place the toast under the broiler to melt the cheese.

Pour Reub into big bowls and place the cheesy toast on top, French-onion-soup style—well, except that there are far fewer onions but still lots of, how do you say, *je ne sais quoi?*

TACO CHICK SOUP

This is a great fire hall soup because, save the marinating time, it comes together in a flash but tastes like it's been simmering for hours. It's so flavourful that you likely won't even need to do the standard salt-and-pepper tune-up before serving, as the salsa takes care of all the seasoning you'll ever need. Olé!

ROUND UP THE GANG

- 2 pounds chicken or turkey thighs
- Cuban Lime Marinade (page 6)
- Butter
- 1 medium or ½ jumbo onion, diced
- 2 celery stalks, diced
- 2 carrots, sliced thin
- Kosher salt and freshly ground black pepper
- 1 orange or red pepper, also diced
- 4 cups chicken broth
- 1 medium jar (3 cups) salsa—I love the smoky chipotle salsa
- 19-ounce can kidney or black beans, rinsed
- 11-ounce can peaches-and-cream corn
- Sour cream, cilantro and taco chips, for garnish

AND TAKE A CHICK TO LUNCH

Marinate the chicken in Cuban Lime Marinade for at least 4 hours, but preferably overnight, to maximize flavours. If you're Speedy Gonzalez, then simply season with a healthy shot of **Fired-Up Santa Fe Spice** (page 5) instead.

Barbecue or broil the thighs over medium heat until cooked through.

Cut the chicken into bite-sized pieces. You measured everyone's mouths ahead of time, didn't you?

Toss the butter into a soup pot over medium heat and get the onions in there, frying them up until caramelized, or, in blue-collar layman terms understood best by people like me, slightly browned.

Pull the celery and carrots from the on-deck circle and toss them in. Season the veggies with salt and pepper and fry until tender-crisp.

The peppers are wanting in on the veggie-fest, so acquaint them with the others and fry briefly, just long enough to slightly soften and flavourize.

Pour in the chicken broth, salsa, beans and corn. Bring your soup to a simmer and get the cooked chicken in there to round out the line-up.

Heat the soup through for at least 15 minutes to combine the flavours—as usual, the longer the meld, the better the soup will be.

Ladle the soup into bowls. Place a dollop of sour cream in the centre of each bowl, stand the taco chips around the inside rim and sprinkle chopped cilantro over top. Talk about presentation! Is this a high-class Tex-Mex restaurant you're running here, or what?

WITH THE FUNNY NAME

Mulligluttony? No. Uhhh . . . Mullet-Tony? Uummm . . . no. Milli Vanilli? Mully-What's-Its-Face? Oh, I can never remember the name of this soup. I guess I'll have to look it up. Let's see . . . oh, yeah, mulligatawny, that's the one. There are many versions of this succulent soup with a hint of curry. Here's mine.

THE FUNKY INGREDIENTS

- 3 tablespoons butter
- 4 garlic cloves—press 'em, hack 'em, let's attack 'em
- 3 tablespoons finely diced fresh ginger
- 4 cups diced onion (about 2 large onions)
- 4 stalks each celery and carrots, diced (about 2 cups of each)
- Kosher salt and freshly ground black pepper
- 2 tablespoons curry powder—don't use the cheap generic stuff
- 1 teaspoon ground cumin—again, quality does make a difference
- 8 cups chicken broth
- About 4 cups cooked chicken or turkey
- 2–3 Granny Smith or other tart apples (or ripe mangos)
- 14-ounce can coconut milk
- Whatever else you're keen on throwing in (do a fridge check while I wait)

AND THE FUNK-I-FIED METHOD

Warm up the butter in a wok over medium heat. Don't brown it.

Work in the garlic and ginger to flavour the butter, but only briefly.

Get the onion, celery and carrots in there, and dust the veggies with 2 teaspoons kosher salt, a few good grinds from the old pepper mill, the curry powder and the cumin. Mix the spicy spices through the veggies.

When the former ground dwellers are slightly softened, pour in about half of the broth and fire up the heat. Boil until the veggies are very soft.

Working in batches—and yes, you really do deserve stunt pay here—ladle the soup into a blender until about half full. Place the lid on the blender with a towel held over top. Now turn your head, wince and *carefully* pulse the blender until the veggies are smooth. Jeff the Know-It-All Chef has burned himself on this more than once, so watch yourself, please!

When all is blended, add it to the remaining soup broth, and bring on the meat, apples or mangos and coconut milk. Heat it all through.

Fine tune the mulligatawny with salt and pepper to boost the flavour quotient.

Consider this your soup base. You can add shrimp, roasted broccoli, red peppers, sautéed zucchini or whatever veggie, meat or seafood suits you— a.k.a. whatever items you need to get rid of in the fridge. Food overboard! The best-before date is approaching quickly—let's use it all up!

Serve your creation over a bowl of cooked basmati rice. If you like, garnish our buddy mulligatawny with chopped cilantro and slices of lime.

SEASON AS YOU GO

I can't stress this enough: season as you go. If you're, say, browning ground beef or sautéing vegetables, give them a little shot of kosher or sea salt, freshly ground black pepper, **Fired-Up Spice** (page 4) or whatever herbs or spices you feel would complement the dish. Seasoning as you go brings out the natural flavour of the ingredients. That may sound like a contradiction, but it's true. If you don't believe me, try a slice of tomato without seasoning. Then try a slice of tomato with a little kosher salt and freshly ground black pepper. See, I told you!

I didn't always cook with kosher salt, but from the day I first gave it a go, I haven't looked back. Buy a box (be forewarned, it is more expensive) and compare it to regular table salt. Taste it raw. Table salt is bitter and often leaves an unpleasant aftertaste. Kosher salt is smooth, without the bitterness. Kosher salt also has large, coarse grains, making it easy to sprinkle.

When it comes to baking, however, I prefer to use sea salt. Again, it's worth the taste test. Sea salt kicks table salt's butt, too.

You may need to add 50 to 100 percent more kosher salt, as it's less salty than table salt. When it comes to sea salt, however, I use the identical amount.

One pet peeve I have is when people don't taste the food I've prepared before seasoning. I always spice the food I make, so chances are the meal doesn't need another shot of salt or pepper. I have no issue with those who try it and then add salt, pepper, hot pepper sauce or other condiments to suit their personal tastes. But please, taste first.

I remember working as a visitor at No. 5 station and being asked to make lunch. I agreed, and prepared a giant batch of hamburger soup for the crew. The moment Kevin sat down, he squirted about a cup of ketchup into his steaming bowl of soup. One of the other firefighters got on his case right away. "Come on, Kevin, Jeff's our guest. He does us a favour and makes lunch for everyone, and you offend him by pouring ketchup all over it."

"I don't need to try it," Kevin answered. "Hamburger soup is always better with ketchup."

Bottom line, you can do like Kevin and take my advice with a grain of salt, or make the switch to kosher and sea salt today. Come on, toss that table salt over your shoulder. It's good luck, you know!

Note: Not recommended for people with hypertension, heart conditions, those having trouble getting into their jeans, bodybuilders taking truckloads of creatine who are already worried about water retention, and four-pack-a-day smokers whose taste buds wouldn't know the difference anyway. Individual results may vary.

SUREFIRE SALADS

JUST CALL 911

I'm honoured when fellow fire chefs call during meal prep and ask for advice. Even though I, too, am in the midst of getting a meal together, I'm always happy to share my opinion. The guys I work with say, "Hey Jeff, you've got another Food 911 call."

"Go ahead, caller, you're on the air," I say with a chuckle.

I'm certainly amused when someone calls Food 911 and asks something along these lines (yes, this was an actual call): "Yeah, Jeff, I'm making your Lemon Poppyseed Salad, and I was wondering . . . we're out of red wine vinegar, we don't have any poppy seeds and we're shy of lemon juice, as well. What do you suggest?"

"Well, if you want to make this recipe, I suggest you go to the store."

On another occasion a firefighter called three-quarters of the way into the cooking time to ask how long to cook the roast he was preparing. The problem was he was using a but-I-got-it-on-sale blade chuck pot roast for a recipe that called for a premium oven roast, and dinnertime was rapidly approaching. I sure wish I could have intervened before that beef became shoe leather.

Though I apparently missed the ceremony, it appears I've been appointed Recipe Troubleshooter and Damage Control Officer. I'm always up for a challenge, so even if it's not my recipe, I'll research the problem and learn in the process. If I happen to be the recipe's author, however, I could also be the scapegoat. "I talked to Jeff, and he said it would work. Don't blame *me*, it's a recipe from *his* book."

Good thing God blessed me with thick skin and a sense of humour. I now see where a cookbook author can be credited for a well-received dish or blamed for a flop—without consideration given to misinterpreted directions or illegal substitutions.

Do feel free, however, to make substitutions to the produce found in this section. If a favourite vegetable or fruit is in season and bursting with flavour, give it a try. You have my permission. If you stray way off course, though, do me a favour and sign the waiver absolving me of any responsibility.

Surefire Salads is slotted between soups and main dishes because salads straddle both lunch and dinner at the fire hall. On a hot summer day, a salad served with barbecued meat or seafood for lunch may be just what the crew ordered. For dinner, no matter the time of year, a salad is a great way to round out a meal, especially as we strive to eat a healthier diet. So, let's go, herbivores, and fire up the big, green, environmentally friendly salad machine!

CAESAR SALAD
FROM SCRATCH

Here's a lighter take on the bottled, creamy, calorie-counter version of Caesar salad dressing that's still full of brash, I-love-garlic taste, aftertaste and, best of all, odoriferous aura. Garlic detoxifies—so it's good for you!

PULL OUT THE FOLLOWING

- 3 anchovy fillets (they come in a flat tin can, just like sardines)
- Milk
- 1 egg—coddling instructions to follow
- ½ tablespoon Dijon mustard—this is what holds our dressing together
- ½ tablespoon Worcestershire sauce—made from more anchovies
- 3-4 garlic cloves, chopped or pressed
- 1 teaspoon Louisiana-style hot sauce
- ½ teaspoon kosher salt
- ¾ tablespoon freshly ground black pepper
- ¼ cup fresh-squeezed lemon juice—no seeds, please
- 1 heaping tablespoon mayonnaise
- ¼ cup extra-virgin olive oil
- 1 head romaine lettuce, washed and spun dry, please
- Grated Parmesan cheese, to taste
- Red onion, in slices or rings
- Croutons—purchased, or better yet, slice up a baguette, spread garlic butter on both sides of each slice and fry or broil to brown
- Bacon bits (well, so much for the low-fat angle! Consider them optional)
- Lemon pepper (optional)

AND FIRE UP THE BLENDER

Soak the anchovies in just enough milk to cover. Let stand for about ½ hour, to absorb any of the extra fishiness from the fillets. Drain.

Place the egg in a greased microwaveable bowl. Beat with a whisk. Cook the egg in 10-second intervals, stirring after each radiation blast, until the egg just starts to solidify in places. We want to keep the egg liquid, yet not totally raw—a food chemist would say about 120°F. Alternatively, I'm told that you can coddle an egg by placing it in rapidly boiling water for about 45 seconds. This is the de-salmonella process.

Get out the blender. Toss in the anchovies, Dijon, Worcestershire, the all-important garlic, hot sauce, salt, pepper, lemon juice, mayo and the previously discussed coddled, sorta-cooked egg.

Get the blender rocking and processing, and while it's running, carefully pour in the olive oil to emulsify—in other words, bring it all together.

Taste the dressing and adjust with salt and pepper, if necessary. Also, if you find the dressing too tart—and remember, it should have a lemony edge—then simply add a little more mayo to smooth it out.

Toss the romaine, Parmesan, onion, croutons and bacon bits (if using) together with the dressing in a bowl. Season with lemon pepper, if desired.

FEELIN'-THE-HEAT

ASIAN NOODLE SALAD

Yeah, I know, that chili-garlic sauce does show up in a lot of my recipes. Guilty as charged. But you know us firefighters, our favourite colour is red and we are asked to handle a little heat now and then, so it only figures.

IT'S THE DRESSING THAT PACKS THE ZZZZZIIPPP!

- ⅓ cup soy sauce
- ¼ cup rice wine vinegar
- ¼ cup peanut oil
- Juice and zest (that's the finely grated rind) of 1 lime
- 2 tablespoons chili-garlic sauce (you can adjust it to suit your taste)
- 2 tablespoons white sugar
- 2 tablespoons toasted sesame oil
- About a 1-inch piece of ginger, grated up well, now
- 4 garlic cloves, minced, pressed or otherwise abused
- A few turns from the old pepper mill

IT'S THE VEGGIES THAT GIVE THE SALAD SUCH COLOUR!

- 10 ounces rice noodles (or linguine)
- 2 carrots, grated
- 1 red or yellow pepper, cut into strips
- ¼ pound mushrooms, sliced into Ts
- 1 bunch green onions
- Chopped cilantro

JUST A TOUCH OF BACK HEAT TO WARM YOU INSIDE

Combine the dressing ingredients and get them off to the fridge so all those eclectic ingredients can funkify . . . that's cooking jargon for *come on, you guys, get together and make lovingly beautiful flavours together.*

Boil the pasta. If you're using the more traditional rice noodles, then simply soak them in boiling water until they're soft. Soaking directions should be printed on the back of the noodle package in Thai.

Drain the softened noodles in a colander and run them under cold water. The idea here is not only to rinse and cool the noodles, but also to drain off as much water as humanly possible.

Chop, grate and in general prepare the veggies for happy salad living.

Bring it all together, man! Place the pasta and vegetables in a bowl, stir up the dressing and pour over top. Toss it like you mean it before serving.

I like to get the salad ready early and let it set up in the fridge while I prepare the rest of the meal. This salad only gets better with time.

Great as a side salad with **Thai Fish Cakes** (page 105) or **Thai-Becued Salmon** (page 102).

HONEY-LIME SALAD

Spinach salad with fruit is a big favourite of mine, and here's yet another twist on this burgeoning trend. It's a little bit different, just enough to offer variety and to keep guests guessing what you have up your sleeve next.

WE'RE MAKING ALMONDS INTO CANDY

- ¼ cup slivered almonds, candied—relax, I'll tell you how to do it
- 1 heaping tablespoon butter
- 1 heaping tablespoon brown sugar

GET THE DRESSING TOGETHER IN A BLENDER AND BLEND

- ⅓ cup peanut oil
- ¼ cup seasoned rice vinegar
- ¼ cup liquid honey (nuke it if you need to)
- 2 tablespoons smooth Dijon mustard
- 1 tablespoon Everybody Goes Pesto (page 144) (you can sub cilantro in the unlikely event that you don't have any pesto on hand)
- 2½ teaspoons lime juice
- ½ teaspoon kosher salt
- A few good grinds from the old pepper mill

GET THE SALAD TOGETHER IN A BOWL AND TOSS

- 10-ounce bag washed-and-ready-to-go spinach leaves
- 3 kiwis, cut into small pieces
- Your choice of mandarin orange segments, mangos, nectarines, peaches, strawberries, bananas—actually, any sweet fruit works well in this salad
- Half a small red onion, cut into long strips

WHAT DID YOU SAY ABOUT CANDYING THE ALMONDS?

Bring a frying pan up to medium-low heat. Add the butter and toss in the almonds. Follow up with the brown sugar. Better keep the almonds moving, so they don't burn.

Once the almonds are light brown, get 'em out of the heat, place them on a plate and get them into the fridge. The almonds will no doubt all stick together, so you'll have to let them cool before breaking them up just before serving them.

There's an added benefit to squirrelling them away in the fridge. It keeps them hidden from the guests/family members/salivating firefighters hovering in the kitchen looking for something to snack on. Keep them out of sight and out of mind. Just don't forget about them yourself.

If the salad is tossed—and it had better be by now; I've warned you once already—simply add the almonds to the mix and pour the dressing over top. Toss, toss, toss and serve.

JEFF-THE-CHEF SALAD

Here's a great, easy, everyday salad that goes with just about anything. It expands easily to feed a crowd, and you can make as many substitutions of your favourite ingredients as you like. There are no rules—just get out your trusty food guide and do your best to cover as many food groups as possible. Whether you're at home or at the fire hall, or looking for a dish to take to a potluck dinner, you'll be hard pressed to find someone who doesn't love this salad.

BLAME THE VEGETABLES FOR THE GREENHOUSE EFFECT

- 1 head iceberg or Boston lettuce (if you're feeding a crowd and you'll be buying more than one head of lettuce anyway, why not mix it up with a variety of lettuces? Iceberg, Boston, romaine, red leaf, etc.)
- 2 large tomatoes, sliced
- 1 cucumber, sliced
- 1 red onion, sliced into slivers
- 1 or 2 carrots, sliced thin
- ½ pound Black Forest or honey ham—you can use sliced or, better yet, buy a large solid chunk and dice it into cubes
- 6 slices turkey bacon, fried crisp, drained and chopped fine
- 4 eggs, hard-boiled and sliced
- Your favourite cheese—I like Swiss, but cheddar is traditional

WHAT'S THE DRESSING?

- ¾ cup prepared whipped dressing or mayonnaise
- ⅓ cup sugar
- ¼ cup white vinegar

YOU KNOW, THIS SOUNDS LIKE A DELUXE BLT IN A BOWL

Wash and spin dry that lettuce, rip or chop it into bite-sized pieces and prepare the rest of the ingredients.

Once the hot stuff is as cool as the cucumbers, get your teammates into a bowl—I'm talking the ingredients here, not your fellow firefighters or family members.

Whisk the dressing together and toss with the salad until coated the way you like it. I love dressing, and according to my wife, I overdo it all the time, which is why I'm leaving it up to you and she's considering leaving me. Ah, but I jest. (I just hope I can hang onto my pension.)

As an optional dressing—I'm talking about the one I grew up on—try **Mom D's Salad Dressing** (coming up next in the program) thinned out a bit with a splash of buttermilk or regular milk. It's delicious stuff!

SALAD DRESSING

Here's another Derraugh family favourite. This recipe dates back to the 1960s and a leaflet passed along by our milkman in the "You can whip our cream, but you can't beat our milk!" dairy truck. It's great on a tossed green salad—with hard-boiled eggs, of course, and why not some bacon, to boot?—or as a sandwich topping in place of mayonnaise or whipped salad dressing.

YOU CAN'T TELL THE PLAYERS WITHOUT A RECIPE

- 4 eggs
- 1 cup sugar
- 2 tablespoons flour
- 1 teaspoon salt
- 2 teaspoons dry mustard
- Pinch cayenne
- ¼ cup water
- ¾ cup distilled white vinegar
- 1 tablespoon butter
- 1 cup light sour cream

HERE'S THE BATTING ORDER—WHISKER UP!

Beat the eggs together in a heavy 1-quart pot—a.k.a. a saucepan.

In a bowl, combine the sugar, flour, salt, dry mustard and cayenne.

Get back into the cupboards and dig out another bowl and combine the water and vinegar.

Mix the wet into the dry ingredients and stir with a whisk.

Let's bring that newly formed combo into the pot with the eggs. Whisk 'em together, then get the heat fired up to medium and bring to a low boil. Once you're there, turn the heat down to simmer and stir constantly with that handy whisk until you get a pudding-like consistency.

Remove the pot from the heat and add the butter. Give it a whisk!

When your combination has cooled down, serve as vanilla pudding for a wildly hilarious practical joke. I mean, add the sour cream.

Store in a plastic container in the fridge. This fits perfectly into a large yogurt container, providing of course that the yogurt has been removed first. You may want to eat the yogurt rather than dump it out. I mean, really, it is the "green" thing to do.

If you're using Mom D's as a salad dressing, thin with milk or even buttermilk until you reach the consistency you're after.

If you happen to be in possession of my rookie debut, *Fire Hall Cooking with Jeff the Chef*, this dressing makes an awesome pinch-hitting effort for the whipped salad dressing called for in the Warm Mushroom Spinach Salad.

PEACHES 'N' PECANS
ROMAINE

As you may already be painfully aware, I'm a huge fan of fruit-based salads, and here's yet another of my many faves. As per the Tossed Salad Accord of 1946, *there is always room for the legal substitution of players. So whether it's in season, out of season and canned, a favourite fruit, a colourful fruit or whatever fruit you happen to have in the fridge, get God's bounty into the game. As long as you have the starters in there, too, you're a surefire bet to win big—in fact, Vegas has you down as a 21-point favourite!*

TOSS IT TOGETHER
- 1 head romaine lettuce
- ½ cup pecans (decadent) or walnuts (more reasonably priced)
- 1 tablespoon butter
- 2 tablespoons brown sugar
- Fresh or canned peaches (or mangos, oranges, strawberries, kiwis)
- Craisins—those trendy dried-up cranberries in a bag

DRESS IT UP
- 1 cup canola oil
- ½ cup white sugar
- 6 tablespoons white wine vinegar—balsamic is a nice touch, too!
- 1 teaspoon kosher salt
- 1 teaspoon dry mustard
- ½ small red onion, chopped (about ⅔ cup)

AND TAKE IT ANYWHERE

Wash the lettuce and give it the spin cycle in the salad spinner. Remember not to overload the spinner, to yield only the driest and cleanest of lettuces. Blast away that dirt, my friend! Get out the pressure washer if you have to.

The pecans (or walnuts) have asked to be candied, so let's do that by melting the butter in a frying pan over medium heat, adding the nuts and dusting them with the brown sugar. Toss the nuts as you go, to keep them from burning, and get them off the heat when glazed.

While the nuts cool, slice up the fruit. Peaches 'n' Pecans is just a guide; use whatever combination of fruit happens to turn your wheels.

Toss the romaine, fruit, nuts, Craisins and dressing together in a bowl.

As far as what to serve with this? Well, the options are endless; this salad is so flexible that it goes with just about anything. Well, maybe not haggis.

CAESAR SALAD

My families at home and at work love Caesar salad, but I must admit I was getting tired of making the same old Caesar over and over, so I decided to throw a curveball and introduce the Southwest to this complacent Roman emperor. Yes, it means a few line-up changes, but the result is a grand slam home run. Chipotle peppers throw the heat, lime juice pinch-hits for lemon, Monterey Jack was picked up in a trade for Parmesan, and those sweet corn bread croutons are battin' cleanup. So rosin up the fork, step up to the plate and give this New Mexican a ride.

HAIL THE MIGHTY CAESAR SANCHEZ

- 1 batch Chili Corn Bread (page 205)—about 4 cups cubed corn bread
- ¼ cup melted butter
- 1 head romaine lettuce
- ⅓ cup bottled Caesar dressing
- ⅓ cup sour cream
- ⅓ cup whipped salad dressing or mayonnaise
- Juice of 1 large lime (or about 3–4 tablespoons lime juice)
- 4–6 garlic cloves, pressed or minced
- 1 or more chipotle peppers in adobo sauce (in your grocer's Mexican foods section)
- ½ medium red onion, cut into thin strips
- Monterey Jack cheese, grated
- Red, yellow or orange peppers, sliced into thin strips
- Bacon, fried, drained and chopped fine

ET TU, JORGE . . . BEWARE THE IDES OF MEXICO!

Fire up the oven to 450°F.

Toss the corn bread cubes in a bowl with the melted butter. Get them spread out on a baking pan and dry 'em up in the oven until nicely golden brown. Set the little suckers aside to cool.

Meanwhile, fill up a sink with cold water, add the romaine, let God's good earth drop from the leaves and move them to a salad spinner for the dry cycle.

Let's get that dressing together. Combine the bottled Caesar dressing with the sour cream and whipped dressing or mayo. Toss in the lime juice and crushed garlic and bring on the chipotles. This is your heat adjustment. You can decide what's right for your taste buddies: 1, 2, 3+ peppers? The adobo sauce the chipotles are packed in combines nicely with the dressing, so you can use it to fine tune the heat as well.

Let's toss it all together, shall we? Romaine, red onion, grated cheese, peppers, bacon bits (if they showed up to play) and our dressing.

Slide the corn bread croutons over home plate for the final play.

Hey, I just had a thought. Why not toss some boneless, skinless chicken breasts or thighs in a batch of **Cuban Lime Marinade** (page 6) for a few hours, show them the Q or broiler and make this a Santa Fe Chicken Caesar main course for lunch or supper?

SO DAMN SALAD

Firefighter Lee Timchuk made this for us at the fire hall and it was such a huge hit that the masses insist on So Damn's making a regular menu appearance. To put a handle on this tasty salad combo, think of a Greek salad, but with the funky twist of fresh dill, Dijon mustard and lentils. So Damn Salad, so named because . . . it's just so damn good! SO, YOU'VE GOT ME SALIVATING, WHAT DO I NEED, DAMN IT?

FOR THE DAMN SALAD

- 1 long English cucumber, in chunky cubes, please
- 1 red onion—go for the 1-inch-square look
- 1 each orange and/or yellow pepper, ditto the above
- 19-ounce can lentils, drained
- Say about 5 ounces feta cheese, finely diced or crumbled
- 2–3 tomatoes, cut in large cubes (or 1 pound grape tomatoes)

FOR THE DAMN DRESSING

- ½ cup extra-virgin olive oil
- ½ cup red wine vinegar
- ¼ cup Dijon mustard
- ¼ cup chopped fresh dill
- 2 teaspoons sugar
- 1 teaspoon kosher salt
- Freshly ground black pepper to taste

AND FOR THE CHEF . . . DAMNATION?

Not a chance. Serve So Damn, and you'll be soaking in praise and elation.

The great part is, it's so quick and easy, especially if the prep chefs are armed with knives and cutting boards and willing to help. Before they get rolling, be sure to remind them to go for that chunky cubed veggie look.

The dressing's a breeze, too. A blender is a good option if you're making it for a crowd. Otherwise, the old bowl and whisk will do. Count on the Dijon mustard to keep it all together.

Toss the dressing and salad together. For added flavour, toss it into the fridge for an hour before serving, minus the tomatoes.

Toss in the tomatoes just before the salad hits the table. If you toss them in earlier, they just might decide to mutiny and sweat out their liquid, thereby diluting your dressing.

By the way, So Damn Salad goes great with marinated chicken—use either **Lemon-Lime Lickin' Chicken** (page 119) or **Lemon-Garlic Marinade** (page 6).

BLACK BEAN SALAD

If you're serving up Mexican or Tex-Mex and looking for a little something to saddle up beside your main dish, then give your cookbook browsing the cease-and-desist order. Here's a tasty, refreshing salad that's like a deluxe salsa. You can serve it as a side dish, use it as a topping for Q'd meats or pad it with either spinach leaves or rotini pasta and serve it as the centrepiece of a laid-back Tex-Mex lunch. Of course, you know what follows lunch—siesta time, amigo!

IT'S A CORNUCOPIA OF COLOURS

- 1 medium orange pepper, diced
- ½ medium red onion, finely chopped
- 1 small package grape or cherry tomatoes, each cut in half
- 1 or 2 jalapeno or habanero peppers, seeds out, chopped very fine—the peppers are your heat control, so respect and use them as you would the Force
- About ½ cup fresh chopped cilantro
- 19-ounce can black beans, drained and rinsed
- ½ cup peaches-and-cream corn—yes, fresh barbecue-roasted corn, painstakingly removed from the cob, would be ideal, but come on!

AND FIRED-UP FLAVOURS

- ¼ cup extra-virgin olive oil
- 1 medium-sized lime—use grated zest and 3 tablespoons juice
- 2 tablespoons orange juice
- 1 teaspoon sugar
- 1 teaspoon kosher salt
- 1 teaspoon ground cumin
- Lots of good old freshly ground black pepper
- 3 garlic cloves, pressed, minced, busted up!

THOSE BLACK BEANS ARE MAKING ME GO LOCO

Wash 'em, rinse 'em, dice 'em and chop 'em—you know the drill. Then toss in the beans and corn.

Organize a get-together for the veggies—are tomatoes a vegetable or a fruit?—in a handsome bowl. Combine the dressing ingredients and toss with the veggies.

This salad likes to sit so it can learn to pronounce its flavours, with a fitting Mexican accent, I should add, so let's give the salad space to do that in the fridge. Tick, tick, tick . . .

For variety, how about some Tex-Mex or jalapeno Monterey Jack cheese sprinkled over top? Or perhaps there's another genetic variation of beans that you'd like to add for contrast, like great northern or white navy beans. Oh, the possibilities! Remember, it's your salad, and you don't have to play by the rules. I say it's best to make your own rules, instead.

CHILI TWIST

Here's a nice, light salad so packed full of flavour and tang that it's unlikely anyone will suspect it's actually good for them. Why, you sneaky chef, you, taking care of your crew just because you care. You can serve this as a side with just about anything Asian or Indian, and you can even serve this as a main lunch dish paired with **Bangkok Orange Wings** *(page 128),* **Tokyo Black Wings** *(page 128) or* **Tender on the Q** *(page 124).*

THAT SWEET CHILI SAUCE IS SURE ROCKETING UP THE CONDIMENT CHARTS

- ½ cup sweet chili sauce (see page 4 if you're unfamiliar with it)
- ½ cup lime juice
- 1 tablespoon brown sugar, or more, to taste
- 1 tablespoon chopped cilantro
- 1 tablespoon minced fresh ginger
- 2 garlic cloves, minced or pressed
- 1 teaspoon toasted sesame oil
- 1 teaspoon sesame seeds

NO, YOU DON'T HAVE TO WAIT TILL SPRING TO ASSEMBLE THIS MIX

- Mushrooms, say about ½ pound
- Spring mix greens, also about ½ pound
- ½ medium red onion, cut into strips
- 1 cucumber, in slices
- Sugar snap peas—eyeball what you think you need
- 1 red, yellow or orange pepper, cut into strips
- 2 cups bean sprouts, washed before using, please!

BUT YOU'D BETTER GET A MOVE ON HERE, CUZ HUNGER IS HOVERING

Let's kick things off by getting the dressing ingredients together and tossing them into the fridge to chill. Depending on the sweet chili sauce you've chosen, this dressing can be quite fired up. If you find it's a little over the top, add more brown sugar to balance it out.

Slice those mushrooms into Ts. Personally, I'm not a big fan of raw mushrooms in salad. If you're like me, then you may prefer to sauté the 'shrooms in a couple of dabs of butter first. A little hit of kosher salt and freshly ground black pepper wouldn't hurt, either. Drain and let them cool.

Then get the rest of the produce pals together in a bowl and add the dressing.

As per the theme of the salad section, feel free to make as many substitutions as you like. Candied slivered almonds and sunflower seeds are a nice touch, as are grape or cherry tomatoes. Basically, whatever happens to be in the pantry or fridge and needs using up is fair game.

THAI COLESLAW

*Here's a salad that goes great along with just about any Asian dish found in this book, and outside this book. Actually, astute cooks and experts in the field of plagiarism will notice that the dressing ingredients are quite similar to those found in **My Pad Thai** (page 162). Yes, I've successfully ripped myself off! Oh, the shame of it all!*

FOR THE DRESS REHEARSAL
- 6 tablespoons peanut oil
- 3 tablespoons seasoned rice vinegar
- 3 tablespoons premium oyster sauce
- 3 tablespoons white sugar
- 3 tablespoons ketchup
- 1½ tablespoons Worcestershire sauce
- 1½ tablespoons fresh lime juice
- 3 teaspoons chili-garlic sauce (in your grocer's Asian food section)

TO BE DRESSED
- 10-ounce bag cabbage coleslaw or broccoli slaw mix
- 1 bunch green onions, chopped
- 2 celery stalks, chopped fine
- ½ cup chopped cilantro
- 1 single-serving package Japanese noodles, any flavour, noodles crumbled
- ¼ cup coarsely chopped peanuts or almonds

THAI ONE ON

Combine the dressing ingredients in a small bowl with your handy whisk.

Pour the bag of slaw into a mixing bowl.

Toss in the onions and celery, and follow up with the dressing ingredients.

Cover the bowl and get it into the fridge to marinate. Overnight is likely best, but you can get away with setting aside at least 2 to 4 hours for this process in order to infuse the slaw with all those wild, diverse flavours.

Just before serving your slaw, introduce the cilantro, noodles and nuts to the other guests and toss them through, to mingle.

Sure, it's a funky slaw, but you know, I have a sneaking suspicion you're going to like it.

MEOW, MEOW, MEOW, MEOW, MEOW, MEOW, MEOW, MEOW!

Back when my son Connor was seven, he asked, "Dad, I'm doing a survey for school. It's for what kind of pizza people love the best. What is your favourite? There are three kinds to choose from: pepperoni, cheese or veterinarian."

"Oh, put me down for a veterinarian," I replied with a chuckle. "In fact, I'll take an extra large cat lover's, please."

DEB'S
DECADENT DRESSING

My wife and I were over at retired firefighter Ken English's house for dinner one night, and his wife, Deb, served a simple yet sensational salad that led me to demand a recipe confession. Deb served this over romaine lettuce with cashews, but it also works great over fruit-based salads like the **Funky Honey-Lime Salad** *(page 54) and* **Peaches 'n' Pecans Romaine** *(page 57). Save perhaps the poppy seeds, chances are you'll have all of the dressing ingredients on standby. With no expensive wine vinegars or olive oils required, this has quickly become a fire hall favourite.*

IT'S TIME TO RAID THE CUPBOARDS FOR . . .

- ¾ cup sugar—we're off to a good start, aren't we? Sweeeeeet!!
- ⅓ cup distilled white vinegar
- 3 teaspoons finely chopped or grated onion
- 2 teaspoons dried mustard
- 1 teaspoon kosher or ½ teaspoon sea salt
- 1 cup canola oil
- 1 teaspoon poppy seeds

OH, AND PULL OUT THE BLENDER WHILE YOU'RE IN THERE

Let's get the sugar, vinegar, onion, mustard and salt together in a blender. Purée the lot, then pour the canola oil in there with the poppy seeds and hit the PLAY button to combine.

RASPBERRY VINAIGRETTE ### DRESSING

TASTES GREAT! LESS FILLING!

- ½ cup extra-virgin olive oil (or canola oil)
- ½ cup raspberry wine vinegar
- 2 tablespoons white sugar
- 2 tablespoons grainy Dijon mustard
- ½ teaspoon kosher salt
- ¼ teaspoon oregano
- ¼ teaspoon black pepper

YADA, YADA, YADA . . .

Combine all ingredients—try using a blender to bring it together. This dressing goes great over a basic lettuce 'n' veggie tossed salad, but much like Deb's Decadent Dressing, it also nicely complements a fruit-based tossed salad. If you're going to go the fruit route, however, go for canola oil instead of the olive oil and double the amount of sugar.

THE LITTLE SIREN THAT COULD

During the pre-Christmas months at the fire house, used toys in various states of disrepair arrive to be passed along to the less fortunate. One such item was a little toy beacon, fashioned after the emergency lights on the fire truck. Not only did the light shine and revolve brightly, but it also had a siren that blared through small speakers at the base.

Firefighter Gary found incessant pleasure in triggering the siren while playing cards in the kitchen of the fire house. Firefighter Guy was annoyed and told Gary to shut it off. But just as we were warned many years ago by our captain at the training academy, once a firefighter locates the button on a crewmate to push, and the crewmate reacts, it only makes the firefighter push it harder and more often. So in typical firefighter style, Gary went to town, playing the siren at any and every opportunity, just to tick Guy off. Finally, Guy snapped and grabbed the toy beacon, threw it to the ground and stomped on it, before leaving the kitchen in a huff.

Gary picked up the siren and gathered the broken pieces. During his examination he discovered that joining two of the bare wires in the pile of wreckage caused the siren to work again.

Later that night shift, at about 2 AM, Guy was wakened by the siren blaring away in the adjacent kitchen. Guy stomped into the room where Gary sat with a knowing smile on his face, touching the wires of the busted up toy together. Guy couldn't believe his ears, so he went to the apparatus floor and grabbed a rubber mallet off one of the trucks. He returned to the kitchen and proceeded to pummel the siren into oblivion. "Good luck making it work now!" he said before returning to the dorm.

As Gary gathered the smashed-to-smithereens device, another member of the crew, Bryan, plotted revenge. "Keep the siren's pieces, Gary, I've got an idea."

The next night Bryan brought a replica of the exact same toy to work. Gary placed the pile of rubble on the table, making it appear that it had been repaired. When Guy entered the kitchen, Gary touched the two infamous wires together in an exaggerated fashion. As he did, Bryan turned on the siren of the new toy he had hidden on his lap under the table. When Gary pulled the wires apart, Bryan shut it off. On and off, on and off the two worked, synchronizing their movements perfectly, driving Guy around the bend. Again Guy stormed out, returning with a pail of water, and tossed the beacon's parts into the drink, as the firefighters suffocated with laughter.

ON THE NIGHT SHIFT

THE DINNER BELL

Heat 'n' Sweet Chicken Thighs 71
Some call it honey-mustard chicken

Hot Chicks in a Big Flaky Blanket 72
Leftover chicken goes upscale

Juicy Roast Turkey 74
Tired of Sahara-dry white meat?

Orange-and-Maple-Roasted Chicken 77
Via the orange and maple trees

Oompahpah Pot Roast 78
Pour that roast a beer

Primo Rib Roast 80
Sear it and roast it, or roast it and sear it

Red Wine Short Ribs 82
A long, slow braise makes for tasty, tender ribs

Raspberry and Rosemary Pork Loin Roast 84
A sweet little piggy!

Rum-Roasted Half Chickens 85
What, Jamaican with that dark rum, mon?

Sizzlin' Salisbury Steaks with Mushroom Gravy 86
Tasty and filling on a budget

Gourmacaroni and Cheese 88
If you think we're talking KD, think again

Slow Cooker Pork Roast 89
Start it before you leave for work

Turkey and Stuffing, All-in-One Meatloaf? 90
Economan's Christmas dinner

We're Havin' Flippin' Duck! 91
You'll flip over this easy roast duck recipe

Wine 'n' Whiskey Beef Ribs 92
These ribs are a-weavin' and a-wobblin'

IT'S A FIRE BOAT! IT'S A FISHING BOAT!

Almond-and-Sesame-Crusted Sole 95
Nuts 'n' seeds are good for your soul, too

Lasagna of the Sea 96
If you're a seafood linguine fan, you'll sure love this

Crab-Stuffed Pickerel Fillets 98
Serve when company's coming over

Fired-Up Calamari 99
What? An appetizer in a Jeff the Chef cookbook?

Potato Chip Pickerel 100
Fish and chips have really come together this time

Psychedelic Salmon 101
I'm having a gourmet seafood flashback here

Thai-Becued Salmon 102
We've taken that tie-dyed salmon to Thailand

Shrimp Goes Couscous 103
No shrink necessary; we're talking wee pasta

Sun-Dried-Tomato-Pesto Pasta with Seafood 104
Shrimp 'n' scallops go uptown

Thai Fish Cakes 105
Make 'em big as an entrée, or mini as an appetizer

Thai-Lapia 106
You put the lime in the coconut . . .

WE'VE GOT A WORKING FIRE!

AROUND THE HALLS IN 40 MEALS

THE DINNER BELL

THE FIRE HALL KITCHEN GOGs (General Operating Guidelines)

I've often been asked, "Who pays for fire hall meals?" Some people are under the impression that meals are part of our benefits package. Not so. We all share in the cost of a meal—not "all" as in "all taxpayers," but as in "all dining firefighters."

Another question I'm often asked is, "Do firefighters take turns cooking?" Well, it depends on the fire house. Some firefighters are better cooks than others, so at some halls you'll find that one chef does all the cooking, while at other halls they take turns. Either way, each meal has a head chef, and depending on how many work at the hall, when it comes to chopping and preparing, one or more firefighters will always lend a hand. They may have a hidden agenda behind their offer to help, however, as being a cook means you don't have to do dishes. "There, I chopped the onions, so count me out on dishes."

How do we decide what to have? To be honest, many menu choices are determined by what's on sale. Enter the grocery flyer. "Hey, look, this store has two-for-one pork roasts on sale. Let's have pork roast the first night and hot pork sandwiches the second night."

Firefighters are bargain hunters, and we don't take kindly to paying retail. Keep in mind that price is one of the three major components of the successful fire house meal, as in "It better be good, it better be cheap and there better be lots!"

Sometimes cravings rule: "Mmmm . . . let's have something greasy."

For some, simplicity and lack of imagination dictate: "How 'bout pizza, like we have every Friday night?"

Perhaps it's a fire hall chef's signature dish that's requested: "You've gotta make those Fallin'-Off-the-Bones Ribs with the Whiskey Barbecue Sauce again."

Or, "I'm on the South Beached Whale Diet, so let's hold off on the carbs."

So really, there is no set rule when choosing a fire hall meal.

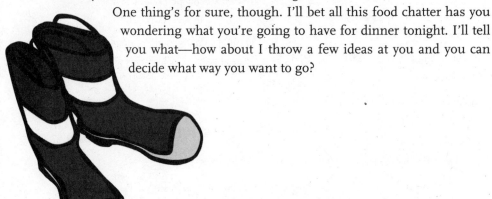

One thing's for sure, though. I'll bet all this food chatter has you wondering what you're going to have for dinner tonight. I'll tell you what—how about I throw a few ideas at you and you can decide what way you want to go?

CHICKEN THIGHS

This is one of those yin-and-yang recipes—it's all about balance. Imagine, if you will, a teeter-totter with Heat (a.k.a. curry) seated at one end and Sweet (a.k.a. honey) seated at the other. Sure, their play starts off nice enough, but suddenly Heat jumps off, causing Sweet to crash to the ground and smash his chin on the handle. Heat laughs ("What a great prank!"), but Sweet isn't amused. Now Heat will have to do lots of sweet-talking to get Sweet back to play with him. Heat can be an overpowering bully in Foodland, and he needs Sweet. When Heat 'n' Sweet choose to play together nicely, our see-saw is in perfect balance. The result is fun food play—and culinary bliss for the delighted diners.

HEAT AND SWEET AREN'T ALONE ON THE PLAYGROUND

- 12 chicken thighs, bone in, skin on or off
- 3 tablespoons butter, divided
- A nice shot of Fired-Up Spice (page 4)
- 1 large onion, coarsely chopped
- 1 cup plain yogurt—try the nice thick Balkan style
- ½ cup soft or liquid honey
- ¼ cup + 2 tablespoons soy sauce
- ¼ cup + 2 tablespoons mild curry paste (or go for hot curry paste and get dispatch to call in another alarm)
- 2 tablespoons prepared mustard
- 2 medium mangos, diced into chunks (or about a pound of frozen mangoes, thawed)

COME ON, YOU IDIOTS, GET ALONG!

Fire up the oven to 400°F.

Place the chicken pieces on a rack in a large ovenproof dish with sides. Spread about a tablespoon of soft butter over the chicken pieces. Dust each with a shot of Fired-Up Spice or seasoning salt. Bake uncovered on the centre oven rack for about 40 minutes.

Meanwhile, melt the remaining 2 tablespoons of butter in a frying pan over medium heat and toss in the onion. Fry for about 10 minutes to caramelize.

Stir the yogurt, honey, soy sauce, curry paste and mustard together in a bowl, and add those beautifully caramelized onions you created.

Remove the chicken dish from the oven. Set the chicks aside, remove the rack and carefully pour off any grease. Get the chicken back into the dish.

Bring on the flavour! Toss the curry sauce over the chicken and bake for an extra 15 minutes, or until the chicken is cooked through and glazed.

Add the mango chunks to the sauce just long enough to heat through. Any longer and they'll get mushy, and that's just not good enough.

Get a lovin' batch of basmati rice onto dinner plates, top the rice with the chicken, mangos and sauce, and for a garnish, well, nothing works better with curry than his good old play pal, cilantro!

HOT CHICKS IN A
BIG FLAKY BLANKET

Hey, those chicks over there are absolutely parched. Could you please pour them a white wine with a 7Up chaser? Yes, that old comfort-food standby, chicken pot pie, is going uptown for a fire hall makeover. We're talking a hen party packed tight in pastry in a firefighter-sized lasagna dish.

FOR THE CRUST AND THE FILLING

- 5 cups all-purpose flour
- 1-pound package all-vegetable shortening
- 1 cup 7Up, Sprite or similar lemon-lime soft drink, cold
- ¼ cup butter
- 4 garlic cloves, minced or pressed
- 2 cups finely diced onions
- 1 cup each finely diced celery and carrots
- 1 tablespoon Italian seasoning
- 1 teaspoon each seasoning salt and kosher salt
- Go to town with the pepper mill
- 1 cup frozen niblets corn
- ⅓ cup all-purpose flour
- ½ cup white wine
- 3 cups chicken broth
- ⅓ cup half-and-half cream
- 6+ cups cooked turkey or chicken, cut into bite-sized chunks

DID YOU SAY ONLY 3 INGREDIENTS IN THE CRUST?

The first 3 ingredients are all you'll need to make the pastry. I like to do it in 2 batches—one batch for the dish lining and the other for the topping. So, divvy the fixings up into 2. Get the flour in a large bowl and cut in the shortening. I like to carve the shortening off in small bits, mixing it with the flour as I go. Then I get the electric mixer in there

and let 'er rip until coarse little balls form. Or, if you're so equipped, use a pastry cutter. Then simply add just enough 7Up for a workable dough.

Form the dough into a ball, wrap it in cling wrap and move it on over to the fridge for a half hour to set up.

While that's happening, melt the butter in a large frying pan and add the garlic. Wait a second, this smells just like . . . a fire hall!

Follow up tout de suite with the onions, celery and carrots.

Let's fire up the flavour quotient by tossing the Italian seasoning, the salts and the pepper in there. Give them a stir to spread them around. Fry the veggies till they give when poked with a fork—a.k.a. tender-crisp.

Get the corn in there for a minute or so, to combine.

Dust the lot of 'em with the flour and work it through the veggies.

Pour in the wine, and follow up with the chicken broth and cream, a little at a time, with a stir or two in between. Don't give up on stirring quite yet; let's keep the pan going until it's bubbling a bit.

The chick chunks want into this flavour party, so toss them in and let them mingle with the other guests.

It's taste-test time. Me, being me, I like to add about ¼ teaspoon of cayenne about now to fire it up, but you can add a little salt if you think it's required. Follow your trusty gut instinct—you know what's best.

You can turn off the frying pan now and let the ingredients cool while you turn your attention to the pastry filling.

Pull out a 9 x 13-inch dish. Give them a shot of cooking spray and set them aside.

Gentlemen and women, start yer ovens at 400°F.

Get the dough out of the fridge and dust your counter and rolling pin with flour, 'cause we're rolling out—the pastry, that is.

Work that rolling pin so you end up with a rectangular pastry a couple of inches wider than the baking dish on each side. You should have lots of pastry to work with, so don't worry if you're being generous.

You may want to enlist a friend here as you carefully pull the crust off the counter, fold it in half and move it into the dish. If it cracks when you unfold it, don't sweat, it repairs very easily and won't leave a scar. Work it so it covers not only the bottom of the dish, but the sides, too.

Pour the cooled filling over the pastry and roll out the second ball of the dough to make the lid. Dip your finger in water and run it along both the top edge of the dish and the pastry edge, to seal it.

Top your dish with pastry 2, trim any excess and, for that "Grandma's pastry" look, use a fork to crimp the edges. Oh, and cut a few slits in the pastry lid— ventilation is as important in cooking as it is in firefighting.

Off to the middle rack in the oven for, say, 20 to 30 minutes, or until nicely browned both top and bottom.

Allow the pie to cool for 10 minutes before serving. A salad would go nicely on the side, don't you think? Serves about 6 to 8.

CHICK CHICK CHICKEN

Ever wonder how a fire hall recipe gets its name? Well, over at No. 11 hall they're serving up Chicklets Catastrophe Chicken . . . tick, tick, tick . . . eventually. Chicklets, a firefighter so named for his awe-inspiring upper row of front teeth, loaded the roaster to the brim with chicken legs 'n' thighs, laid on the sauce and put it in the oven assuming the cooking time would be the same as it would be for only four pieces of chicken spread out on a much smaller dish at home. When the chicken hit the firefighters' plates, visions of salmonella danced through their heads, and all meals were returned to the kitchen. The undercooked chicken was then nestled back in the roaster for another hour of hungry firefighter cooking time. They've been requesting Chicklets' Catastrophe Chicken—the pink-free version—ever since.

JUICY ROAST TURKEY

And now, a word about brining: terrific! There's nothing worse than dried-out white meat on a turkey. But not to worry, I have a few tricks up my sleeve when it comes to cooking up a big, succulent bird. This trio of tips includes the garlic-herb butter stuff, flippin' the bird and brining.

Brining means soaking the turkey in salt water overnight. You know how salt helps us humans retain water? Well, it's basically the same principle. Let's see, if I remember my grade 10 biology correctly, I believe we're talking reverse osmosis in action. Salt water allows the turkey's cells to retain moisture, keeping the big guy plump and juicy. As a bonus (much like with koshering), the salt draws blood out from the bird, and that makes for a clean, handsome turkey.

LIFT YOUR AXE OVERHEAD AND, IN ONE FLUID MOTION, STRIKE

- 14-pound turkey (approx.)—fits perfectly in my roaster, how about yours? Oh, and don't use a Butterball turkey for this brining exercise
- 1 cup each kosher salt and brown sugar for every 4 quarts (about a gallon) cold water
- About ½ cup garlic butter with herbs, store-bought or homemade (just add crushed garlic to butter or margarine and toss in some fresh poultry herbs or Italian seasoning)
- Fired-Up Spice (page 4)
- 1 jumbo onion, quartered
- 1 head garlic, cloves peeled and left whole
- 2 celery stalks and 2 carrots, cut into big chunks
- 1 cup dry white wine (or sherry)
- 10-ounce can chicken broth
- 10-ounce can consommé
- half-and-half cream, as needed
- Freshly ground black pepper

BRINE, BRIIIIIIIIIIIINE IS ON YOUR SIDE . . . YES, IT IS

You'll need to locate a stockpot, pail or bucket large enough to lodge Tom the turkey. Do the dry-dunk-tank fit test.

Got one? Let's go! Pour water to about the halfway mark on the container and add the salt and brown sugar, stirring to combine.

Ease Tom into his sweet saltwater bath and add water until it just covers the big bird. The brining has begun. Off to the fridge you go, Tommy, for a sleepover.

Remove Tom from the liquid about an hour before his date with destiny and thoroughly rinse him inside and out. Not to worry, the salt has penetrated our friend; we're only washing off the excess here. Pat the big guy dry with paper towels—or should that be beach towels?

Mix up the garlic butter with Italian seasoning or poultry herbs. Get your finger under the skin that covers the breast meat, working your way to the other end of the turkey. Place a couple of tablespoons under each side, spreading it out to cover each breast.

Fire up the oven to 350°F (325 for convection).

Place the bird on a rack in a roaster. Brush garlic butter over the breast side of the bird and lightly season with Fired-Up Spice.

Surround the turkey with onion, garlic, celery and carrots. Now that the veggies are lying in the gutter, let's pour the wine over them.

Get our buddy into the oven, breast side up, and cook uncovered for 30 minutes.

It's workout time. Let's get that appetite rolling! Remove the bird from the oven and, with a ratty old pair of oven mitts—or good mitts guarded by paper towels—grab each end of the bird and flip it over so the bird is now breast side down. I like to get someone to slip a piece of greased aluminum foil onto the rack so the breast skin doesn't stick when it's time to flip it back over.

Turn the oven down to 325°F. Roast our buddy uncovered for about 2 hours, basting Tom with pan juices every 30 minutes. We're now at the 2½ hour mark. Tick, tick, tick . . .

Take a break from your company; it's time for another flip. Get the mitts ready—remember, lift with the legs, not the back! Get the bird breast side up, baste liberally, and get it back in the oven, uncovered, for another ½ hour

to 45 minutes, or until browned and cooked through.

One of those digital meat thermometers would come in handy now. Poke one into the meatiest part of the thigh. When it hits 165°F, the turkey's ready.

Remove Tom and set him aside, tenting him with foil to keep warm. Let him sit for half an hour. Allow no diner to gobble before it's time.

Meanwhile, remove the veggies from the pan juices, but keep the garlic handy; we're not done with it yet. Place the juices in a measuring cup, wait for the key separation and spoon off the fat.

You could simply convert these juices into gravy by getting them boiling in the pan and thickening with a cornstarch-and-water combination, or you could follow my lead and cheat. Here's how.

Depending on the amount of gravy you're making, choose to use only about ½ cup of the richest pan juices. Get the juices back in the pan where they belong, add the chicken broth and consommé and bring it all to a boil, scraping any of those little brown bits off the bottom of the roaster to flavour the gravy.

Move the gravy over to the blender with the reserved roasted garlic and black pepper. Cover and carefully blend. If the gravy is quite dark, which is likely, simply add a bit of half-and-half cream until the desired beige colour is attained. A taste test is in order.

If the gravy is a little thin for your liking, combine 2 tablespoons cornstarch with ¼ cup water and add it to the gravy a bit at a time, stirring constantly until you attain the desired consistency.

Now we're talking juicy roast turkey, served with a delicious gravy that makes it positively juicylicious!

Serve with the equally delicious **Stuffing on the Side** (page 195).

THE MAGICAL MEAT PROBE

I finally gave in to the advancement of modern technology and picked up a digital meat thermometer.

I was skeptical at first—I mean, I never trusted the used and abused analogue ones we have at the fire hall. Besides, I'd been taught by firefighter chefs to judge the doneness of meats by look and feel. For example, I knew that a roast turkey or chicken was ready to yank from the oven when the skin pulled back on the ends of the legs, the leg 'n' thigh wiggled loosely and the thigh juices ran clear. With a beef or pork roast I went by approximate cooking times based on other roasts I'd cooked, by the shape of the roast (a basketball roast would take longer to cook than a cylindrical roast) and by gut instinct.

But, alas, life is so much easier with a meat probe, *especially* an accurate one with the readout appearing *outside* the oven. My current model has a little wire leading from the probe out of the oven or barbecue to the magical unit poised on the counter. Better yet, there are now cordless ones available, and they're cheap. So now I not only know when the meat is done, but I also know how close it is to being done, so I can time the rest of the meal. Of course, the probe is only as good as its calibration and condition—kitchen gadgets take a beating in a fire hall—so it's always a good idea to use your tried-and-true examination methods and instincts as well, to ensure that your meat is cooked properly.

Always remember that meat continues to cook once it's removed from the oven, and its forward momentum is directly related to the heat of the oven, so expect the temperatures to climb 5 or 10 degrees as the meat rests, especially if the oven was blazing. That's why recipes recommend that you rest roasts loosely tented with foil for a good 15 to 30 minutes before carving. Otherwise you're just going to let all those succulent juices escape, instead of letting them relax and finish their final job inside the roast.

If you don't own a meat thermometer, give in like I did, and get one. You'll be glad you did.

ORANGE-AND-MAPLE-ROASTED
CHICKEN

Here's a great way to funkify your next roast chicken dinner. Give it the Asian-orange-meets-maple-syrup treatment. The bonus is the unique gravy this bird dishes up.

ASK NOT WHAT YOUR CHICKEN CAN DO FOR YOU

- Approximately ¼ cup butter or margarine
- 6 garlic cloves, minced or pressed
- 2 tablespoons minced fresh ginger
- 1 5-pound roasting chicken or 2 3-pound fryers, rinsed and patted dry
- Fired-Up Spice (page 4)
- 1 large orange, cut into 4 segments
- ¼ cup pure maple syrup
- 1 tablespoon sweet soy sauce
- 1 tablespoon seasoned rice vinegar
- 1 teaspoon chili-garlic sauce
- 1½ cups orange juice
- 1 tablespoon cornstarch combined with 1 tablespoon water

RATHER, ASK WHAT YOU CAN DO FOR YOUR CHICKEN

Fire up your oven to 400°F.

Mix the butter with a few cloves of the minced garlic and 1 tablespoon of the minced ginger. Work your fingers under the skin of the chicken breast to loosen things up, and place a heaping teaspoon of garlic/ginger butter between the skin and breast.

Rub the butter all over the outside of the skin, as well.

Season the inside and outside of the bird with Fired-Up Spice.

Fire the orange slices into the chicken's cavity, truss the bird and get it onto a roasting rack and bake breast side up, uncovered, for 20 minutes.

Meanwhile, whisk together the maple syrup, soy sauce, rice vinegar, remaining tablespoon of ginger and chili-garlic sauce. Heat in a small saucepan, reducing until the sauce coats the back of a spoon—we're looking to give it a little body.

Turn the oven down to 375°F and remove the boid from its roasty nest.

With a couple of sheets of paper towels protecting your oven mitts, carefully flip the bird over so the thighs are now on top. This'll help the bird cook evenly.

Pour the orange juice into the pan and bake for 45 minutes to 1 hour. Baste the bird with the maple syrup sauce at the 30-minute mark. Don't let the drippings in the pan go dry; add OJ or water to the pan, as needed.

Flip the bird to breast side up, baste with sauce and bake until the meat thermo in the thigh hits 165°. Baste often for a great glaze.

Let the chicken rest for 10 to 15 minutes while you make the gravy.

Move the gravy to a small saucepan and heat it to boiling. Slowly add the cornstarch/water mix until it reaches the desired consistency. Give it a taste test and the old "salt-and-pepper-the-way-you-like-it" treatment.

OOMPAHPAH POT ROAST

What gives this pot roast the oompahpah, you ask? Well, empty your stein, because we need a bottle of your finest brew. Not a beer lover? Not to worry—chances are you won't even notice there's beer in this gravy. Rest assured, you won't blow a no-no on the Breathalyzer, either, because rumour has it that the alcohol burns off during cooking. It's all about taste . . . and just wait until you taste this!

BEER AND HIS ROASTING BUDDIES

- 2 tablespoons grainy Dijon mustard
- 2 tablespoons brown sugar
- ½ tablespoon horseradish
- 4-6 garlic cloves, minced or pressed
- 1 12-ounce beer—I like a dark lager, but any beer will do
- 6 tablespoons olive oil—not all at once; 2 at a time
- 4- to 5-pound pot roast—I like a boneless blade or cross rib
- Kosher salt and freshly ground black pepper
- ¼ cup red wine or water
- 2 tablespoons butter
- 2 cups coarsely diced onion
- 1½ cups each coarsely diced celery and carrots
- 1¼ cups consommé soup or beef broth—as in a 10-ounce can

I'M LOOSENING UP THE LEDERHOSEN AND GOING IN!

Simply combine our marinade ingredients. That's the mustard, brown sugar, horseradish, garlic, beer and 2 tablespoons of the olive oil.

Move the roast into a zip-top freezer bag and add that tasty marinade to the roast. Squeeze out the air and seal it up.

Allow the roast to marinate overnight to suck up the flavours. You don't have to marinate the roast, but I figure the longer it sits in the beer, the more ideas this roast is going to get about tasting great!

About an hour before show time, get that roast out of the marinade and onto the counter to rest. Don't toss that marinade; we need it!

Pat the roast dry with paper towels so it will brown, and dust that hunk of meaty madness with salt and pepper.

Place another 2 tablespoons of the olive oil in a Dutch oven over medium-high heat. Get out the oven mitts covered with paper towels and lay the roast in the oil to sear. Move it around to brown on all sides. Watch for splashing grease—hence the all-important forearm-protecting oven mitts. Fire mitts and a turnout coat will also do. It's safety first in the kitchen.

Remove the roast to a safe haven, like a plate, add the red wine to the pan, and use a wooden spoon or some such implement to scrape those flavour-laden brown bits off the bottom.

Pour the wine 'n' bits into a bowl or cup. Don't toss them out, they'll be making a taste-enhancing comeback.

Fire up the oven to 325°F.

Place the butter and the last 2 tablespoons of the olive oil into the Dutch oven over medium heat. When the butter melts, get the onions in there to soften and caramelize, and follow up with the celery and carrots. As always, dust those veggies with salt and pepper to bring out the flavours.

Move the veggies to the side of the pot and nestle the roast in there.

Now, let's reintroduce the red wine 'n' bits and the beer marinade to the meat 'n' veggies along, with the consommé soup, and bring it all to a boil.

Transfer the hot tub party to the oven for 2 hours of fun.

Flip the roast over, reduce your oven temp to 275°F and roast for another 1½ to 2 hours, or until the roast is very tender.

Remove the roast from that funky broth and let it stand, loosely covered in foil, for about 15 minutes before carving.

While it rests, pour the gravy into a large, heat-safe measuring cup or bowl. The grease should rise to the top so you can tip the cup slightly and ladle or siphon it off with a turkey baster.

Pour the gravy back into the Dutch oven, bring to a boil and reduce for about 10 minutes to concentrate the flavours.

Get out the blender—*how many pots, pans and kitchen aids are we going to use here, Jeff?*—and pour half the gravy into the blender. Place the cover on the blender with a tea towel over top. *Carefully* pulse the blender to purée. Repeat with the other half of the gravy.

Get the gravy back into the Dutch oven *again* and do the salt-and-pepper routine to correct any seasoning omissions you may have made.

Serve with your favourite veggies and a whack of mashed potatoes. Be sure to make a depression in the middle of the spuds so you can create a Mt. Gravy lava flow. *Sooo good!*

THICKEN IT UP!

Is your sauce or gravy a little thin? Need to tighten it up? Well, there are a few approaches you can take. The traditional "mom's gravy" method is to combine flour with enough water to make a light paste and add it to the bubbling liquid. You can also do like the French, and combine equal parts melted butter and flour (called a roux) and toss it in with the bubbling sauce or gravy. The upside to this one is that you get the flavour boost of butter; the downside is that you also get the calorie boost. Or you can go Asian and add equal parts water and cornstarch to the liquid. For each application, just make sure you let the liquid boil for a bit after you add the thickening agent, and add only a bit of the thickener at a time until you get the consistency you're after.

Need to both tighten and lighten a sauce or soup in colour, but not calories? Try adding some cream.

PRIMO RIB ROAST

Really, roasts are easy to cook. Just season them up, pop them in the oven and leave them be until they're ready. But when you spend upwards of $50 on a cut, you hope and pray that the recipe you've chosen will result in prime rib roast perfection. I've included two variations for you to try: **Sear First, Slow-Roast Later** *and* **The Reverse Sear.**

FOR EITHER METHOD YOU'LL NEED . . .

- 6-pound prime rib roast—a nicely aged, nicely marbled (not lean) AAA cut makes a big difference in flavour and tenderness
- Lots of garlic, cut into matchsticks
- 2 heaping tablespoons grainy Dijon mustard
- 1 heaping tablespoon creamy horseradish (or 2 teaspoons regular horseradish)
- Lots of freshly ground black pepper
- Dried thyme
- 1 jumbo onion, in thick slices (optional)
- Kosher salt

SEAR FIRST, SLOW-ROAST LATER

Take the roast out of the fridge about 2 hours before its date with the oven. Pat dry with paper towels. With a small paring knife, make cuts in the roast just big enough so you can plunge those garlic matchsticks into the meat.

Mix the Dijon mustard and horseradish together and paint it onto the roast, excluding the bone side. Top with pepper and thyme. I tend to hold back on the salt at this point, but don't worry, it'll get a generous hit of kosher salt just before the roast hits the heat.

Fire up the oven to a rip-roarin', ready-to-roast 450°F.

Pop the roast on a rack in a shallow roaster, rib-side down—that's how a standing rib is built to stand—or on a bed of onion slices in a shallow roaster. Add ½ to 1 cup water to the pan to cut down on splatters during the all-important searing process.

Sprinkle some kosher salt over top and let 'er rip for 30 minutes.

Turn the oven down to 200°F, but don't open the door. You want the roast to come down from the sear slowly. Bake the roast for an additional 2½ hours, or until a meat thermometer reaches the desired level of doneness. Personally, I like my roast pink, not blue, and definitely not dried out and brown, so I'll take it out when it gets to about 135°F.

Cover the roast with foil and set it out on the counter to rest for 20 to 30 minutes before carving. I know, everyone's on your case to serve it right away, but the juices in the roast really need to rest.

THE REVERSE SEAR

I was inspired to try this method by one of my favourite food writers, Alton Brown. It sure makes sense at home or at the fire hall if you're working the night shift, as you can get the day crew to pop your roast in the oven in the afternoon without having to worry about their forgetting to turn down the oven from the opening sear. Believe me, firefighters have good intentions, but if they get a call, or a sporting event or activity causes their minds to wander, your roast may be in serious trouble. The reverse sear puts you in total control, as you add the browning sear at the end of the slow-roasting process. Ideally, you'll want to use one of those hi-tech, yet inexpensive digital meat thermometers, either cordless or with the braided cord that exits the oven and plugs into a temperature display that sits on the counter. I'll tell you, it sure makes for easy monitoring. You're in command of this incident now!

SLOW-ROAST FIRST, SEAR LATER

Get your roast out of the fridge 2 hours before its date with destiny. Pat it dry and stuff and season your beefy buddy just as you would in the Sear First, Slow-Roast Later method.

Start your oven off at 225°F. Place the roast rib-side down on a rack or a bed of onions in a shallow roaster, but don't worry about adding water to the pan. Insert a meat thermometer in the roast's centre.

Pop the roast in the oven and immediately turn it down to 200°F. (If you started it at 200°, opening the oven door would take you down to 175.)

Let the roast do its thing. We're looking at a guesstimated arrival of about 1 hour per pound. Don't open the oven to peek; you want to maintain that low temperature. Cooking the roast is as simple as checking out the meat thermometer every once in a while.

When the thermometer reaches about 120°F, take the roast out of the oven and cover it with tin foil. The roast will likely climb about another 5° as it rests.

Turn the oven up to 450°F, and when it's up to temp, get the roast back in there, uncovered, for about 10 to 15 additional minutes, to brown it. You're looking for a finishing temperature of about 135°F for medium-rare. Adjust the temperature targets depending on the level of doneness you prefer. Keep in mind that the temp of the roast will climb again after you pull it out of the oven a second time.

Re-cover the roast with foil and set out on the counter to rest for about 20 to 30 minutes before slicing. Hey, you've got potatoes and veggies to prepare anyway, so if the Alarm Gods are willing, this should work out perfectly.

RED WINE
SHORT RIBS

Short ribs can be amazingly tasty, but there are definitely a couple of secrets behind cooking them successfully. Finding good short ribs that aren't too lean or too fatty can sometimes be a challenge, but braising them low and slow in a flavour-infusing liquid like red wine and broth boosted by onions, celery, carrots, garlic and tomato sauce is easy. Oh, and wait till you taste the gravy you'll get by puréeing all but the ribs in a blender when the roasting is done. Mmmmmm!

TELL YOUR BUTCHER, "I NEED YOUR BEST SHORT RIBS!"

- About 5 pounds short ribs
- About 2 teaspoons Fired-Up Spice (page 4)
- About 2 teaspoons Italian seasoning
- 1 teaspoon dried thyme
- Kosher salt and freshly ground black pepper–a light dusting, as usual
- ¼ cup canola oil
- 10-ounce can chicken broth
- 2 tablespoons each olive oil and butter
- 2 cups diced yellow onions (about 1 medium onion)
- 1½ cups each diced celery and carrots (about 3 each)
- 6 garlic cloves, peeled but left whole
- 10-ounce can consommé
- 3 cups Merlot (or other dry red wine)
- 1 cup tomato or spaghetti sauce

TELL YOUR GUESTS, "BONE APPETITE!"

Fire up your oven to 300°F.

Let's get those ribs dried off a bit with paper towels. We do this so they'll get with the program and brown up nicely for us.

Move the ribs into a big bowl and toss them with a shot of Fired-Up Spice, Italian seasoning, thyme, salt and pepper.

Heat the canola oil in a large Dutch oven over medium heat. In two batches, brown the ribs completely on all sides.

Drain off any oil, get the pot back on the stove and add the chicken broth. Bring it to a boil and get scrapin', my friend. Those little black bits on the bottom of the pan mean *flavour*!

Pour the broth off into a measuring cup or bowl, but don't chuck it out!

Place the olive oil and butter in the Dutch oven, and stir-fry the onions, celery, carrots and garlic until the veggies soften a bit. Toss in a little kosher salt and pepper for bonus flavour points as you go.

Get the broth 'n' bits back in there, plus the ribs, consommé soup, wine and tomato sauce, and bring the big batch of lovin' fun to a light boil.

Cover the Dutch oven and place it in the oven for 3 blissful hours.

If your Dutch oven is overflowing or you've gone and doubled the recipe, you can use a covered roaster instead.

Hey, you've got time for a workout

here. The question is, do you have the will? Not to worry, I'm not here to judge, I'm simply here to help you make supper.

Tick, tick, tick . . . time's up! What time is it? It's options time. The choice is yours. You can remove the ribs, let the sauce cool a bit and cover and refrigerate the ribs and the sauce separately. Then the following day, simply crack the Dutch oven pot open and scrape off the congealed layer of fat from the top. Heat up the sauce on the stovetop, picking up the action below at "Get the Dutchie . . ."

Or, if you're pushing this recipe right through, then remove the ribs to a safe, warm spot and skim off any fat from the liquid.

Get the Dutchie rolling on the stovetop. Fire it up to full boil ahead and keep it there for about 15 minutes. The goal here is to reduce the sauce, thereby intensifying the flavours. As you know, we're all about flavour.

Now let's move half the sauce *carefully*—because I care about you, you're special to me—over to a blender.

Purée the sauce—yes, veggies and all—and place the sauce back in the Dutch oven *once again!* Do the same with the other half.

Here's your chance to do the old taste test and a final salt-and-pepper treatment, as you see fit. Get the ribs back in there to coat them in that tasty gravy sauce. Heat it through and we're finally ready to rock.

Serve the ribs over roasted garlic mashed potatoes or egg noodles. A little chopped fresh parsley would be great sprinkled over top.

By the way, this recipe makes *lots* of sauce—actually more of a gravy. So why not put the leftover sauce aside and freeze it? Serve with roast beef, meatloaf or meatballs—whatever you like. It's great!

THEY'RE AT THE POST

When I'm planning a meal, I'll often ask firefighters what they like and dislike. The answer I inevitably get is, "Anything but liver." I respond with my stock answer: "Not to worry, I have a couple of rules that I follow. I don't cook Disney characters—except Donald Duck—and I don't do internal organs."

There are those, however, who love "a river of liver," and then there are those who have found alternate uses for this slimy beast. Yes, at No. 1 fire hall years back the boys initiated the exciting spectator sport of liver racing. Side by side the combatants stood as they each tossed a hunk of liver against a wall or piece of porcelain (use your imagination here). If thrown properly, the liver would stick and then ever so slowly slide down the wall, leaving a less-than-appetizing trail behind. No wonder it's such a popular choice among fire house diners.

RASPBERRY AND ROSEMARY
PORK LOIN ROAST

I picked this gem up from Angela Peterson when we worked together—or, as we called it, co-conspired—at No. 1 station. This was one of Ang's go-to meals, a great yet simple blend of flavours she developed out of what she had on hand at home one day. Tasty tender pork with gravy that's sweet and so good! Best to plan a day ahead for this one.

THERE'S A PIG LOOSE IN THE RASPBERRY PATCH!

- Say about a 3- to 4-pound pork loin roast
- 1 cup raspberry syrup (in the supermarket with the pancake syrups)
- ½ cup white wine vinegar
- 2 tablespoons fresh rosemary, chopped coarsely (or 1 tablespoon dried rosemary)
- 4-6 garlic cloves, cut into matchsticks
- Fired-Up Spice (page 4) and freshly ground black pepper

THAT PIG'S A LITTLE SWEETIE, OR AT LEAST SHE'S GOING TO BE

If your roast is a boneless loin, take the butcher's twine off and open it up so more surface area is exposed to the marinade. Toss the pork in a freezer bag with the mix of syrup, vinegar and rosemary, and send it off to the fridge for about 24 hours.

An hour before oven time, get the roast out on the counter so it can psych itself up for all the heat it's about to endure. *Sure wish we firefighters got that kind of time to prepare.* Preheat your oven to 400°F.

Pat the roast dry with paper towels, but reserve the marinade. Drying the roast off will help it brown. If you separated the roast, it's time to tie it back together. You can even stuff the roast with dressing, if you'd like.

Place the roast on a rack in a roaster, poke a knife into the top of the roast and distribute matchsticks of garlic into the meat. Poke, poke, poke, fill, fill, fill. Season the roast with Fired-Up Spice and pepper.

Get the roast into the oven, uncovered, for 20 minutes to sear the outside.

Remove the roast from the oven and turn the temp down to 350. Top the roast with the reserved marinade and loosely tent with foil. Back in you go, pal!

Check the roast periodically and add a little water if the bottom of the roaster starts to dry out and burn. Roast until the meat thermometer reaches 160°F (I know, some prefer 170) or until juices run clear.

Let the roast rest 15 minutes before carving. Ang likes to add an envelope of pork gravy mix to the roast drippings along with the starchy water that the potatoes were boiled in. A little salt and pepper to taste, and maybe a little cornstarch and water added to thicken the gravy as it bubbles away on the stove. Make the call, guys, dinner is ready! Pigs to the trough!

RUM-ROASTED
HALF CHICKENS

Sure, poultry skin has fallen out of favour with some, but I guarantee that even die-hard—I know, ironic if they did—dieters will be fighting over the skin basted with this glaze. Just the look of the mahogany-coloured glaze will get them salivating and, as I often remind you, presentation is everything. Okay, maybe not quite everything, as the sweet scent and flavour accented by a kick of rum push this recipe over the top.

CHICK IT OUT

- 3 tablespoons butter or margarine
- 3 garlic cloves, minced or run through the press
- 1 teaspoon Italian seasoning
- 2 3-pound frying chickens, split in half
- Fired-Up Spice (page 4)
- ½ cup brown sugar
- ¼ cup dark rum
- 2 tablespoons ketchup

JUST BAKE IT AND BASTE IT

Fire up your oven to 425 rip-roaring degrees.

Make up a wee batch of garlic butter by combining the butter, garlic and Italian seasoning in a bowl. You can adjust the seasoning if you like, as long as you promise me you'll think *bite* when you test it.

Rinse the chicken with cold water and pat dry with paper towels.

Work your finger under the skin on the breast and get a loaded teaspoon of garlic butter in there. Yes, our flavour pocket's been planted.

Spread the garlic butter over the outside of the chicken's skin as well, and season it up with Fired-Up Spice.

Place our half chickens on a rack in a shallow roaster and move them into that warm, inviting oven, roasting uncovered for 45 minutes.

Get our glaze together by combining the brown sugar, rum and ketchup.

Yank the chicks from their hot-house, brush the glaze generously over them and roast for, say, another 5 minutes or so.

Glaze again, then roast for approximately 5 minutes more, or until the leg joint is loosey goosey and a meat thermometer jabbed into the thigh reads 165°F.

Here's an option for you. If the Q season's on, after the oven roasting is completed, do the glazing finale by getting the chickens over the unlit side of a fired-up barbecue and finish them with the sauce as you would in the oven-glaze method. Bonus flavour points are sure to be had!

Let the chicken stand for 5 to 10 minutes before serving.

This glaze also makes an awesome quickie barbecue sauce. Try it on Q'd chicken pieces, pork chops or ribs and guests will be licking their fingers with delight. Let's just hope they washed their hands before dinner.

SALISBURY STEAKS

On one of my many road tours I visited No. 4 station, where the hall's captain, Ted Jaworski, a.k.a. Jawsman, asked, "Hey Jeff, what are you cooking us on nights?" "I don't know. Any requests?" I replied. "Yeah, how about Salisbury steaks with gravy and mashed potatoes?" I'll admit, it wasn't my specialty, but where there's a will, there's a way. By the way, this meat mix also makes great burgers.

I'M NOT A CHEF . . .

- 1½ cups finely diced onion
- 3 tablespoons butter
- 2 eggs
- ½ tablespoon Worcestershire sauce
- ½ tablespoon prepared mustard
- ½ head garlic, pressed or minced
- 1 teaspoon Fired-Up Spice (page 4) or seasoning salt
- ½ teaspoon pepper
- 1½ cups bread crumbs or bread
- 1½ pounds lean ground beef
- 1 pound ground pork

FOR THE MUSHROOM GRAVY

- 3 tablespoons butter
- 1 medium onion, cut into half rings
- 1 pound mushrooms
- ½ teaspoon each kosher salt and freshly ground black pepper
- 2 teaspoons Italian seasoning
- ½ cup red wine
- 2 tablespoons flour
- 2 cups beef broth or consommé
- ½ cup sour cream

BUT I PLAY ONE AT THE HALL

In a frying pan over medium heat, sauté 1½ cups onion in the butter until caramelized (about 10 minutes).

In a mixing bowl, whisk together the eggs, Worcestershire sauce, mustard, garlic and spices. When the onions have cooled down a bit, toss them into the egg mix and combine.

I'm a big fan of fresh bread crumbs, as going fresh allows me to choose the bread—usually homemade. Just get out your trusty food processor or one of those little mini-choppers and toss in the bread, crusts and all, and chop it up; don't worry about getting it super fine.

Bring the beef and pork to the veggie party, making sure to distribute each evenly. Toss the bread crumbs in and work the ingredients through the meat without over-handling, which can toughen your burgers. If it's too moist, simply add more bread crumbs. If the mix is too dry, then add a bit of milk. You should easily have enough to make about 8 fake megasteaks.

Get those Salisbury steaks on the barbecue (the preferred method) or under the broiler (choice number 2), or panfry them (good old traditional style).

While that's happening, let's get going on the gravy. Melt the butter in a large frying pan over medium heat and toss in the second batch of onions.

Once again, we want those onions to cough up their sugars and caramelize. Brown 'em a bit in the pan for maximum flavourtude, Dudie!

Bring on the mushrooms, dust with the salt, pepper and Italian seasoning and give them a good go in the pan.

Pour in the wine and get that heat going to medium-high, to reduce. If you can get it to the point where there is no more moisture in the pan, then you're a better man than I am.

Otherwise, dust those veggies with the flour, work it through nicely and introduce the beef broth, whisking as you go to blend your gravy.

Onwards and upwards we go as we reduce the sauce to bring out those incredible flavours. To finish, work in the sour cream with a whisk and give it the old salt-and-pepper taste test.

Pour the mushroom gravy over the Salisburys and it's go time!

THE FRESH HERB DEBATE

This is how I approach fresh herbs, and if you don't like my opinion, well then, Tiger Williams is waiting for you outside in the parking lot. Parsley and cilantro are no-brainers. Use them fresh, or turn in your spatula. They kick the living daylights out of their tasteless dried derivatives, and they are plentiful and cheap. However, you can't say the same for fresh herbs such as oregano, basil, rosemary, thyme, tarragon, etc., *unless* you aren't one of the budgetarily challenged, you grow your own or you're serving at least a portion of them in their uncooked state—such as in a pesto, where they must be fresh.

A favourite method of cooks with far more culinary knowledge and grey matter than I is to place half of the fresh herbs in a soup, stew or pasta, etc., while it cooks, while reserving the other half to sprinkle over the food just before serving. This technique makes for great presentation, and you get a taste of both that cooked-in goodness and that wonderful freshness.

But there's a price to pay for that decadence, and firefighters in particular don't like to pay for ingredients that can be easily substituted for free with part of their station kitty—as in dried herbs. Therefore, the following equation is the one I follow more often than not, at work and at home. Dried herbs + cooking liquid + time = great taste and frugal economy. I really don't see a huge taste-versus-cost advantage to using fresh herbs in this application, but perhaps that's just me. As for substitutions, I generally go about 1 teaspoon dried for 1 tablespoon of fresh herbs in recipes, though you can certainly adjust that to taste.

Oh, and one more thing. I much prefer coarse dried herbs over the crushed-up fine powders.

AND CHEESE

If you can whisk a whisk you can make a cheese sauce, and if you can make cheese sauce you can make Gourmacaroni and Cheese. Make it plain for the unappreciative kids, or go full-bore deluxe for a tasty cornucopia of flavours.

MAKE THIS MAC & CHEESE

- 1 tablespoon canola oil
- 8 slices of turkey bacon or ham
- 2 tablespoons butter
- 1 medium onion, diced
- 2 celery stalks—dice them up, too
- About ¼ pound mushrooms—T them up!
- Italian seasoning, kosher salt and freshly ground black pepper, to taste
- 2 tablespoons each butter and flour
- 1½ cups 2% or whole milk
- Cayenne to taste
- About 1 pound grated Tex-Mex, cheddar or your fave cheese
- 2½ cups uncooked macaroni
- ½ cup fresh bread crumbs, mixed with 2 tablespoons melted butter

AND YOU'LL THROW THAT STORE-BOUGHT STUFF OUT!

Get the canola oil going in a frying pan. Toss in the turkey bacon and cook over medium heat, turning often, until browned. Crisp it up a bit! Remove the bacon, dice it up and let the pan cool slightly.

Once the pan's chilled a bit, add in a couple of tablespoons of butter. Follow up with the onions and fry until lightly browned, then soften the celery and finish with the 'shrooms. A light dusteroo of Italian seasoning, salt and pepper will boost the flavour.

Now that the adult additives have been prepared and set aside, let's get going on the cheese sauce. Melt the butter over medium heat and bring on the flour. Get the whisk whisking to combine. That's a roux now.

Slowly add the milk a bit at a time, combining with the whisk until it all comes together. The white sauce should be starting to bubble and thicken about now. Season your sauce with kosher salt and a dash of cayenne.

Bring on about half the cheese, whisking until melted and smooth.

Meanwhile, boil the macaroni till cooked al dente. Drain and toss with the cheese sauce.

Cue the oven, 350°F, please.

To make a barebones, "ew-what's-that"-free version, simply add the bacon and top with the rest of the grated cheese (lay it down pizza cheese style) and bake in a suitably sized casserole dish for about 20 minutes.

For the adult—a.k.a. gourmet—version, get the bacon and veggie mix into the cheese/mac sauce and lay down the remaining grated cheese. Top it off with the bread-crumbs-and-butter mix and bake in a casserole dish, uncovered, for 20 minutes, or until nicely browned on top.

SLOW COOKER
PORK ROAST

True, I am the cook, and I am a little slow, but that isn't what I'm talking about here. It's time to get out the Crock-Pot. No, not the crackpot; you know, the slow cooker you got for a wedding present, the one still unopened in its box. Simply brown the meat and pop the ingredients in the low-and-slow machine in the morning, and by the time you're back from work, supper's ready!

FIREFUCIUS SAY, EAT TILL IT HURT!

- 4- to 5-pound pork shoulder or loin roast
- 5 garlic cloves, cut into matchsticks
- Our surefire pork seasoning combo of Fired-Up Spice (page 4) and dried basil
- 2 tablespoons each vegetable oil and butter
- 10-ounce can cream of chicken soup
- 10-ounce can consommé
- 1 Package dry roasted garlic and onion (or just onion) soup mix
- ½ cup white wine (or dry sherry)
- ¾ cup each diced onion, celery and carrots

I CAN'T BELIEVE I ATE THE WHOLE THING! ATTA BOY!

Dry the roast off with paper towels. Poke holes in the top of it with a knife and stuff with garlic. Season with a hit of Fired-Up Spice and dried basil.

In a large frying pan over medium-high heat, bring on the vegetable oil and butter. Carefully place the roast in the pan and sear on all sides—a couple of minutes on each side should do.

Combine the remaining ingredients in a bowl and whisk them together.

Shoot a little cooking spray in the business end of the slow cooker, and place the nicely browned roast into the level 1 staging position.

Top with the broth ingredients (i.e., all the other stuff). This part of the recipe can be done the night before, to reduce morning stress levels. Just stash it in the fridge overnight.

In the AM, set your slow cooker to low and cook for 9 hours, covered.

What on earth are you going to do for 9 hours? You'll think of something, I'm sure. Hopefully, goodness wins the battle over the lure of evil.

Remove the roast from the bath and tent it with foil to keep it warm.

While the roast rests, carefully move the gravy with veggies into a blender.

Cover the blender and, exercising a little caution, pulse a few times, then increase your speed to purée until the gravy is smooth.

The purée of veggies should take care of thickening the gravy, but if it seems a little thin, simply move it to a saucepan, bring to a light boil and slowly add a combo of about a tablespoon of cornstarch to 2 tablespoons of water.

Salt and pepper the gravy to taste, or do like so many do and salt and pepper everything without even tasting it first! Oh, sorry, I think I struck one of my own nerves.

TURKEY AND STUFFING,
ALL-IN-ONE MEATLOAF?

Imagine, if you will, the delicious flavour of turkey and stuffing all in one very afford-
able bite. This recipe covers all the bases! As a bonus, it's a snap to make, and an easy
sell to any musclehead in your hall or home who appreciates your using turkey due to
its renowned low fat/high protein count.

THIS LOAF'S FOR YOU!
- 1 head garlic—not a clove, the full head
- About 1 tablespoon olive oil
- About 2 tablespoons butter
- 1 apple, peeled, cored and diced
- 1 medium onion, diced
- 2 celery stalks, diced as well
- Kosher salt and freshly ground black pepper
- 1 teaspoon dried sage
- Bring us 2 of your beaten, your abused eggs
- 1 cup good old plain yogurt
- 6-ounce box packaged stuffing (seasoning packet included)
- 2 pounds ground turkey or chicken

PASS THE CRANBERRY SAUCE!
Fire up your oven to 350°F—that's 200 kilometres centigrade.

Peel the loose paper-like skin off the outside of the head of garlic and place the head, whole, on a small sheet of foil. Drizzle a tablespoon or so of olive oil right in the middle of the head. Fold the foil around the head, seal the top, place it on a baking pan and send our little fragrant package of joy off to the oven for about 30 minutes.

Back at the kitchen island, let's prep the fruit 'n' veggies.

Warm up a frying pan over medium heat. Add the butter and toss in the produce. Sprinkle a teaspoon or so of salt, a little pepper and that dried sage for flavour booster.

Set the veggies aside when they've reached the point of softening. Oh, and once the garlic has cooled off, squeeze it out of its skin and mash it up.

Get your butt back to the handy kitchen island and add the eggs and yogurt to a large mixing bowl. Make the fruit 'n' veggies feel welcome, and that includes the flavourful, breath-enhancing garlic, and toss in the stuffing. Combine them briefly, then round out your cast of characters with the lead actor (the turkey), who's lurking in the fridge, and give the pepper mill a brief workout with a few grinds of fire-me-up.

The plot thickens. Fire up your oven to 350°F. Grease a large bread pan and snuggle in the turkey and his supporting cast, nice and tight. Sure, the mixture is quite moist, but relax, that's the way we want it.

For the final act, make that loaf pan the centre of attention in that oven of yours for 1 hour to 1:10 or until cooked through.

Ah, ah, ah! The show's not on until you let the loaf stand for at least 10 minutes. The loaf isn't being arrogant or difficult; it just needs to set up. Try telling that to a hungry crew!

FLIPPIN' DUCK!

If there's duck on the menu in a restaurant, I'm all over it as my first choice. Not only do I love the flavour, but until quite recently it's been an item I haven't cooked nearly enough at home. This recipe has changed all that. Duck isn't difficult to roast; you just need some patience, a little intervention and a willing fork.

THAT'S IT?

- A 5- to 6-pound domestic duck, excess fat trimmed off the tip and tail
- Fired-Up Spice (page 4)
- Sweet soy sauce, a.k.a. *kecap manis*

DUCK IT!

If your duck was frozen, make sure you not only thaw it out, but dry the duck thoroughly by patting it down, like you're a cop and you suspect the duck is packing heat. After the paper towel treatment it's also a good idea to place the duck on a rack and store it uncovered for several hours in the fridge, to dry the skin even further.

Bring your oven up to speed, 250° F —yes, that's hot enough.

Pull out your fork and prick the duck's skin all over, say about 15 times per side. Don't stab into the meat, just into the skin, so the duck will release its fat when cooked. This is the key, as duck is notoriously generous in the fat department. Add ¾ cup of water to the roasting pan, to reduce splattering.

Truss the duck with butcher's twine like you would a chicken (a.k.a. tie the bird together), sprinkle with Fired-Up Spice and place in the roaster breast side up. Roast, uncovered, for 1 hour.

This is the first of 4½ hours, so budget accordingly.

Remove the duck from the oven and flip it over, breast side down now (with oven mitts covered with paper towels), and get it back in the oven.

Repeat that scenario each ½ hour for a total of 4 hours. If you don't think the duck is releasing enough fat, prick the skin a little more along the way, to help the getting-lean-and-mean cause.

Remove the duck from the oven and fire up the temp to 350°F, 'cause it's time to crisp up Daffy's skin.

Give the duck another flip—you should be going breast side down here.

My favourite approach is to brush sweet soy sauce all over the duck—or try your own favourite glaze—but you can go the naked route, too. Hey, I'm talking about the duck here! Oh, come on, at least wear an apron!

Roast for 15 minutes and then flip to breast side up. Brush liberally with the sweet soy sauce and roast for a final 15 minutes or until done. The longer you roast it, the crisper the skin, but it's a fine line because we want our duck juicy inside, too. Tastes as good as it looks. Just ducky!

WINE 'N' WHISKEY
BEEF RIBS

Are you looking for mouth-watering, restaurant-style beef ribs in a tangy sauce? Well, I believe you've come to the right place, as this is the home of the boozy beef rib.

TO THE BUTCHER, SUPERMARKET AND LIQUOR MART WE GO

- 2 cups red wine
- ¼ cup canola oil
- 14 beef rib bones (2 racks)—you can cut each rack in half, to fit a roaster
- 2 carrots, 2 celery stalks and 2 medium onions, coarsely chopped
- 1 head garlic, broken up into individual cloves
- 2 tablespoons peppercorns
- 8 cups beef or chicken broth (or use bouillon cubes mixed with hot water, as a shortcut)
- 3 cups ketchup
- 1 cup rye whiskey or bourbon
- ½ cup honey
- ⅓ cup brown sugar
- ¼ cup molasses—preferably fancy
- 3 teaspoons dried oregano
- 1+ teaspoon red chili flakes

LET'S TAKE THAT COW OUT FOR A FEW DRINKS

Combine the red wine and canola oil and marinate the ribs in 2 large zip-top freezer bags for at least 2 hours, or even overnight, in the fridge.

Fire up your oven to 300°F.

Place the ribs and marinade in a large roaster. Nestle the vegetables, garlic and peppercorns in there as well, and pour the broth into the roaster until the liquid is about halfway up the sides of the ribs.

We're ready to braise! Cover the roaster and bake for about 2 hours, depending on size.

Now, let's mix up the sauce. Just whisk the ketchup, whiskey or bourbon, honey, brown sugar, molasses, oregano and chili flakes together in a saucepan. Simmer for 15 to 30 minutes or so, long enough to allow flavours to meld.

When you can just pierce the ribs with a butter knife, bring on the sauce.

Remove the ribs and cut them into individual bones. Dump the braising liquid—its layoff notice is out. (Not to worry, it got a severance package.)

Go to town with the whiskey sauce. Don't stop until the ribs are pretty much swimming in that temptingly tangy concoction.

Get the ribs back in the covered roaster for another hour at 300°, giving the ribs a flip at the halfway point. Those heifers are soaking up the flavours now! Dare we declare them (*hick-a-mooooooooooo!*) hammered?

Lift the cover from the ribs and give them another sauce baste. You can bake them, uncovered, for 15 more minutes, broil them or, the Utopian option, barbecue them. The idea here is to caramelize the sauce on the ribs without drying them out. Beware the temptation to overcook!

GIVE A GUY A BREAK . . . IN

I was working the night shift at the fire hall one Christmas Eve while my family attended church. During the service some Good Samaritan smashed out the passenger-side window of our car and ran off with my wife's new camera. Yes, our home was filled with glad tidings of joy as we realized the true meaning of Christmas—that it's better to take than to receive.

Since the holidays are also the season of sharing, I took the glass fragments to work a couple of weeks later. While the other firefighters slept—I mean, worked—I snuck out to our rookie Dean's brand new SUV, rolled down the driver's window, spread the broken glass out over the driver's seat and floor mats and tossed a screwdriver onto the driver's seat.

At shift change Dean exited the hall only to return seconds later, incensed. "*#%@*!!! My truck was broken into!*"

I nonchalantly wandered out from the kitchen to see what all the ruckus was about, as members of our crew and the relieving crew—none of whom were in on the joke—followed Dean to his truck to inspect the damage.

"Hey, there's a screwdriver on the seat," Bruce observed. "They must have tried to steal your truck and someone scared them off."

"It sure is clean around the window, no glass fragments at—" Keith said, before I elbowed him the shush sign. Thankfully, Dean was so busy inspecting his truck that he missed Keith's observation. Once Dean was satisfied that nothing was missing, he started cleaning up the broken glass. "That's just brutal," I said, straight-faced, consoling my downtrodden coworker as he dumped the broken glass into the garbage. "It's just like with my car. You can't have anything new, because someone is always there to ruin it for you."

"So what do I do now?" despondent Dean asked, shaking his head.

I explained that he could drive straight to a glass repair shop and call the insurance company from there to make a claim. I also told him that it would cost him his deductible, $200, and that he'd also have to fill out a police report.

Once Dean completed the interior cleanup he slid behind the wheel of his truck. As I stood holding the driver's-side door open, Dean fired up the motor. When he put it in gear I rolled up his window, and as I closed the door I wished him a good day. Dean was completely confused. "How did you . . . ? What just . . . ?" he sputtered as the rest of the crew inside—clued in by Keith—roared with laughter. "*What just happened here?*"

Yes, I had to explain it to him.

IT'S A FIRE BOAT!
IT'S A FISHING BOAT!

THE BUCKET BRIGADE

Water fights are commonplace in fire halls throughout the world. Whether it's a bucket of cold water thrown on unsuspecting firefighters, ice water tossed at a showering firefighter or a length of 1¾-inch fire hose stretched into the kitchen to knock playing cards out of the hands of firefighters embroiled in a heated Hearts game, water is here to play. It's *everywhere*, so you'd better bring a spare set of clothes to work, because you're going to need it.

One day as the water war—I mean, apparatus floor washout—wrapped at No. 1, Lee went out to one of the trucks to back it into the hall. I noticed that one of the compartment doors was open, so I raced out to close it before he ripped it off backing in. Having saved the truck from certain destruction, I walked back into the hall and—*splash!* Ryan had climbed to the roof of the hall above the overhead doors and doused me from above.

The same hit man is famous for another set-up. Ryan asked Dean to come out to his truck in the parking lot to show him something. After their chat, Dean walked back across the parking lot to the hall. He spotted a (strategically planted) football at the edge of a huge puddle—a lake, really—that often formed in a low spot in the lot after it rained. As Dean leaned over to pick it up, Ryan floored his truck. Dean turned his head just as Ryan ploughed through the puddle, sending a tsunami wave that *buried* Dean in a wall of water. Gotcha!

I love this one. A water fight erupted one day at No. 6. Everyone was getting soaked, with the exception of Jaws, who was hiding from the battle in the floor watch booth. One of the guys stood outside the booth and demanded that he come out and get saturated like everyone else. "I'll tell you what," Jaws responded. "I'm wearing my dress uniform. Let me get into my fatigues and you can give it to me."

Jaws ran upstairs and got changed. When he came down he was immediately drenched. "All right, are you happy now?" Jaws asked his assailant. With that, Jawsman went back upstairs, got changed back into his dress uniform and resumed his duties. At the end of the day, his attacker screamed from the change room area, "Hey, what the hell? My clothes in my locker are all soaking wet. Jaws, you changed into *my* clothes!"

Well, I don't know about you, but all this water talk has me craving seafood, so let's head to the fire hall kitchen and see what the catch of the day is.

ALMOND-AND-SESAME-
CRUSTED SOLE

Being the fried fish fin-atic that I am, I'm always looking for new breading ideas. One firefighter suggested I try almonds, while another raved about sesame seeds as a coating. So, in my quest for decadence, I decided to bring the two ideas together and top the fish off with a tasty lemon-infused hollandaise sauce.

OH, THAT FISH IS A GOOD-NATURED SOLE, THOUGH A LITTLE NUTTY

- 1 cup almonds (any size or shape)
- ½ cup sesame seeds
- 2 pounds sole fillets (or pickerel, pollock or similar mild white fish)
- Fired-Up Spice (page 4)
- All-purpose flour
- 2 eggs, beaten with 2 teaspoons water
- Packaged hollandaise sauce (simply follow the package directions)
- 1 tablespoon fresh (or bottled) lemon juice
- Peanut or canola oil
- Butter
- Asparagus, woody ends snapped off
- Kosher salt, freshly ground black pepper and cayenne, to taste

WHY, IT'S SO CRUSTY IT'S ALMOST A CRUSTACEAN

Pull out the food processor or blender and mash up the almonds until fine.

Once you've mulched the almonds, combine them with the sesame seeds. I like to maintain a mix of about 2 parts almonds to 1 part sesame seeds.

Sprinkle both sides of the fish fillets with our old standby, Fired-Up Spice.

Dust the fillets with just enough flour to coat and absorb the moisture.

Get the fillets to the edge of the egg wash pool and demand that they walk the plank one by one. Come on in, guys, the egg wash is great!

Now, let's finish up by dredging them in the almond/sesame combination. Set aside in the fridge.

While the fish sits, let's get that fine-tasting hollandaise sauce together, adding the lemon juice to give it a little extra zip.

Heat up a large frying pan over, say, medium to medium-high heat and cover the pan's bottom with about a quarter inch of oil. When the oil comes up to temperature, get the fillets in there and cook the wee fellas until lightly browned on both sides and cooked through.

In a separate pan, heat a couple of tablespoons of butter to medium-high and get the asparagus in there with a little salt and pepper. Fry until the asparagus just reaches the tender-crisp stage—try checking it with a fork to be sure.

Hey, we've got the green light to plate our masterpiece. Let's start with a helping of **Lemon-Pesto Jasmine Rice** (page 192). Top the mound of rice with the fish fillet, then the asparagus and, for the grand finale, the hollandaise sauce with a light sprinkle of salt, pepper and cayenne to fire it up!

LASAGNA OF THE SEA

You may recognize this sauce from the Linguine of the Sea recipe back in Fire Hall Cooking. *My buddy firefighter Gale Osterman has used this sauce to top stuffed manicotti in her quest for extreme decadence, so I figured that if it works there it should do likewise in lasagna. And does it ever, with a few small modifications. To boost the delectability quotient, we've made this a four-cheese lasagna, but not to worry, my calorie-conscious friends, it's all low-fat cheese!*

WHAT IS THIS, THE SEA OF CHEESE?

- 2 tablespoons each olive oil and butter
- 1 medium onion, chopped fine
- 3-4 garlic cloves, minced or pressed
- Kosher salt and freshly ground black pepper
- 1 red pepper, slivered
- 1 cup celery, diced (or mushrooms, sliced into Ts)
- ½ tablespoon Italian seasoning
- ⅓ cup flour
- 1 cup dry white wine—I like those little 1-cup bottles
- 3 cups chicken broth
- 2 5-ounce cans baby clams—be sure to reserve the juice, don't toss it!
- 8-ounce package light cream cheese, at room temperature
- 2+ teaspoons chili-garlic sauce
- 1 pound crab-flavoured pollock
- 1 pound large shrimp, out of their shells and cut in half
- 12–16 whole-wheat lasagna noodles— depending on size of lasagna dish
- 1 pound light ricotta cheese
- 2 eggs—give them a beating
- ½ cup freshly grated Parmesan cheese— much better flavour than the tubed stuff
- 2 cups grated light mozzarella cheese (or even a 4-cheese Italian blend)

LAYERS 1, 2, 3, PLUS THE FINAL TOPPING—OF ALL THINGS, CHEESE!

Get the olive oil and butter going in a large saucepan over medium heat and sauté the onions and garlic until nicely softened. You know, a little hit of salt and pepper would sure add to the experience.

Intro the other veggies, plus the Italian seasoning. Sauté the veggies until they are fork tender, and then dust with the flour.

Pour in the wine and let it reduce; the flour will help in that department.

Follow up with the chicken broth and clam juice (but not the clams). Simmer for 30 minutes.

Drop the cream cheese into the sauce in wee pieces a bit at a time, whisking the sauce together as you go until blended and creamy.

Let's fire it up! Drop in the chili-garlic sauce, combine and taste-test. You can also add salt, pepper and more Italian seasoning as you see fit.

Spoon off, say, about ¾ to 1 cup or so of the sauce and set it aside.

Bring on the clams, pollock and shrimp and heat through. It should only take about 5 minutes for the shrimp to turn pink—your cue to quit.

Meanwhile, get those noodles boiling. When they're completely cooked, dry them off with paper towels to minimize the water content.

We've got a cheese layer planned for this baby, so let's get the ricotta in a bowl with the eggs and Parmesan and mix them together.

I think it's time to get the assembly going. Fire up your oven to 350°F. Remember that sauce I told you to set aside? Well, spray a 9 x 13-inch lasagna dish with veggie spray and lay down about half of the seafood-free sauce.

Top with your first layer of noodles. Warning: déjà vu coming up . . .

Next up, it's the seafood sauce. Get half of it on those lasagna noodles.

Top with another batch of pasta and get the cheesy middle happening. Spread out the ricotta mixture evenly and top with another noodle layer.

The rest of the seafood sauce wants in, so let's give in to its demand.

Top with more noodles. That was predictable, wasn't it?

I hope you hung onto the remaining seafood-free sauce. If so, spread it out over the noodles and top your creation with the mozzarella cheese.

Bake till it's bubbling and lightly browned on top. We're talking about ½ hour or so, unless you decided to make it ahead and refrigerate it before baking. If so, add 15 minutes or so to the tally.

Let the lasagna set up on the counter for 10 minutes before slicing.

WATERWORLD

Some 15 years ago, Johnny the rookie was asked to bring his video camera to work at No. 1 under the guise that his crewmates would take video footage of him in his new working environment. Did they ever. Once the camera made its way into enemy hands, John was paged to the private phone housed in a phone booth on the apparatus floor.

"Water rescue drill up," was heard over the fire hall's PA system.

Once Johnny entered the booth, the boys backed the water rescue truck up against the door. "Very funny," Johnny thought with a chuckle. But the prank was only starting to roll, as was the film in John's camera. Up to the roof of the booth one of the pranksters climbed, and up and over the opening at the top dropped a fire hose flowing at 125 gallons per minute. The water rose as quickly as Johnny's level of alarm. Once the water reached chest level, however, the pranksters pulled the truck away and water *poured* out of the booth.

Shaking his head and laughing as he inspected his flooded fatigues, good-natured Johnny was met outside the booth by the captain, who shook his hand and said with a wink, "Welcome to No. 1."

PICKEREL FILLETS

Here's a recipe guaranteed to push the envelope of decadence. Not just flavour decadence, but presentation, too. When company is coming over, this is one of my favourite dishes to make. It's like a tasty lemon-garlic fish fillet wrapped around a crab cake. So delicious! Come on, get on it, get stuffed!

THE STUFF TO STUFF

- A whack of butter
- ½ cup finely chopped yellow or white onion
- ¼ cup each finely chopped celery and red pepper
- ½ pound crab-flavoured pollock (or real crab, if you can swing it)
- ¼ cup whipped salad dressing or mayo
- ½ tablespoon prepared mustard
- ½ cup Italian bread crumbs
- 2 tablespoons Parmesan cheese
- 2 tablespoons chopped fresh parsley
- 2 pounds pickerel or sole fillets, bones removed
- 2 toothpicks for each fillet
- Juice and zest (that's the grated rind) of 1 lemon

ROLL 'EM

Melt a tablespoon or two of butter in a frying pan over medium heat. Toss the onion, celery and red pepper in and sauté until softened. Set aside to cool.

In a good-sized bowl, add the remaining ingredients except the fillets and lemon. Toss in the veggies once they've cooled off a bit. Combine the ingredients with your hands. If the mixture seems too dry, add a little extra shot of salad dressing and/or mustard to hold it together.

Roll the crab mixture into individual cylindrical shapes, about the width of the fillet you're about to stuff.

Lay out the fillet and, starting at the wide end, lay down the crab and roll up the fillet jellyroll style. Stab a couple of toothpicks into the fillet to hold it together. Good stuff!

Stand the fillets up on their sides in a greased ovenproof dish, keeping them close together so they'll hold their shapes. At this point you can cover and send them to the fridge if you have other things to do.

When mealtime draws near, heat up your oven to 350°F. Melt 2 tablespoons of butter in the microwave. Introduce the zest and juice of the lemon to the butter and combine.

Brush each fillet (but not the stuffing) with the lemon butter.

Bake for approximately 30 minutes or until the fillets flake easily. Feel free to baste the fillets with lemon butter every 10 minutes.

Serve with a dollop of tartar sauce strategically placed over the stuffing.

Aaaaaaaaghhh! Oh, sorry, I forgot to tell you to remove the toothpicks before putting this taste treat in your mouth.

FIRED-UP
CALAMARI

Calamari is a breeze to cook—quick, easy, and delicious. I'll even show you how you can make this into a lunch special. With me? Let's proceed.

SQUIDWARD WE GO

- ½ cup all-purpose flour
- 1 tablespoon cornstarch
- 1 teaspoon paprika
- ½ teaspoon dry mustard
- 1/8 teaspoon cayenne
- ¾-pound package calamari rings, defrosted
- 2 cups peanut or canola oil (you need an oil that can handle the heat)
- Salt, to taste—best make it sea salt or kosher
- Lemon wedges, for serving

RESISTANCE IS FUTILE

Let's get the flour, cornstarch, paprika, dry mustard and that fiery blast of the red devil cayenne combined in a bowl.

Toss the calamari rings in the flour mixture about a dozen or so at a time. The rings have a tendency to flatten, so do your best to work the flour into the middle of the rings, but don't get too stressed out, as they do tend to co-operate and open up when they hit the hot oil.

Fire up the deep fryer, or do as I do, and carefully pour 2 cups of oil into a sturdy wok and bring it up to 375°F. The temperature is important, as we are only going to cook the little fellas briefly. Fry them too fast, and they won't be cooked through; too slow, and you'll be chewing on rubber. If you happen to be lucky enough to have one of those high-temperature candy thermometers, dip it in the oil for testing.

Get the squids in the hot tub until they turn a nice golden brown—we're talking about a minute or so. Fish them out and place on a paper towel-lined plate or strainer. Toss with salt.

You can serve them basic Italian style and simply squeeze fresh lemon juice over top, or go Greek and serve them with tzatziki sauce.

To make a nice **Spicy Tzatziki Sauce**, combine a finely diced long English cucumber with 2 cups plain yogurt, 2 tablespoons extra-virgin olive oil, 2 teaspoons lemon juice, 1 teaspoon kosher salt, 2 teaspoons dried dill weed, 2 cloves minced garlic and 1 teaspoon **Fired-Up Spice** (page 4). For maximum flavour, let it sit in the fridge overnight.

You could even serve the squids 'n' tzatziki in pitas, or toss the calamari over a fresh Caesar salad. Oh, the possibilities are endless. Get me one of those lobster-eating bibs—my mouth's watering here.

POTATO CHIP PICKEREL

My wife had a group of work friends over one evening while I was working the night shift—and, really, what better time for her friends to visit? Anyway, the next day a big bag of leftover salt-and-vinegar chips was staring me down just as I was looking for something to make for supper. For some reason—best known to my devilish subconscious—I thought, "How about crushing up those chips and breading some pickerel fillets with them?" This became an instant hit at home, as my daughter Elizabeth commented, "Dad, that is the best fish you've ever made!" Only problem with this fish dish is, I'll betcha can't eat just one!

TALK ABOUT YOUR FISH 'N' CHIPS

- 8-ounce bag salt-and-vinegar potato chips
- 2 pounds pickerel (a.k.a. walleye—or try any mild white fish)
- Old Bay seasoning
- Paprika
- All-purpose flour
- 2 eggs plus 2 tablespoons water
- Canola oil for frying

I'LL HAVE A PLATE OF PIPING HOT PICKEREL RIGHT NOW!

Let's pull out the food processor and put it to work. Even one of those little mini processors will do, though you'll have to do more batches. If you don't have either modern-day appliance, you've qualified for manual labour, so get out your tried-and-true rolling pin and go to town on the chips.

Whoa! Hang on! I should have mentioned, do not eat any of the chips. It's clinically proven to be humanly impossible to simply sample potato chips. Once you start there's no looking back. That means a ruined appetite, unsightly pounds, cellulite monsters and guilt trips.

Dust the fillets on both sides with a little Old Bay seasoning and paprika.

Run 'em through the flour station so they have a light coating of the white stuff. Give 'em a little shake to dump the excess.

Next up it's the egg wash, so dip the fillets through to evenly coat.

Those tempting potato chips are calling you: "Eat me, eat me!" Don't listen to them. Place the fillets on the crushed chips, coating evenly.

Warm up a frying pan (I like the non-stick variety) over medium to medium-high heat and pour in a light layer of canola oil.

Once the oil is up to pan temperature, get the chipped-up fillets in there and lightly brown both sides, cooking until the fish just reaches the point where—*you know what I'm going to say, don't you?*— it starts to flake.

As for sides, I have a sinking suspicioun you're thinking french fries. Personally, I'm going the rice route, but from a pairing point of view, you have a valid point. Oh, and be sure to floss the chips out of your teeth!

PSYCHEDELIC SALMON

"What we had in mind was breakfast for 400,000!" Oh, sorry, I was having a Woodstock flashback there. How's that possible? I was only 10 years old! Wait a second, do I hear Jimmy Hendrix playing "The Star-Spangled Banner"? Well, now that we're way off course, here's a great recipe that got its name the morning after its creator, firefighter Scott Atchison, served it to his crew, when the captain complained about the weird dreams he'd had. With nothing else to blame, they figured it must have been the salmon. So, fire up the Q to 11, this salmon's ready to rock! Oh, say, can you see . . .

HEY, WHERE ARE THE MUSHROOMS, MAN?

- ¼ cup + 2 tablespoons soy sauce
- ¼ cup extra-virgin olive oil
- ¼ cup brown sugar
- 3 tablespoons minced, crushed or otherwise rudely violated garlic
- Juice of 1 lemon, plus additional lemons for serving, if desired
- Lots of freshly ground black pepper
- 1 large salmon fillet (about 3 pounds)
- Fired-Up Spice (page 4) or seasoning salt

THE ONLY ONE GETTING HIGH HERE IS THE BARBECUE

Get the marinade together by combining the soy sauce, olive oil, brown sugar, garlic, lemon juice and pepper.

Marinate the fish for half an hour in a glass or other nonreactive dish on the counter. Dust with the Fired-Up Spice or seasoning salt.

Wrap the fillet and about half the marinade completely and tightly in aluminum foil. You really don't want the marinade to leak out onto the Q, or on the family room rug on the way to the Q.

Fire up the barbecue to high. High, like sky-high, incinerating, man!

After the flare-ups die down (thanks here to the fire crew who cooked fatty burgers yesterday), place the salmon package on the Q. Man, there must have been a sale on regular ground beef. We might have to put in a second alarm!

Expect your cooking time to be about 10 to 12 minutes per inch of salmon thickness, depending on the heat your Q throws. You can also bake this baby if the weather's not co-operating. See directions on page 102 for **Thai-Becued Salmon**.

Not to worry, you want the marinade to caramelize on the salmon. In fact, if you nailed this recipe Atch style, Salmy may be slightly blackened. Be sure not to overcook, however, as salmon is known to dry out if you leave it on too long. So once Salmy starts to just flake in the centre, make sure you march him from the Q to the dinner table.

Serve with bonus lemon quarters.

THAI-BECUED
SALMON

I've taken Atch's amazing **Psychedelic Salmon** *(page 101) over to the Far East for a little Thai tune-up. The result is a surefire hit that's a little bit sweet and a little bit tangy. Oh, and you've also got a baking option, explained at the end of the recipe. Mmmmmm, this fish is delish!*

THOSE THAILANDERS SURE LOVE THEIR FISH

- ½ cup sweet soy sauce (see page 4)
- ¼ cup sweet chili sauce
- ¼ cup peanut oil
- ½ head of garlic, cloves minced or pressed
- 2 tablespoons minced fresh ginger
- Juice of 1 large lime (or about 2 tablespoons bottled lime juice)
- Chopped cilantro—toss ¼ cup in with the marinade and have more on hand for serving
- 1 large salmon fillet, say about 3 pounds
- Limes for serving

EVEN IF IT IS ATLANTIC SALMON

Let's bring the sweet soy sauce, sweet chili sauce, peanut oil, garlic, ginger, lime juice and cilantro together and call it our marinade. Pour it over the salmon fillet housed in a nonreactive dish—like glass or Pyrex—and let it rest for about half an hour. Now you can proceed to the Q or fall back on the baking option.

Wrap the salmon plus some of the marinade tightly in foil. I also like to set a bit of the marinade aside after the fish has soaked in it, and boil it for 5 minutes in a saucepan on the range, not only to thicken it slightly, but more important, to kill any naughty bits that it may have picked up from the fish. This is more likely to happen with chicken or beef, but I say let's be safe out there on the culinary playground.

Fire up the Q to high, and once it's heated up, bring on the salmon.

Note: the salmon cooks very quickly on high. It may be ready less than 10 minutes after it hits the Q. Once the salmon just starts to flake in the centre, it's go time, my friend—as in, let's go eat!

Serve the Thai-Becued Salmon topped with the marinade you boiled briefly earlier (warm it up again if it's cooled off) and another hit of that cilantro. Oh, and why not place lime quarters on the side of each plate? As we've discussed many times before, never underestimate the power of presentation.

Baking option: Simply cover the dish with foil and bake the salmon with marinade at 450°F for about 20 minutes, or until Salmy just starts to flake in the centre.

A **Feelin'-the-Heat Asian Noodle Salad** (page 53) would be a nice complement to both the Psychedelic and the Thai-Becued Salmon. Hey, and what about a hearty batch of **Lemon-Pesto Jasmine Rice** (page 192) and some of that tasty **Asian Orange Asparagus** (page 183)?

SHRIMP GOES COUSCOUS

Captain Garry Pinette passed this recipe on to me with the caveat, "This recipe is absolutely fabulous, Jeff. See what you can do to fire it up." I did make a few minor changes, but really, when a recipe rocks, why mess with it?

COUSCOUS—A FINE GRAIN, SO EASY TO MAKE

- You're going to need garlic, so bring a head along
- Get out the butter and extra-virgin olive oil
- ½ cup each finely chopped onions, celery and carrots
- Kosher salt and freshly ground black pepper
- ¼ cup white wine
- 8 ounces bottled clam juice
- 28-ounce can diced tomatoes in their juice
- 2 cups couscous—I like the whole-wheat variety
- 2 pounds large shrimp, peeled, tails on—you know, you could give the little guys a flavour infusion of freshly ground black pepper, say about 2 teaspoons kosher or 1 teaspoon sea salt, plus a shot of Greek seasoning
- Grated zest and juice of 1 lemon
- Chopped fresh parsley
- Chopped green onions

THE SHRIMP ARE GOING TO TAKE A BUTTERY GARLIC BATH

Mince up 4 to 6 cloves of the garlic. In a large saucepan, bring 2 tablespoons each butter and olive oil up to medium heat and toss in the garlic for a flash, about 20 seconds, to infuse that great garlic flavour. Then bring on the onions, celery and carrots.

Season the veggies with salt and pepper to taste, and keep them rocking and rolling along until they're soft.

Pour in the wine, followed up by the clam juice and tomatoes. Bring to a boil, and then turn the range down to a simmer for about 10 minutes.

Carefully, and I mean this, *carefully* pour the contents into a blender, cover with the lid and a towel for extra-safe measure, and pulse the contents until all of the veggies are smashed up and silky smooth.

Pour the purée—here in English Canada we say pure-eh?—back into the pot and bring the couscous in from the on-deck circle.

Cover the pot and let it stand off the heat for about 10 minutes or so.

While you wait, you will work. Melt ¼ cup butter along with its good buddy ¼ cup extra-virgin olive oil in a frying pan over medium-high heat.

Mince up another 6 or 8 cloves of garlic and toss in, followed up closely by the shrimp. Fry until the shrimp is happily pink. Please don't overcook the little guys or you'll be eating Rob-bob-ob-bi the Rub-bu-ber-man.

Toss the shrimp with the lemon zest, lemon juice and parsley.

Serve by laying down the couscous first, followed up by the shrimp, and top the order off with the chopped green onions.

SUN-DRIED-TOMATO- WITH SEAFOOD
PESTO PASTA

Here's a decadent dinner that guests will think you've been preparing all day. Between you and me, though, you'll likely be able to bang this one off in about half an hour, depending on the number of interruptions you happen to receive.

ONCE UPON A TIME, IN AN ITALIAN FISHING VILLAGE

- 1 cup oil-packed sun-dried tomatoes—drain the oil, please
- 1 cup fresh basil leaves (parsley could be substituted)
- 2 tablespoons lemon juice
- 10 garlic cloves in total, minced—4 for the pesto and 6 for the seafood
- 1 teaspoon kosher salt
- Several good grinds from the pepper mill (about ½ teaspoon)
- Extra-virgin olive oil (about 9 tablespoons in total)
- ⅓ cup Parmesan cheese, plus more for garnishing
- 1 medium onion, diced
- 1 zucchini, sliced
- 1 red pepper, sliced into strips
- About ½ pound mushrooms, T'd up
- 3 tablespoons butter
- 1 pound each bay scallops and peeled shrimp (tails on, though)
- 1 pound linguine or favourite pasta, cooked
- Cherry or grape tomatoes
- Parsley for garnish

THE PRINCESS ASKED, "HOW DO I MAKE-A THE PESTO?"

Where did I put that dusty old food processor? Oh, here it is. Let's load 'er up with the sun-dried tomatoes, basil, lemon juice, 4 garlic cloves, salt and pepper. Pulse it a few times to break it all down.

When you've managed to mulch it up nicely, turn the processor on to GO, drizzle in ¼ cup olive oil and follow up with the Parmesan. Leave the machine be with all the contents on board, as more processing lies ahead.

Stir-fry the onions in 2 tablespoons olive oil until softened. Bring the zucchini, pepper strips and mushrooms into the fold, sprinkling the veggies with a little salt and pepper as you bring out their flavours. Set aside.

In a large frying pan over medium-high heat, add 3 tablespoons each olive oil and butter. Once melted, toss in 6 garlic cloves, the scallops and shrimp, and cook till the shrimp is pink and the scallops are translucent.

Remove the seafood, and pour the broth into a measuring cup. Now, head back over to the food processor and hit the GO button. Slowly pour about ⅔ cup of the reserved broth in with the pesto until well combined.

Add the pesto to the cooked pasta and toss through. Bring on the veggies and tomatoes, and welcome the fashionably late seafood. Toss, toss, toss.

Garnish with parsley and additional Parmesan cheese, as desired.

THAI FISH CAKES

A wise Thai man—hiding behind the thinly veiled reality of a dimwitted Canuck firefighter—once said, "Try them as an appetizer, serve them for lunch, or even for your evening meal. And don't forgot a few dollops of the **Sweet Chili Tartar Sauce.**

ESCAPE FROM THE TIGER AND INTO THE CROCODILE!

Or, as we North Americans say,

OUT OF THE FRYING PAN AND INTO THE FIRE!

- 1 tablespoon butter
- ⅓ cup minced red onion
- 1 pound boneless, skinless white fish fillets, cubed (basa, pickerel, sole, or tilapia)
- 1 cup fresh bread crumbs
- ¼ cup packed chopped cilantro
- 1 egg
- 2 tablespoons sweet chili sauce—not chili-garlic sauce—think sweet!
- 2 tablespoons oyster sauce
- 1 teaspoon brown sugar
- Peanut oil

MAN WHO WALK THROUGH TURNSTILE SIDEWAYS IS GOING TO . . .

Get the butter going in a frying pan over medium heat and caramelize the onions—in other words, lightly brown them till they sugar.

Get the fish fillets into a food processor and chop 'em up fairly fine.

Add the onion, bread crumbs, cilantro, egg, sweet chili sauce, oyster sauce and brown sugar to the food machine. Hit GO and combine.

Move the fish combo to a mixing bowl. You may find you need to add more bread crumbs if your mix is too wet. As an option, you could also add a little flour to help dry your creation out. You're looking for a mouldable consistency here, like dough—but not the monetary kind.

Form the mixture into patties—you should get 6 to 8, depending on the size you're after (main course vs. appetizer).

Let the patties sit in the fridge for at least ½ hour or even overnight to set up. It makes for an easy meal when you get home after a long day.

Get your favourite large frying pan humming over medium heat. Toss in enough peanut oil to easily cover the bottom.

Place the fish cakes in the hot oil and fry until golden brown on both sides and cooked through. Place the cakes on a rack to drain off any oil.

Serve with . . .

SWEET CHILI TARTAR SAUCE

- ¼ cup mayonnaise
- 1½ tablespoons fresh lime juice
- 1 tablespoon sweet chili sauce—or more, to taste

Simply mix everything together.

THAI-LAPIA

*Tilapia is a deliciously mild, firm-fleshed fish that's a pushover for any taste you intro-
duce it to. To fire up the flavour quotient we're going to poach the fish in a curried
coconut milk sauce along with onions and sweet peppers. It's an easy, gorgeous gourmet
dish you can prepare in minutes.*

THE THAILANDERS

- 1 tablespoon peanut oil
- ½ jumbo onion, sliced into strips
- 1 red, orange or yellow pepper, in strips
- Kosher salt and freshly ground black pepper
- Tilapia fillets—4 work well, but however
  many you can fit into a large frying pan
- Fired-Up Spice (page 4)
- 1 tablespoon fish sauce (in your grocer's
  Asian food section)
- 1½ tablespoons curry paste—or
  2 tablespoons for rip roaring!
- 14-ounce can coconut milk—stir contents
  together to combine
- 1 ripe mango (or a tart apple), chopped into
  bite-sized squares
- Chopped cilantro and lime quarters, for
  garnish

. . . ARE SHOWING THE TILAPIA A LITTLE THAI HOSPITALITY

Select your favourite frying pan, size
extra-large if you have it. Fire it up over
medium heat, and get the peanut oil
in there. Follow up with the onion and
pepper, dusting the veggies with about
½ teaspoon each salt and pepper as you
go. Stir-fry the vegomatics until they
reach the crucial tender-crisp stage.

Meanwhile, dust both sides of the
tilapia with a hit of Fired-Up Spice.

Drop the fish sauce into the frying
pan with the veggies (do not inhale!),
followed by the curry paste, and work
it through the veggies till the curry
coats them.

Better turn on the range fan unless
you want your place to smell like the
Bangkok Diner for the next few days.
Oh, but it's a great odour, isn't it?

Move the veggies off to the side to
make room for the fish and introduce
the tilapia. Uh-oh, the veggies are feeling displaced and deeply hurt, so to
avoid expensive therapy, let's cuddle
them over top of the fillets.

Pour in the coconut milk and turn
the heat down to an active simmer—
a.k.a. a light boil—and poach the fish
for a couple of minutes.

Bring on the mango and continue to
poach till the fish just starts to flake.

Serve over **Caribbean Couscous** (page
186). I know, Thailand isn't anywhere
near the Caribbean, but this combination will work well for you, regardless.

Top your creation with cilantro and
lime quarters for squeezing.

This recipe is also great with basa
fish. The only issue here is that you'll
likely be able to squeeze only 2 of those
massive fillets into a frying pan.

THE GREEK FETA
FISH DISH

I spied an unfamiliar frozen fish at the supermarket one day, and being that it was not only on sale but yielding in bonus Air Miles, I picked it up—typical cheap firefighter! Once home I did my research. Cape Capensis fish dwell in the deep, cool, unpolluted waters off the west coast of South Africa. Similar to cod, this fish is meaty and quite tasty on its own. But you know me, "quite tasty" just isn't good enough, so we're taking C.C. to Greece for a fired-up taste vacation.

GREEK'S ANATOMY

- 1½–2 pounds Cape Capensis, a.k.a. hake (or cod)
- Fired-Up Santa Fe Spice (page 5) or Old Bay seasoning
- All-purpose flour
- Extra-virgin olive oil
- 4 garlic cloves, minced or pressed
- 1 small red onion, sliced into strips
- 2 celery stalks, diced
- 2 peppers (yellow and orange look nice in this dish), cut into strips
- 1 small zucchini, sliced
- Kosher salt and freshly ground black pepper
- 2 teaspoons Greek or Italian seasoning
- 28-ounce can diced tomatoes
- ¾ cup diced or crumbled feta cheese—I like the one with herbs
- Chili-garlic sauce (optional)
- Chopped fresh parsley

COME ON, CAPE CAPENSIS, TIME FOR A SWIM IN THE MEDITERRANEAN!

Defrost the fish and pat it dry. Season the fillets with a healthy dose of Fired-Up Spice on both sides. Dust the top and bottom with a light coating of flour, to help the fillets brown as they fry.

To make the sauce, pour 2 tablespoons of olive oil into a large frying pan over medium heat.

Add the garlic, onion and celery and fry until tender-crisp. Then bring on the peppers and zucchini and dust the veggies with salt, pepper and seasoning. Stir-fry for a couple of minutes.

Introduce the tomatoes and get things bubbling lightly, then add the feta.

Allow the cheese to melt in the sauce for a few minutes, and give it the old taste test. Hmmmm? A little salt and pepper, perhaps? Or, if you're like me, toss in a shot of chili-garlic sauce to fire your feta fish up.

Meanwhile, let's get a large, non-stick frying pan going over medium to medium-high heat. Pour in enough olive oil to coat the pan and bring it to temperature. When the bath is drawn, page the fish to the pan.

Fry each side of the Cape for approximately 3 minutes, or until nicely browned and about ready to flake. You may need to do two batches.

Plate the fish fillets over rice, top with the feta sauce and garnish with parsley.

TILAPIA FISH

Pesto has so many great uses that it's certainly worth having a batch made up and stored in the fridge in a tight-sealing container. You can go the store-bought route or, even better, try the **Everybody Goes Pesto** *(page 144). This fish dish may be quick and easy to prepare, but it looks and tastes gourmet.*

THE FISH AND THE FLAVOUR ENHANCERS

- 2 pounds tilapia (or try pickerel, sole, Cape Capensis or basa)
- Seasoned flour—3 parts flour to 1 part Fired-Up Spice (page 4)
- 2 tablespoons melted butter
- 4 garlic cloves, minced—garlic butter and fish? Oh, yeah!
- 1 cup dry white wine
- 3 tablespoons Everybody Goes Pesto (page 144) or store-bought basil pesto
- Grated zest and juice of 1 medium-sized lime
- Olive oil and more butter, for frying

YOU'LL HAVE THIS FISH DISH ON THE TABLE IN NO TIME

Dredge the tilapia fillets through the seasoned flour, being sure to shake off the excess. If you're like me, your shirt now sports white blotches. It's okay, a little water on that flour should solve the problem . . . No?

Meanwhile, get the prep-chef *(oh, sorry, you don't have one, either?)* to combine the melted butter, half the minced garlic, the wine, pesto, lime zest and lime juice. Set the mix aside.

Get that oven going at 200°F.

Let's get a nonstick frying pan heated up to medium, add a tablespoon each of olive oil and butter, plus the remaining garlic for bonus flavour points, and get the fillets rocking. Once the fish is a nice golden colour (2 to 3 minutes, depending on thickness), flip and cook until the fish is opaque—in other words, cooked through.

Let's keep the fillets warm on a plate in a slow oven—not slow as in tardy or dense, slow as in not too hot.

Repeat the fry-them-fillets-up procedure until all of the fish is cooked.

Don't rinse out the pan. Simply pour off the excess oil the environmentally friendly way, into a tin can. But you know what? We want to savour the flavour of all those brown bits on the bottom of the frying pan, so you can leave them there as a foundation to build our sauce on.

Pour the wine mixture into the pan and cook until reduced to about half of its original volume. Yes, a little flavour intensification is in order.

Pull those little fillies from the oven and top them with the pesto wine sauce. Yes, it's that easy. Tonight's fire hall fish special is done!

THE NICKNAME GAME

Ever wonder how firefighters get their nicknames? Jeff the Chef goes without saying, but I was labelled Crash as a rookie after I smacked up one of the fire trucks on an icy day. It took a long time to live that one down.

For some firefighters, their nicknames reflect their physical appearances, and this can be less than flattering. Take, for example, Boney, Manchild, Unibrow, Mouse, Dog Face Boy, Possum and T Rex (short arms). There's also a veritable Hollywood who's who of look-alike celebrities: Gollum, Borat, Grimace, Klinger, Harpo, Sammy Davis Jr., Homer Simpson, Ned Flanders, Mr. Bean, and Howdy Doody, to name a few.

Nicknames can also relate to a firefighter's cranial being. For example, Freak, Shady, Squeeky, Sybil, Cement Head, the Brain and Pepsi (empty from the neck up). Or how about my buddy Crabby, also known by the anto-name, Happy?

For others, their handles are abbreviations or mispronunciations of their last names—Jaws, Kozo, Bobko, Bod, Dilly, Horse, Daffy Duck and Cabbage Head.

For the chosen few, their monikers are reflections of their work ethics: Harley (looks good but hard to start), Willow (big, useless tree, not good for climbing or anything else) and Blister (only shows up after the work is done).

Then there's a chief by the name of Wilson who, years ago, rolled his car while responding to an alarm. Any guesses what his nickname was after the incident? Flip Wilson.

A firefighter burned in a house fire came back to work from his injuries clearly aware of the equation Tragedy + Time = Comedy. The name he made up and proudly wore on the back of his turnout coat? BBQ BARRY.

Earlier in the book I mentioned Chicklets, named after his impressive row of chompers. Like me, his nickname also changed, but not due to his culinary skills. The day before the firefighters' golf tournament, Chicklets called the golf course to reserve two carts under his last name, Chatterly. When he showed up at the course he searched through the names posted on signs on the back of the carts, but couldn't find his anywhere. He didn't figure it out until the carts pulled away and he spotted two remaining units bearing the name Chad Turdley. In a show of good sportsmanship, he kept the sign on his cart all day.

Suffice to say that thick skin is required to be a firefighter. If you get branded with a nickname you don't like, it's best just to ignore it and hope it goes away, because if you react to it, the nickname is surely yours for life.

WE'VE GOT
A WORKING FIRE!

THE FIRE HALL DISHWASHER

Remember at the circus when the little car pulls up into the centre ring and 36 clowns pile out? That sums up a load of dishes in the fire hall dishwasher. Firefighters will do *anything* to avoid having to wash a dish by hand, and that means cramming as much into the dishwasher as humanly possible. Pots, pans, baking sheets, humongous mixing bowls—they all get wedged in there. Oh sure, the sprayer arms won't spin, but it's all in the name of saving energy—firefighters' energy, just in case we catch "the big fire."

Not to worry, though, firefighters will throw in five times the required detergent to make up for it, so it all balances out. Hook up the EKG, stat! The dishwasher is ready for its stress test. But hey, when you're the chef you do the cooking and they do the cleanup, so it's best just to let it go.

Back in the pre-dishwasher days at No. 1 hall, one firefighter would wash and 15 guys would line up single file to dry—you'd grab a dish, dry it, put it away and go to the back of the line. Yes, that's one guy working and the rest watching—I know, typical city workers. Pranksters would take pots that had just been washed and put them back in the wash pile. The pots would get washed four or five times before the washer finally clued in.

If you think the dishwasher takes a beating at a fire house, check out the barbecue. Memo to kitty men: buy the Q with the lifetime warranty. Then, when the Q croaks after six months—a lifetime in a fire hall—you can return it for a new one.

If you're lucky, the firefighters who used the Q before you scraped the grill. If you're dreaming, they dumped the ashes (accidentally, mind you, when they were moving it and one of the wheels fell off and the Q tipped over). Under no circumstances will the previous chef have cleaned out the burners. Burners plugged with burger grease rule at the fire house!

But don't let the condition of your hall's barbecue get you down. Accept the harsh reality of passive Q maintenance, and either clean the grill yourself or keep the status quo and forge on undaunted. No matter which barbecue fork in Q road you take, I have a big batch of recipes for you to try. Even a few funky ideas beyond the ordinary to get on the grill, including a variety of wings from around the world. So come on, let's get this fire started!

CHICKEN PIZZA

While discussing the next night's meal at the fire hall, pizza was suggested. I named such eclectic pizzas as Pacific Rim, Thai, Greek pesto, etc., but our captain wasn't too keen. "I don't know, Jeff, better make at least one pepperoni and mushroom for me. I might not like those other weird ones." So I did as ordered. Ironically, the cap's big beef of the evening was that he didn't want to eat the pepperoni and mushroom pizza, because "After eating the other weird pizzas, it just tasted too bland." So be bold and adventurous, deviate from the norm and try something new like barbecued chicken the next time you're thinking pizza.

FOR EACH LARGE PIZZA, YOU'LL NEED . . .

- 1 tablespoon Fired-Up Santa Fe Spice (page 5)
- 1 tablespoon brown sugar
- 8 chicken thighs (or 2–3 breasts)
- Half a large red onion, cut into strips
- 2 tablespoons butter
- Kosher salt and freshly ground black pepper
- 1 red, orange or yellow pepper, cut into strips
- Pizza dough—try the Beer 'n' Pizza Dough (page 136) or use prepared pizza crust, tortillas or, a favourite of mine, panini bread
- Olive oil
- Your favourite BBQ sauce—try the sauce from the Wine 'n' Whiskey Beef Ribs (page 92)
- 1 pound Monterey Jack or Tex-Mex cheese, grated

FIRE UP THE Q!

Combine the Fired-Up Santa Fe Spice and brown sugar, and rub over both sides of the chicken.

Barbecue until the juices run clear. Cut the chick into bite-sized pieces.

Meanwhile, sauté the onions with the butter, salt and pepper over medium heat until they caramelize.

Toss in the pepper strips and slightly soften. Remove and let cool.

Stage your toppings in the on-deck circle. Turn your barbecue down to medium heat. Brush a light coating of olive oil on the grill and lay your pizza crust down on the Q. Close the lid.

When the dough bottom takes on a nice golden brown crust (it'll only take a minute or so), pop any bubbles that form on the top of the dough with a knife and flip it over.

Time is money here, so let's go to town on the toppings. I'm sure you know the routine by now—barbecue sauce, meat, veggies and cheese.

Close the lid, turn off the burner under the 'za and don't give up on that pizza until the cheese melts. If you find that the bottom is getting too crispy too quickly, then you can move the pizza to an upper rack in your Q until the crust and its toppings are both happy, happy.

Alternately, try the **Coffee Can Pizza** barbecue method (page 112), or simply bake your pizza in an oven at 425°F for 15 to 20 minutes.

COFFEE CAN PIZZA

In a mad Internet surf for the best way to barbecue pizza, I came across a video that suggested placing the pizza on coffee cans. Having tried several different ways to grill a 'za—some producing Cajun-blackened crusts—this one made perfect sense. The idea is to get the pizza up and away from the harsh reality of the blazing grill grate where crusts can incinerate before the cheese gets a chance to melt. With this method, the cheese gets to the top of the Q, where the heat's hanging out, resulting in an evenly cooked pizza top and bottom. As a bonus, much like beer can chicken, this is a unique technique that is sure to impress—unless of course you knock the pizza off the cans and onto the grill.

THIS PIZZA IS GOING TO GET A RAISE!

We're going to need pizza dough, and the ideal route to take is the **Beer 'n' Pizza Dough** recipe (page 136). Oh sure, you can buy store-bought crusts for laziness—sorry, I mean convenience.

For a thin crust that, as a bonus, delays the cooking of the crust even longer, try the freeze method in the Beer 'n' Pizza Dough recipe.

Assemble 4 empty 1-pound coffee cans. Cut the bottoms out, making them as open as possible to allow maximum airflow under the pizza pan. If the lid on your Q won't allow enough room for coffee cans, try using 3 or 4 28-ounce tin cans, the ones you'd find canned tomatoes or fruit in.

Preheat your grill to about 450°F. That's if the thermometer on your Q isn't broken, cracked, unreliable or smoked over and thereby illegible.

Make up your favourite pizza on a pizza pan that fits in your barbecue when the lid's closed. I like to dust the pan with a little cornmeal or flour, to keep the pizza from sticking. I suggest keeping the crust very thin, sautéing your vegetables ahead of time to keep the moisture down and, as difficult as it may be, resisting the natural firefighter temptation to load on the toppings. Too many toppings will result in uneven cooking and disappointed, albeit stuffed, diners. Lean and mean wins with this pizza.

Your pizza will likely cook quickly, say in about 5 to 10 minutes, and I say "about" much like a weatherman will predict a "mix of sun and clouds"— to vaguely cover all the bases and still sound like I know what I'm doing!

Keep your eyes on the crust. If the crust bake still beats the cheese melt— didn't I warn you not to pile on the toppings?—simply finish it up under your oven's broiler.

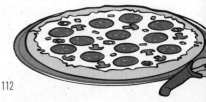

BARBE-SKEWERED
RED SNAPPER
WITH ORANGE SEAFOOD SAUCE

I borrowed the "shish kebab the snapper" barbecue technique from the late, great fire chef David Viljacic and teamed it up with my wife Lori's famously unique orange seafood sauce. Sure it's quick and easy, but with gourmet results.

HERE'S WHAT YOU'LL NEED TO GIVE THAT SNAPPER SOME SNAP

- Wooden skewers
- 1 small jar seafood sauce
- Equal amount sugar—simply use the seafood sauce jar to measure
- Equal amount orange juice
- 1 teaspoon kosher salt or, more appropriately, ½ teaspoon sea salt
- ½ tablespoon cornstarch combined with 1 tablespoon water
- 2 pounds red snapper fillets
- Fired-Up Spice (page 4) or seasoning salt
- Olive oil

FISH KEBABS, JEFF? WHAT MEDS ARE YOU ON, MAN?

Soak the skewers in water for at least 30 minutes to 1 hour, so they don't burn up when they hit the Q.

Get the seafood sauce, sugar and orange juice into a small saucepan, stir 'em up and bring to a light boil. Add salt to taste.

Introduce the cornstarch-and-water mix a bit at a time until you get a slightly thickened, sauce-like consistency.

Cut the fillets into pieces approximately 1½ to 2 inches wide by 6 inches long. Some will be bigger, some will be smaller.

Now, I know what you're thinking.

How are the fillets going to stay on the skewers without falling through the grill and causing you to turn the smoky air blue in frustration? Well, take a Stresstab and maybe even a little shot from the adult medicine cabinet if you feel the need. Not to worry, the firm flesh of the red snapper fillet is perfect for shish kebabs.

So let's skewer the snappers. Start at one end of the 6-inch piece and wind your way in and out of the fillet 3 or 4 times, being sure to stretch the fillet out as you push it along the skewer.

Dust the fish with a light sprinkling of Fired-Up Spice.

Fire up the grill to medium-high, and when it's warmed brush on a little olive oil so the fish doesn't stick. Cooking spray also works, but our legal counsel has instructed me not to recommend it to you.

Place the skewers on the grill, cook for about 3 minutes and turn them over. Brush with sauce as you would barbecue sauce, and cook for another 3 minutes.

Flip them over again and give the top side the sauce treatment. Q until the fish just starts to flake.

Serve over your favourite rice dish and top with the remaining sauce.

COUNTRY PORK RIBS

You won't believe how good these ribs smell as they bake in the oven. It must be the beer. If the wonderful odours don't make up for the guilt you experience wasting a beer in a recipe, perhaps the taste of these moist, tender, tangy ribs will do it for you. If you like your ribs meaty, there's nothing like the meat-to-bone ratio of country pork ribs—all the flavour of barbecued ribs without the waste.

RUB 'EM UP FIRST

- 3 tablespoons Fired-Up Santa Fe Spice (page 5)
- 3 tablespoons brown sugar
- 1 rack (about 5 pounds) country-style pork ribs
- 12 ounces beer
- 1 medium onion, cut into slices
- Barbecue sauce—I have a few suggestions for you

THEN START 'EM SLOW IN THE OVEN BEFORE BLASTING 'EM ON THE Q

Combine the Fired-Up Santa Fe Spice and brown sugar in a bowl. Rub the combo over the ribs, covering all sides—be generous, now.

Place in a 9 x 13-inch lasagna dish, cover with cling wrap and send them off to the fridge for at least 8 hours, or even overnight.

Warm up your oven to 275°F.

Place a small rack in a roaster. Make it a cooking rack with just enough height to get the other rack, this being the rack of ribs, out of the liquid ingredients . . . Oh, and if you don't mind my saying, nice rack!

Pour the beer over and around the ribs. Top the rib rack with the onions.

Bake, covered, for 3 hours, basting once or twice if you happen to be around the house while it cooks. If not, don't worry about it.

Remove the ribs from the oven and smother them with your favourite barbecue sauce. Try **Blasko's Mango-Chipotle Barbecue Sauce** (coming right up), **A Hint of the Orient** (page 124) or the **Whiskey Barbecue Sauce** (page 92).

To finish the ribs let's go to the grill, or to the broiler if the weather just isn't co-operating, as in another wicked Canadian winter day.

Grill the ribs over medium heat for about 15 minutes (much less time if you're broiling), being sure to flip the ribs over at least twice, giving them a fresh baste of sauce after each flip.

Allow the ribs to sit on the counter for 5 or 10 minutes before slicing into portions. A rack generally separates between ribs into 4 good-sized portions. So that means a rack serves 4 chomping-at-the-bit firefighters, 1 Gulliver or 16 Lilliputians.

Serve with additional warmed-up barbecue sauce.

BLASKO'S MANGO-CHIPOTLE
BARBECUE SAUCE

I bumped into one of my favourite fire hall chefs, Chris Blasko, a while back and asked him what was new and exciting. His answer was this fabulous barbecue sauce, which to him makes all other Q sauces obsolete. I gave it a go, and I'm with Chris, this sauce is a surefire way to boost your Q meat, especially pork, with its slight sweet-and-sour element.

THE INGREDIENTS ARE FEW, BUT THE FLAVOUR IS MIGHTY

- 1 medium onion, diced
- About 1 tablespoon butter
- 3 garlic cloves, chopped or run through the press
- 1 large or 2 small fully ripe mangos, diced
- 1 cup of your favourite store-bought barbecue sauce, or better yet, if you have a batch of sauce (from Wine 'n' Whiskey Beef Ribs on page 92) made up, then here's a great way to use it up
- ¼ cup apple cider vinegar
- 1 or 2 (I like 2) canned chipotle peppers (small can in your grocer's Mexican food section)

WHAT? I CAN ACTUALLY MAKE AN EXOTIC SAUCE THIS EASILY?

In a small saucepan over medium-low heat, brown the onion in the butter until very soft and caramelized.

Get the garlic and mangos in with the onion and continue cooking until the mangos are soft. This won't take long, especially if they're very ripe.

Move the onion, garlic and mangos to a blender. Bring on the barbecue sauce, apple cider vinegar and chipotle peppers, tossing in about a tablespoon or two of the adobo sauce the chipotles come packed in—that ought to fire it up! Hit PLAY on the blender.

If the earth, moon and stars are in perfect alignment, your sauce should be good to go as is. However, if you want to do some minor adjustments, now is the time. The sauce should, as I mentioned, have a slight sweet-and-sour flavour. A dab or two of bonus apple cider vinegar will boost the sour; a little sugar or a dash of bottled mango juice will bring on the sweet. As always, cooking is all about balance.

Need more kick? Take up tae kwon do. I mean, look no further than those fiery, smoky chipotles and adobo sauce. Bring on another chipotle and blend away, or simply add the adobo sauce a bit at a time until your face bursts into flame—I mean, until the sauce is sufficiently spicy.

Bring me your ribs, your pork tenderloins, your huddled chickens ... and lather them up with the Mango-Chipotle Barbecue Sauce.

BOOT-SHAPED BURGERS

No, we're not talking firefighter boots. The name has nothing to do with the actual shape of the burgers. We're talking burgers inspired by the boot-shaped country of Italy. You know, bella burgers!

THAT'S A SPICY MEAT-A-PATTY

- 1 large egg
- ¼ cup Everybody Goes Pesto (page 144) or store-bought basil pesto
- 1 pound hot Italian sausage—that ought to fire things up
- 1 pound lean (definitely not extra-lean) ground beef
- ½ cup Italian-seasoned bread crumbs
- Black pepper or cayenne
- Fresh-sliced Mozzarella cheese—not that processed nonsense, please!
- Garlic butter (optional)
- Burger buns—Italian style would be ideal
- Sautéed sweet red onion slices—you know, caramelized by frying
- Tomato slices and romaine lettuce
- Caesar salad dressing

BELLISSIMA, BABY!

Beat the egg in a bowl and add the pesto. Whisk the two together to combine. If you don't want to go the pesto route, try mayonnaise instead.

Get the sausage meat out of the casings. Pull off bits of sausage meat and toss them in a second bowl, alternating with bits of ground beef. This will make for an even mixture.

Dust the meat with the bread crumbs, and work the egg/pesto in with the meat 'n' crumbs. Toss in additional bread crumbs if your mixture is too wet. If it's too dry, simply add a bit of milk. Remember the Golden Rule of burgermeistering: don't over-handle the ground meat or it will make for dense, tough burgers. Our goal is light, moist burgers, not hockey pucks.

By the way, don't worry about salting the meat, as the flavour boost is already in the pesto, bread crumbs and sausage. However, a little pepper couldn't hurt—or cayenne, if you're really adventurous.

Form the meat mix into patties, place on waxed paper and file them into the fridge on a tray for an hour or more to allow the burgers to set up.

Grill the burgers over medium heat until completely cooked through.

I'm thinking that if we happened to allow a little mozzarella cheese to melt on top of each patty, that would certainly be appropriate.

Hey, and why not remain on theme and spread a little garlic butter on the burger buns and toast them onto the Q while you're at it.

Garnish your burger with sautéed sweet red onions, tomato slices, romaine lettuce and, say, a little Caesar dressing or mayo. Would you like spaghetti with that?

FALLIN'-OFF-THE-BONE-ALREADY
RIBS

At evening shift change, firefighter Laura Duncan started to prepare ribs for her shift's dinner, and it led to group discussion about the best way to cook ribs. Really, there are so many methods it's ridiculous, and everyone has their tried and true favourite. Boil 'em, braise 'em, bake 'em, barbecue 'em—the list goes on. Laura's way is to season the ribs, wrap 'em in foil, and bake 'em low and slow before finishing them on the grill. The only problem with this recipe, as she says, is "getting them onto the barbecue without having them fall apart." Yes, Martha, that's a good thing.

GIVE THE RACK A CRANK

- Equal parts Fired-Up Santa Fe Spice (page 5) and brown sugar
- As many racks of those baby backs as you need—½ rack each for the general populace, 1 pricey rack per glutton—I mean, firefighter
- Your favourite barbecue sauce—the one from Wine 'n' Whiskey Beef Ribs (page 92), Blasko's Mango-Chipotle (page 115) or A Hint of the Orient (page 124).

COME ON, RIB LOVERS, LET'S WRAP 'EM, BAKE 'EM AND GET 'EM ON THE Q

Combine the Fired-Up Santa Fe Spice and brown sugar. Rub the mix on both sides of the ribs and wrap them in cling wrap. I like to let the rub sit on the ribs overnight, or for at least an hour, but if time is tight then skip the cling and go straight to the aluminum.

Fire up the oven to 300°F.

Unwrap the ribs. Lay out sheets of aluminum foil and spray one side with cooking spray. Wrap the ribs in foil with the meaty side up. Secure so the moisture will have a hard time escaping. *Aha! The secret's revealed.*

Place the foil-wrapped racks on a baking sheet. Get the ribs into the baker and let them go for about 2 to 2½ hours, or until the bones pull back on the ribs about a quarter inch and the meat is very tender. Keep in mind that cooking times will vary depending on the size of the racks. I hate to say it, but I must: in this case, size does matter.

Now, fire up the barbecue, and lather the ribs in sauce. Q them just long enough on each side to get those happy grill marks happening. Give them a quick baste again, and Q them to caramelize the sauce.

If it's wintertime, simply bake the ribs for 15 minutes more, uncovered, or place under the broiler, but only long enough to give them some colour.

Let the fall-apart ribs stand for 5 minutes before serving.

This technique also works well with St. Louis-style spareribs—in other words, the trimmed rectangular cut of spareribs. Your buddy the butcher will know. In the unlikely event that he doesn't, then pick a rack of spareribs and instruct the band saw operator to rip 'em right down the middle.

TURKEY BURGERS

The big worry with turkey burgers is that, due to their low fat content, they'll dry out on the grill. Well, here's an idea: how about infusing that lean, mean ground turkey with a little feta cheese to boost the juiciness quotient? Here's a simple-yet-delicious burger with a nice hint of the Mediterranean.

COME WITH ME TO THE FRIDGE FOR . . .

- 2 tablespoons olive oil
- 1⅓ cups finely diced red onions
- 1 cup diced red, yellow or orange pepper
- 2 pounds ground turkey
- 1 cup crumbled feta cheese—I like the packaged variety with sun-dried tomatoes and oregano already added
- 2 teaspoons dried oregano—going Greek means more oregano!
- 6–8 garlic cloves, run through the old press, please
- Let's call it a dusting of seasoning salt
- Lots of that freshly ground black pepper
- Pita or focaccia bread or buns
- Tomato slices
- Romaine lettuce
- A choice of sauces—coming right up

OUT OF THE FRIDGE AND INTO THE FIRE WE GO!

Bring a frying pan up to medium heat, swirl in a little olive oil and follow up with the onions. Let's fry for about 5 to 10 minutes to brown them up.

Browned yet? As in caramelized and nicely sweetened? Then add the peppers to the onions and soften them up, too.

Let the veggies chill for a few minutes, and once you deem them cool enough to handle, add them to a mixing bowl and follow up with the turkey, feta cheese, oregano, garlic and the salt and pepper to taste. Well, not really to taste. You wouldn't taste raw meat. Just use your judgment, culled from countless years of experience manning the Q.

Get your hands all ooey gooey and mix the ingredients until combined. Form them into patties, get them on a plate and send them off to the fridge for about an hour or so to set up.

Get those burgers on the preheated Q over medium to medium-high heat for about 5 minutes per side, or until cooked through.

Serve the burgers on pitas, focaccia bread or bun topped with even more sautéed red onions, sliced tomatoes, lettuce and your choice of **Spicy Tzatziki Sauce** (page 99; the traditional Greek solution), Caesar dressing, like the one on page 52 (call it the Italian influence), or good old mayo (conservative North American).

LEMON-LIME
LICKIN' CHICKEN

Here's a great blend of flavours, a twist of tang balanced with a hint of sweetness, a healthy bite of garlic and as much cayenne pepper as you're willing to fire up. So, get that chick into a relaxing bath, and when time's up, say "Off to the barbecue you go, girlfriend!"

THE ¼ CUP IS GOING TO GET A WORKOUT HERE

- ¼ cup lemon juice—real or not so real
- ¼ cup lime juice—ditto the above
- ¼ cup olive oil—I'm partial to extra-virgin, but regular will do
- ½ cup brown sugar—that's 2 x ¼ cup
- 2 tablespoons prepared mustard
- 2 tablespoons Everybody Goes Pesto (page 144) or store-bought basil pesto
- 4–6 garlic cloves, minced or pressed
- ½ tablespoon kosher salt
- ¼ teaspoon, more or less, cayenne
- 4 chicken breasts (or 8-10 boneless thighs)

THAT FREEZER BAG IS GOING TO BE THE FLAVOUR GYM

Simply whisk all of the ingredients together in a bowl. The mustard will help it stay together. Move the mix along to a freezer bag, drop in the chicken and let it sit in the fridge for 4 to 24 hours before barbecuing.

Goes great with a **Caesar Salad from Scratch** (page 52), **Santa Fe Caesar Salad** (page 58) or **So Damn Salad** (page 59).

A PROFOUND COMPLIMENT FROM ANOTHER SATISFIED DINER

One of my former captains, Jo Van der Horst—one of the many firefighters who *truly* enjoy their food and are equipped with the physical stature to back up that claim—sat down at the fire hall to dine on a hearty plate of barbecued ribs. As per my method of operation, the ribs were lathered in a thick coating of sauce from the **Wine 'n' Whiskey Beef Ribs** (page 92). It was a sight to be seen. Jo was firing through his plate of ribs as sauce dripped from his hands, chin and jowls onto not only his plate but his stout-cut uniform shirt, pants and even the glasses hanging from a chain around his neck. He looked like we'd fired the sauce through a fan at him! When he finally came up for air he paused to comment, "You know, this is really good, and I'm not usually a sauce guy."

Could have fooled us, Big Guy!

Q THE SIZZLING SHRIMP

Anytime is a good time for shrimp, especially now that you can purchase them zipper-back style, deveined, split and ready to peel. Here's a quick way to serve up those sawed-off little runts with a minimum of fuss. Oh, you could skewer them before you put 'em on the Q, but I prefer to do them in a barbecue basket because it just so happens that I'm in a lazy, inertia-challenged mood today and I just feel like taking the easy way out. Sue me, I'm on days off.

SHRIMP AND HIS TASTY FLAVOUR-BOOSTER BUDDIES

- 2 pounds large shrimp
- 4 garlic cloves
- ½ tablespoon kosher salt
- 2 teaspoons dried oregano (leaf, not ground)
- 1 teaspoon sweet paprika
- ½–1 teaspoon cayenne—set your flame level accordingly
- Freshly ground black pepper—give your mill a few good bump 'n' grinds
- 2 tablespoons extra-virgin olive oil
- 2 tablespoons lemon juice
- Grape tomatoes—you can Q these, too, if you like
- Parsley—the fresh stuff, chopped up nicely
- Lemon wedges

SPEAKING OF FLAVOUR BOOSTERS, LET'S FIRE UP THE SMOKY Q!

If your shrimp are frozen—the most likely scenario—then simply toss them in a sink full of cold water. If you left your dinner decision to the last minute, don't worry, they'll shed their ice in a flash.

Peel the shrimp, leaving the tails on so they won't curl up on you.

Pull out the garlic press and squeeze about 4 good-sized cloves through the unit to extract that glorious nectar in praise of Odoriferous the Greek God of Garlic. Worship him, for he is great and makes stuff taste good!

Bring the garlic and the spices together in a small bowl and stir them all together with a fork or small whisk. I smell spicy!

Get the olive oil in there, mix it all up and bring on the lemon juice.

Stir it together—it should resemble a thick sauce—and call the shrimp in from the hold of the fishing boat. Marinate the shrimp for 30 minutes.

Fire the Q up to medium-high, get the Q basket over the grill and add the shrimp. Stir them around every minute or so until they're pink. Don't overcook them; we don't want any little rubber dudes for dinner.

Serve with grape tomatoes, parsley and lemon wedges for squeezing.

Q2

For a Southwestern twist, all you have to do is substitute lime juice for lemon and add 1 teaspoon of ground cumin to the mix.

WITH TROPICAL SALSA
PESTO HALIBUT

Halibut is great on the barbecue because its firm flesh holds together nicely without falling through the grill, much like a steak. Here's a great way to fire it up. Give the halibut a pesto-marinade flavour infusion, Q it and serve it hot, hot, hot off the grill topped with the fruity, sweet Tropical Salsa.

HALIBUT IS HAPPY TO TAKE ON ANY FLAVOUR YOU SEND ITS WAY

- 1 cup Everybody Goes Pesto (page 144), with variations (see below)
- 1 cup extra-virgin olive oil
- 4 halibut steaks—fresh are best, if possible
- 1 mango, diced—I know, that core in the middle is a pain in the . . .
- 2 kiwis, diced
- 1 cup pineapple tidbits, drained
- ½ banana, sliced and sliced again
- ½ cup finely diced red onion
- 2 jalapeno peppers, seeded and diced very fine
- ⅓ cup cilantro, chopped
- 1½ tablespoons plum sauce
- 1½ tablespoons lime juice
- ½ teaspoon chili-garlic sauce (optional)
- Kosher salt and freshly ground black pepper, to taste

NO "JUST FOR THE HALIBUT" JOKES, PLEASE!

Make up a batch of Everybody Goes Pesto, using lime juice instead of lemon, and rather than using only ½ cup cilantro, let's go for a full cup and drop the basil. I've even made this pesto with the cilantro plus arugula subbing for the parsley. Very earthy, very tasty and very funky!

To make the pesto into a marinade, add the extra-virgin olive oil and mix.

Marinate the halibut with the pesto in a zip-top freezer bag in the fridge for 1 to 4 hours. Turn the fish several times while marinating.

Let's make the Tropical Salsa. Combine the mango, kiwi, pineapple, banana, red onion, jalapenos, cilantro, plum sauce, lime juice and chili-garlic sauce. Oh, and a little salt and pepper. Toss the salsa and then toss it in the fridge for 30 minutes to 1 hour.

Fire up your grill to medium-high. Grease the grill lightly with olive oil.

Grind pepper over both sides of the halibut steaks. By the way, if you'd like to go sans marinade—as in naked—then simply season the fish with pepper and a little sea salt, to bring it back to its roots.

Get the halibut on the grill or in a grill basket for about 5 minutes a side, depending on thickness. Olive oil can cause flare-ups, so keep an eye on it.

When this former sea dweller is opaque in the middle and just starts to flake, you're there. Do your best not to overcook and dry it out.

Serve the Pesto Halibut steaks topped with the Tropical Salsa.

STEAK MARINADE

As you'll see in the intro to Fire Sides, I may not know much about wines, but one thing I do know is that red wine is served with beef. Wouldn't it make sense, then, to marinate the cow in red wine, to complete the circle of grapes and beef?

PUT THE WET STUFF ON THE RED STUFF

- ½ cup red wine
- 6 tablespoons Dijon mustard
- 2 tablespoons each soy sauce, olive oil and brown sugar
- 6 garlic cloves, minced or pressed
- 2 teaspoons horseradish
- 2 teaspoons coarsely ground black pepper
- 2 teaspoons dried thyme or tarragon

Combine all of the ingredients with a wire whisk and get the liqui-mix into a large zip-top freezer bag with sirloin or other premium steaks. This should be enough bathing liquid for 2 pounds of moo. Marinate for at least 4 hours, or even overnight for maximum flavour penetration.

WE EAT, WE SLEEP, WE FIGHT!

When friends and fellow firefighters alike take shots at our proud profession, they invariably focus on two so-called fringe benefits: permission to sleep during night shifts when we're not busy and the great meals we share together. Oh, I've heard a few of them over the years.

"Eat till you're tired, sleep till you're hungry."

"Pig out, pass out!"

"It's one of the two professions where you earn your living on your back."

"What's your schedule? Is that two lunches, two dinners and four days off?"

Or, as now-retired Captain John Webster would explain it, "Two days out of eight I get up to go to work. Two days out of eight I get up to go home from work. The other four days I get up whenever the hell I want."

John would also remind those who felt we had it easy that "sometimes we're busy at calls, and sometimes we're busy doing nothing. But make no mistake about it, we're always busy at the fire hall."

Here's another self-description of our vocation, one that applies in many ways to the police and armed forces as well: "Firefighting is hours of boredom interrupted by moments of sheer terror."

Or, as one firefighter was known to say, "If it weren't for the calls, the danger at fires, the threat of exposure at medical calls and the awful sights we see, this would be the perfect job."

SOUTHWEST CHIPOTLE 'N' LIME
MARINADE

Back in my early twenties I spent two months in Mesa, Arizona, training for an upcoming bicycle-racing season. After riding some 50 or 60 miles one day, my training partner and I, in a mad state of hunger, hit the local all-you-can-eat Mexican restaurant. Barely allowing time for flavour to register with our taste buds, we powered back multiple portions before our insides knew what hit them. The following morning, well, let's just say that I couldn't sit down on my bike. Since then I've learned to temper my attack on spicy foods and to make food with enough bite to satisfy most, while hoping that it isn't too hot to turn off some. Here's a great steak marinade that features the fiery fire hall combo of heat and smoke, thanks to the chipotles.

OUT THERE ON THE TEX-MEX RANCHER'S PLAIN IS . . .

- About 2 pounds sirloin, flank or skirt steak
- 2-3 limes, juiced (about ½ cup or so)—bottled lime juice will also work
- Oh, and about 2 teaspoons grated lime zest
- 3 tablespoons olive oil
- 6 garlic cloves, minced, pressed and violated
- 2 chipotle peppers, with about 2 tablespoons of the adobo sauce they're packed in, more or less, to taste
- 1 tablespoon brown sugar
- 1 tablespoon ground cumin
- 2 teaspoons kosher salt
- Freshly ground black pepper
- ½ cup chopped cilantro (or 2 teaspoons ground coriander)

INSIDE THAT RANCHER'S KITCHEN THE PLAN IS TO . . .

Get those steaks into a zip-top freezer bag, combine all of the marinade ingredients and pour them over the steaks. Squeeze the air out of the bag, and off the steaks go to the fridge for 4 hours minimum, but since more is more better—*smack! Ouchhh! That smarts . . . !* You're not going to believe this, but my grade 7 English teacher just whacked me with a ruler. Yes, she's still watching over my shoulder and can't believe I'm a published writer. I'm surprised, too!

Sorry, let's try that again. Since more is better *(wince . . . good, she's nodding now)* an overnight soak will fire it up even more.

If you like the steak 'n' marinade, why not go firefighter deluxe and try it with the **Working-Fire Steak** recipe, which is coming up on page 126.

TENDER ON THE Q

I absolutely love pork tenderloin. It cooks up quickly, tastes delicious and is solid meat—no bone, no fat and no waste. As long as you don't overcook it, it's a winner. However, as my buddy Captain Mike Dowhayko says, "The big problem with this cut is when firefighters look at their plate, their eyes bug out, as all they spy is an eight-ounce portion, and wonder where the rest is. Once they tie into the tenderloin, however, they see how filling it is." Here's an easy way to make tenderloin on the Q with a delicious barbecue sauce, inspired by the recipe genius of firefighter and restaurateur Eddie Yuen.

A HINT OF THE ORIENT Q SAUCE

- 10-ounce jar hoisin sauce
- Equal parts barbecue sauce and ketchup
- 2 tablespoons honey—soft or liquid

SORRY, NO FRUIT ON THESE LOINS

- 2 pork tenderloins
- Fired-Up Spice (page 4), seasoning salt and freshly ground black pepper

JUST A DELICIOUS Q SAUCE

Get our sauce together by combining the hoisin sauce, barbecue sauce, ketchup and honey.

Get the pork tenderloins on the carving board and, armed with a small sharp knife (with Band-Aids lined up in the first aid staging area), surgically remove the silver skin from the loins. Don't omit this step.

Season the tenderloins with a light dusting of equal parts Fired-Up Spice, seasoning salt and pepper.

Fire up the Q to medium-high. Once it reaches the desired temperature, get the tenderloins on the grill and give them some barbecue-induced colour.

I want you to treat the tenderloin as if it's a small roast that has 4 sides that all must be cooked evenly. Rotate the loins so all sides take on those groovy looking grill marks.

As you rotate the tenders, get the barbecue sauce on the cooked sides of the loins. You can turn the Q down if they're getting too dark too fast.

The key is to cook the tenderloins until the centres are still slightly pink. What I like to do is press down on the tenderloins to test for doneness. If they give slightly before bouncing back, I consider them done. If they feel like mush, more time is needed. If they're rock solid, then you're going to want to get out the dental floss, because you'll need it to rid your teeth of the stringy pork lodged between your molars. Allow 20 to 30 minutes, depending on the size of loins and the Q temp. If you have a meat thermometer handy, you're looking for an internal temperature of 145 to 150°F.

Tent the loins with foil and wait 5 minutes before slicing them into medallions.

TRIPLE-SPICED BARBECUED
HALF CHICKENS

That chicken, it's a pushover for any flavour it comes in contact with. That's why we're going to whack it three times before it hits your dinner plate. First with a sweet spicy rub, then with a mop sauce on the Q, and finally we'll ambush that hot chick with a fired-up fast attack of barbecue sauce.

ROUND UP
- 1 or more whole fryer chickens, about 3 pounds each

HERE'S THE RUB
- 1 part Fired-Up Santa Fe Spice (page 5) combined with
- 1 part brown sugar

HERE'S THE MOP
- 1 cup apple cider vinegar
- ½ medium onion, diced fine
- 1 teaspoon each kosher salt and dried red chili flakes

AND HERE'S THE BARBECUE SAUCE
Go for the **Whiskey Barbecue Sauce** (page 92) or for **Blasko's Mango-Chipotle Barbecue Sauce** (page 115) or **A Hint of the Orient** (page 124).

HEY! THIS CHICK IS GETTING READY TO SPLIT
With a sharp knife, or even better, a sharp pair of poultry shears, cut the chicken right in half between the breasts and along the backbone.

Lay the chick down on the cut sides. Attack the chicken halves with a generous shot of the sweet and fiery spice rub. Let the chicken sit for at least ½ hour, to allow the flavours to set up.

Fire up the barbecue. When it reaches operating temperature, turn off one side of the Q and place a catch basin—an aluminum lasagna tray works great here—on the off side. The on side should be medium-high.

Oil the grill with a light bit of olive oil. Or, if you love theatrics and agree to sign the waiver relieving me of any responsibility, use cooking spray.

Place the chicken skin sides down on the lit side just long enough for it to gain some colour and, of course, inherit those wonderful pro-grill marks.

Flip the chick onto the cut sides, and place over the unlit side of the Q, with the legs facing the lit side of the Q, keeping the breasts facing away.

Barbecue for about 50 minutes, keeping the chicken moist with a light brushing of mop sauce every 10 minutes or so.

When the chicken is nearly done, baste liberally with your chosen BBQ sauce, and Q until the chicken is cooked through.

To oven bake, cook the rubbed chick, uncovered, at 375°F for 1 hour. Top with sauce and cook for another 10 to 20 minutes or until done.

WORKING-FIRE
STEAK

I was thinking of calling this Tex-Mex Steak, but being that it's one of my fluke creations, I tagged it Working-Fire Steak. Much better than Pot-of-Food-on-the-Stove Steak, Fire's-out-on-Arrival Steak or False-Alarm Steak. We want action here! Combine all these hot and spicy flavours with the on-the-edge-of-disaster excitement of a fiery flambé and, adrenaline junkies, this steak's for you!

A SOUTHWESTERN STEER AND HIS SIDEKICKS

- Let's say about 2 pounds prime sirloin steak
- Southwest Chipotle 'n' Lime Marinade (page 123)
- 3 tablespoons butter or margarine
- 1 jumbo onion, cut into strips
- 1 orange, yellow or red pepper, in strips
- About ½ pound mushrooms—sliced
- ¼ cup tequila (optional)
- ¾ cup of your favourite salsa—try chipotle
- ¾ cup salsa-ranch dressing
- Fresh cilantro—chop, chop!

WHERE THERE'S SMOKE, THERE'S FIRE

Toss the steaks in a freezer bag, add the marinade, zip it up and toss it in the fridge overnight. The steak is having a sleepover in the smokehouse with those smoky chipotles. Let 'em be.

Get the steaks out of the fridge for an hour before flaming them.

Toss the butter into a size-large frying pan over medium heat and add the onions. Allow, say, about 10 minutes for the criers to caramelize.

Bring on the peppers and mushrooms and get them softened. You know, you could do this on the side burner of your Q if you're so equipped.

Fire up the Q, and get those steaks just the way you want 'em. I like to show each side of my steak a hot fire and then turn the Q down to medium and cook the steaks through to their happy place. For me that would be a nice, pinky medium-rare.

Move the veggies to the side of the frying pan and get the steak in there.

Pour the tequila over the steak, with a pot lid handy in case things get away on us. Once the tequila starts to bubble, carefully ignite its vapours. Whooossshhhhhhhhhh! Oh yeah, we've got a working fire now!

Once the conflagration dies down— *tell me it's not getting into the cupboards,* **I told you to have a lid handy!**—remove the steak.

Let's add the salsa and the salsa-ranch (or plain ranch) dressing to the veggies and heat through.

Allow the steaks to laze around for 5 minutes or so on a cutting board.

Then slice the steaks against the grain into ¼-inch strips.

Serve the steak topped with the tasty sauce and garnished with cilantro.

WINNIPEG RED WINGS

Is this a sad, desperate attempt to bring NHL hockey back to Winnipeg? Sorry, sports fans, we're talking tasty wings finished in a tangy red sauce. Pomegranates are all the rage in the antitoxin world, so let's bring a healthy blast to these little flappers for great between-periods eating action.

ON THE WINGS

- 3-4 pounds chicken wings or drumettes
- Seasoned flour—3 parts all-purpose to 1 part Fired-Up Santa Fe Spice (page 5)
- A little olive oil treatment for the grill
- 2 cups pomegranate juice—it can be a blend, like the pomegranate and blueberry, pomegranate and tangerine, etc., from your grocer's shelves
- ½ cup sugar
- 2 tablespoons cider vinegar
- 6 garlic cloves, minced or pressed
- 1 teaspoon Fired-Up Santa Fe Spice (page 5)
- 2 tablespoons pomegranate juice combined with 1 tablespoon cornstarch

DON'T WORRY, I'LL COACH YOU THROUGH IT FROM THE BENCH

If the tips are still on the wings, clip them off and toss them out. Cut the wings in half, right at the joints. This will make the cooking and chowing down processes a little easier.

Mix the flour and Fired-Up Santa Fe Spice together and toss the wings in to lightly coat them.

Fire up one side of your barbecue to medium-high, and once heated, brush the grill on the other side with a little olive oil. Spread the wings out on that unlit side.

Q the wings until browned all over, about 40 minutes, turning once.

If baking instead, then fire up the oven to 400°F, spread the wings out on a rack placed in a shallow roaster and bake for 30 to 40 minutes. Keep the oven firing, because we're gonna need more heat.

Add the juice, sugar, cider vinegar, garlic and Fired-Up Santa Fe Spice to a small saucepan. Bring to a boil and reduce the sauce to about half (about 1¼ cups). If you're unsure, go to the toolbox and bring out the measuring cup and pour the sauce into the cup as you go. Slowly add the pomegranate/cornstarch combo to the boiling sauce till slightly thickened.

If you Q'd the wings, now's the time to fire up the oven to 400°F.

Once the Q'd wings are ready to rock, place them in a mixing bowl and pour the sauce over top. Toss them through to coat. If you baked the wings, you can sauce them up right there in the roaster.

For the Q'd wings, spray a 9 x 13-inch lasagna dish with cooking spray and toss in the wings 'n' sauce. Roast them, uncovered, for 10 to 12 minutes, or until the wings are nicely glazed and cooked through.

WINGIN' IT AROUND THE WORLD—
TALK ABOUT VARIETY!

Why not use the **Winnipeg Red Wings** *cooking technique and, for a nice bit of fun, take your pick from this eclectic bunch of sauces? Hey, you can just about have wings every night of the week now!*

BEIJING BROWN WINGS—
a.k.a. Honey-Garlic Wings

- ½ cup honey
- ¼ cup soy sauce
- 3 tablespoons rice wine vinegar
- 4–6 garlic cloves
- 2 teaspoons chili-garlic sauce
- 1 tablespoon cornstarch mixed with
  2 tablespoons water

Get the first 5 ingredients in a saucepan, bring to a boil, then slowly add the cornstarch/water combo, to thicken. Toss the wings in the sauce and finish baking till nicely glazed and cooked through.

TOKYO BLACK WINGS—a.k.a.
Teriyaki Wings

- ¾ cup bottled teriyaki chicken marinade or teriyaki sauce
- 3 tablespoons honey
- 1 teaspoon chili-garlic paste (or more if you like it fiery)
- 1 teaspoon ginger powder (or 2 teaspoons ginger paste)
- 1 tablespoon cornstarch mixed with
  2 tablespoons water

Get the first 4 ingredients in a saucepan, bring to a boil, then slowly add the cornstarch/water combo, to thicken. Toss the wings in the sauce and finish baking till nicely glazed and cooked through.

BANGKOK ORANGE WINGS—
a.k.a. Sweet Chili-Garlic
Wings

Let's get out that wonderfully wicked sweet chili sauce (check it out on page 4 if you're not familiar with it) and lay it on the wings full strength for the final bake.

For garnish, hey, a little chopped cilantro would be nice.

BUFFALO RED-HOT WINGS—
a.k.a. My Mouth's a Working
Fire!

Combine ⅓ cup each Louisiana-style hot sauce, brown sugar and melted butter or margarine. To pour more heat on the fire, simply add more Louisiana hot sauce to the mix.

As per the Winnipeg Red Wings recipe, baste the wings in this fiery sauce and then give them the final bake to finish.

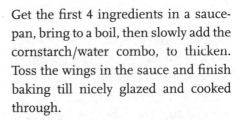

KAHLÚA-Q'D WINGS

It's unclear whether Kahlúa's routes trace back to Mexico or the Arab Republics, but regardless, we're giving it a bit of a funky Asian/Hawaiian treatment today. With that in mind, we should have called these Melting Pot Wings. Given the price tag on a bottle of Kahlúa, I can't see your making this at the fire hall on a regular basis unless you made out like a bandit at the duty-free. But at home, or for special company, ignore the budgetary restraints and go for gold!

I SEE THE KAHLÚA, BUT WHERE'S THE MILK?

- 3 pounds chicken wings or drumettes
- ¾ cup Kahlúa—it's not just a liqueur anymore
- ½ cup sweet chili sauce (you can look it up on page 4)
- ½-1 tablespoon cornstarch
- 3 tablespoons pineapple or orange juice

BETTER STRETCH OUT THE HOSE, I THINK WE'VE GOT A FIRE!

For the wings, please refer to the handy cooking instructions found in **Winnipeg Red Wings** (page 127). Depending on the season, you can either barbecue them or fake it in the oven. Go have a look at the recipe and follow it right up to the point where the sauce enters the picture. Come on, it's easy, I'll wait for you here . . . go! I'm not going anywhere, I promise.

Oh, you're back, nice to see you again. I told you it was easy. Now for the Chili Kahlúa Sauce, simply combine the Kahlúa with the sweet chili sauce in, of all things, a saucepan. I think you'd better get out a wire whisk to bring them together; that'll work best.

Meanwhile, stir the cornstarch in with the pineapple or orange juice.

Bring the sauce to a low boil and slowly, as in a bit at a time—and remember, I'm watching you, always watching you—add the cornstarch mixture until your sauce slightly thickens.

Get those Q'd wings into a mixing bowl and toss in the Chili Kahlúa Sauce. Spray a 9 x 13-inch dish with cooking spray, and get those sauced-up, culturally confused wings in there and bake for another 10 minutes, or until they're nicely glazed and cooked through.

As for pairing these wings with an adult beverage, well, let's see . . . hmm-mmmmmm . . . the answer appears to be a question, how now brown cow?

THAT MEAN OLD GARLIC PRESS

As I mentioned earlier, firefighters are exceedingly tough on dishwashers and barbecues, but that's just the tip of the icebox. At No. 11, a firefighter purchased a "guaranteed for life" garlic press for the fire hall kitty. He'd been using it at home for months and had been telling his crew how indestructible the unit was. Another firefighter, keen to take it for a test drive, placed a head of garlic in the processor, squeezed the trigger and broke the unit on its very first press.

When it comes to the danger factor in the kitchen, the handy-dandy garlic press ranks right up there with pot handles that burn and knives that cut. I can't begin to count the number of injuries I've had preparing food. Back in my rookie firefighter days, my daughter Stephanie noticed a large scab on the bottom of my forearm and asked, "Dad, what's that on your arm?"

"That?" I replied as I inspected the mark. "Oh, I burned myself at work."

"Oh no!" Stephanie exclaimed in worry. "What happened?"

"Well, I was taking the lasagna out of the oven . . ."

The examples are many. Recently at No. 1, I put a huge pot of water on the gas stove and turned it on high. A few minutes later Kozo walked down the hallway and said, "Oh, does it ever smell like gas in here."

"It looks like some of the pilot lights on the stove are out again," I replied as I lit the pilot on the element beside the pot of water. WHHOOOSSSHHHH!!! Unbeknownst to me, the element I'd placed the pot on hadn't been lit *until now!* All the built-up gas ignited at once. My eyelashes were singed shut, my eyebrows looked like they'd been waxed off and my hairline receded even further.

Yes, firefighting is a dangerous profession. But one scenario attacks me even more often than chopping jalapeno peppers without gloves and absentmindedly taking a bathroom break: using the garlic press. It never fails. I load it with a clove, squeeze, and the garlic juice squirts me right in my eyes. Rendered blind, I stumble through the kitchen as if splattered with battery acid, wincing and voicing expletives.

By the way, if your garlic press ever gets plugged—which can happen if you overload it—don't look into the barrel as you squeeze the trigger wondering why it isn't working. *It's not worth it, man!* Really, a garlic press should come with safety glasses.

I know what you're thinking: an orangutan would catch on to kitchen safety faster than I ever will. What did you say you do for a living again, Jeff?

AROUND THE HALLS IN 40 MEALS

BE THE GUEST CHEF

I swear I spend half my time in the fire hall kitchen in a mad search for pots, pans, cheese graters, garlic presses and whisks. No item, it seems, is ever put back in the same place twice by crewmembers on any of the four shifts.

When I work at another fire house as a visitor, I'm *really* lost. Without fail, some essential instrument, spice or condiment will be missing, leading me to ad lib my way through meal prep. In addition, soup pots and saucepans with warped, paper-thin bottoms and worn-out Teflon, and knives as sharp as *[insert name of current airhead celebrity here]* are particular sore spots for me.

Yes, cooking in another fire hall has its challenges. Years ago, firefighter Eddie Yuen was sent to No. 20 station to fill in for a tour. "All right!" I thought. "The best chef on the job is coming to visit. I'm sure he'll be happy to cook for us." Well, not quite. You see, Eddie spent his off hours at his family's Peking Chinese Restaurant. Truth be known, Ed was looking for a break.

Fast-forward to the present and, I'll be honest, I sometimes cringe when I visit a hall and a firefighter says, "Hey, I'll bet Jeff will cook for us." Invariably I'm put on the spot to come up with a surefire lunch or dinner idea. Expectations are high, and I know I'd better come through with a winner to preserve my limited reputation. In the fire house cooking world, you're only as good as your last screw-up, so the pressure is on.

But there's more. As a visitor, you often don't know what the guys will, won't or can't eat. Try as you might, you sure can't please everyone. As if it isn't hard enough to put together a meal everyone will eat at home, a fire hall can sometimes take picky-eaterdom to a whole new level.

Give me a crew of adventurous, appreciative eaters, a well-stocked kitchen with no shortage of easy-to-find tools and I'm a happy fire chef. Ah, but I dream! Bottom line to this rant: I can sure sympathize with Master Chef Eddie now—though I must admit to having a hard time staying out of the kitchen when I'm not the chef.

Speaking of touring around and adventurous eating, that's what this chapter is all about: eclectic foods—funky recipes that'll help you bring the world home to your house or fire house. So leave the traditional fare behind, and set sail with me on a culinary journey around the globe. Bon voyage!

FAR EASTERN
A SPAGHETTI

Well, that's what we call it at our house. Italy meets China in this quick, tasty dish. We're talking ground beef and veggies starring in a stir-fry featuring that great ginger-beef flavour, without the big ginger-beef price tag!

FOR THE SAUCE, ROUND UP . . .

- 10-ounce can consommé
- ½ cup premium oyster sauce
- 2 tablespoons each soy sauce and rice vinegar
- 1 tablespoon brown sugar
- 2+ teaspoons chili-garlic sauce

LOOKS LIKE THE LINGUINE'S BROUGHT ALONG A POSSE

- ⅓ pounds linguine, cooked
- 4 tablespoons peanut oil, divided and conquered
- 2 tablespoons ginger, finely minced
- 2 garlic cloves, minced, smashed or otherwise violated
- 1 medium onion, coarsely chopped
- 1 pound lean ground beef—no violence please, it's suffered enough
- 2 carrots, sliced on the bias, as in at 45°
- 2 cups celery, ditto the above (get out your grade 7 geometry set)
- 1 red pepper, sliced into strips
- About ¼ pound mushrooms, sliced into Ts
- 1½ tablespoons cornstarch combined with 3 tablespoons water

DUEL AT DINNER TIME!

Let's start by combining the sauce ingredients in a bowl and setting them aside. Do it now, so you won't be scrambling while the stir-fry is on.

If you haven't cooked the linguine yet, well . . . *get moving, pal!*

Heat your wok over high heat. Where there's smoke, there's a need for peanut oil, so toss in 2 tablespoons oil, then the ginger, garlic and onion. Keep that great-smelling trio moving, to avoid browning.

After about 20 seconds, introduce the ground beef and fry it up until the beef is browned. Remove the beef to a strainer and drain off the fat.

Wok still rockin'? Then let's get another shot of peanut oil fired up, and add the "must have been cut by a finishing carpenter" carrots and celery.

Stir-fry for about a minute, and then add the red pepper and mushrooms.

Bring on the sauce ingredients—it's flavour-injection time!

Let's re-add the beef 'n' onions, to reheat. Keep that spatula moving, now!

Once the veggies are tender-crisp, bring the noodles to the party.

As your creation bubbles in the wok, intro the cornstarch slurry a bit at a time until the sauce attains the desired thickness, and it's supper up!

AUSSIE-RULES CHICKEN

Ah yes, the boneless, skinless chicken breast, the picture of health—high protein and low fat. Hmmmm, what can we do to make it sing with decadence? Hey, I know, let's turn it over to the Aussies and see what magic they can work. This dish never fails to impress at home, at the fire hall or in the outback.

SHOULDN'T WE BE TALKING ABOUT A KANGAROO, HERE?

- 4 boneless, skinless chicken breasts, slightly flattened
- Fired-Up Spice (page 4)
- All-purpose flour
- Butter and extra-virgin olive oil, for frying
- 1 cup sweet onions, diced fine
- 1 cup mushrooms, sliced into Ts
- 1 cup sweet peppers, cut in short, skinny strips
- 6 slices turkey bacon, cut in half—keeping with the poultry motif
- ½ cup prepared mustard
- ½ cup soft or liquid honey
- ¼ cup mayonnaise—don't tell me, the non-fat variety? Nawwwww . . .
- ¼ cup light corn syrup
- 2 cups (low-fat, maybe?) Monterey Jack or nacho cheese, grated

GOOD ON YA MATE! GOOD IN YA, TOO!

Sprinkle both sides of each chicken breast with Fired-Up Spice and then dredge it through a light coating of flour. Fair dinkum!

In a large frying pan over medium heat, add a couple tablespoons each of butter and olive oil. Get those chalky breasts in there and fry until browned on both sides. Remove the breasts to a greased 9 x 13-inch dish. Hang onto a couple tablespoons of the drippings for what's up next.

What's next is getting the onions, mushrooms and peppers into the same pan you fried the chicken in. Yes, those drippings make for bonus flavour.

Meanwhile, add a touch of olive oil to a completely different frying pan brought to medium heat. Let's fry that turkey bacon, turning it fairly often, until it's happily browned. Don't overcook it, or it could get leathery.

Let's build the Aussie sauce. Whisk the mustard, honey, mayo and corn syrup together and dump it all over the chicks.

Fire that oven up to 375°F.

Cut the bacon strips in half and top each chick with 2 to 3 strip halves.

The onions, mushrooms and peppers would like to ride atop the breasts as well, so get them into position. Just what kind of monstrous chicken breasts are you building, Dr. Frankenchef?

Bake the deluxe Aussie breasts for about 10 minutes.

Top the breasts with a whack o'cheese—yes, I'm serious—and bake them for an additional 20 minutes or until the chicken is cooked through.

BEEF BOURGUIGNON

French cuisine was certainly Julia Child's specialty, and this is one of her most imitated recipes, which is why I'm getting on board to give it a shot with a simplified fire hall version. Talk about a full-bodied stew—this is amazing!

LET'S WINE AND DINE THAT COW

- Olive oil
- ½ pound lean bacon (i.e., more pink than white), cubed
- 3 pounds stewing beef, cut into about 2-inch squares
- Fired-Up Spice (page 4)
- Get that pepper mill grinding! Work it, baby!
- All-purpose flour
- 2 jumbo onions, chopped into cubes
- 1 mega-big carrot, coarsely chopped
- Kosher salt to taste
- 3 cups dry red wine—bourguignon is traditional; I like a Merlot
- 2 10-ounce cans (2½ cups) beef consommé (or beef broth)
- 2 tablespoons tomato paste
- 4 garlic cloves, minced or pressed
- 1 teaspoon dried thyme
- 1 pound of those mini carrots
- 1 pound mushrooms, cut into thick Ts
- Italian seasoning, to taste

UH-OH, OUR COW'S ABOUT TO GET A LITTLE TIPSY—.08+++++++

Fire up your oven to 325°F.

Get a Dutch oven or large saucepan on the range, heat it up to about medium and toss in about a tablespoon of olive oil.

Bring on the bacon and render it down until crisp. By the way, Julia refers to this pork fat as a lardon. I think I'll just let that one be.

Remove the bacon with a slotted spoon to a paper-towel-lined plate—but hang onto those flavour-laden drippings, we'll need them.

Dry the stewing beef with paper towels. Dry beef fried in the drippings in an uncrowded pan will allow it to brown. We want that, so . . .

Toss the beef in a mixing bowl and sprinkle those little nuggets with a healthy dose of Fired-Up Spice and pepper. Dust and toss the beef with flour until lightly coated all over.

Toss batches of beef into the drippings to brown them up. When each batch is ready, place it in a mixing bowl.

Sauté half of the onions and the mega carrot for a few minutes in the same pan. A little salt and pepper couldn't hurt, eh, Julia?

Bring back the bacon and beef and add them to the veggies. Stir through to combine.

Place the red wine, consommé, tomato paste, garlic and thyme in there, and get the stew rolling with a little heat. Once the stew starts to boil, give it a stir, cover and move it to the oven.

For the next 3 hours, simply *forget about it!*

Actually, make that 2½ hours. Here's what I need you to do ½ hour before the stew has stewed. Get out a frying pan over medium heat, add a couple of tablespoons of butter and sauté the remaining onions until nicely browned. Julia would refer to this as caramelizing.

Meanwhile, steam the mini carrots until they just start to get tender.

Add the mushrooms to the onions, toss in a little salt and Italian seasoning to spice them up, and sauté briefly. Set the veggies aside.

Remove the stew from the oven and set it back on the range. You have 2 decisions to make, based on your innate sense of what's good and stewy.

Decision 1: If the gravy in the stew needs thickening, then turn the range on to get the stew bubbling, and combine 2 tablespoons each of melted butter and flour (a.k.a. a roux) and add it to the gravy to thicken.

Decision 2: Does the Beef Bourguignon need a flavour boost? If so, give it the old salt-and-pepper-to-taste treatment.

Introduce the onions, mushrooms and carrots to the stew and stir them through. Serve over a batch of smashed potatoes.

Just like soup, this stew is even tastier the second day. With that in mind, why not make it up a day in advance? Simply refrigerate it right in the Dutch oven after the 3-hour baking period. That is, of course, after you let it cool down. But you knew that, didn't you?

Before serving the day-old stew, skim off any congealed, fridge-formed fat from the pot and move the pot to the stovetop. Then simply pick up the recipe action back where I asked you to sauté the remaining onions.

Heat the stew thoroughly, stirring often to avoid Sticky Burned Pot Bottom Syndrome. Just wait till you taste this stew. A winter classic!

NO NEED TO TORTURE ME—I HAVE NO SECRETS, HONEST!

Did you know that Julia Child was a spy? I'm not kidding. Julia worked for the American spy agency that preceded the CIA before she learned the secrets of French cooking. Google it if you don't believe me. It's an interesting story.

Speaking of secrets, when I worked with Doug Rogowski at No. 3 station, Doug would take a recipe home that he enjoyed at work and ask his wife, Tammy, to replicate it. When she did, Doug would actually have the gall to taste it and say, "It's good, but it just doesn't taste the same as Jeff's."

This led his lovely bride—a very good cook in her own right—to accuse me of purposely leaving out one or more vital ingredients in my recipes. I stand before you, my hand on *Mastering the Art of French Cooking*, pleading not guilty! It became a running joke. "Hey, Doug, here's a recipe to take home to Tammy. See if you can figure out what I omitted this time."

BEER 'N' PIZZA
DOUGH

You know how great beer and pizza are together. Well, why not get the beer right into the pizza? Splashing it all over the pizza isn't an option, unless you like your pizza runny or your drinking problem is that you happen to spill a lot. No, instead of water, we're using beer in the pizza dough. The result is a dough that holds together nicely, rolls out easily and crisps up beautifully when you bake it. I can hear Homer now: "Mmmmmmmmmmm . . . Beer 'n' Pizza DOHHHHHHHH!"

BEER, WONDERFUL BEER

- 1 cup + 2 tablespoons beer—it doesn't have to be Duff
- 1½ tablespoons extra-virgin olive oil
- 1½ tablespoons honey
- 1 teaspoon sea salt (table salt can be substituted)
- 1½ cups whole-wheat flour
- 1½ cups all-purpose unbleached flour
- 2 teaspoons fast-acting yeast

BET YOU WON'T STOP AT ONE

Get the above ingredients into your bread maker in the order listed. Hit the dough cycle, and go find something else to do for the next 1½ to 2 hours. A workout might not be a bad idea, depending on what you're planning to top the pizza with. Life is all about balance.

Fire up your oven to 425°F.

Flour your counter and rolling pin and roll out your dough.

As a nice touch, lay down a little cornmeal on the pizza pan before stretching the dough over top.

Top with your favourite fixin's and bake for 15 to 20 minutes or until lightly browned, top and bottom.

THE FREEZE

For a thin crust, do like revered fire hall pizza-ologists like Ken Laramee and Romeo "Petizza" Petite do, and stretch your pizza dough over floured pizza trays and send them off to the freezer overnight. Then, when your stomach starts to emit angry, impatient hunger sounds the following day, you're already halfway to pizza heaven.

Don't let the dough defrost; simply top your frozen dough with your fave ingredients and dispatch it to the oven, tout de suite. Since it's frozen, the dough will have no time to rise, resulting in a thin, thin crust.

For added crispiness, Ken Laramee suggests placing the frozen crust and toppings right on the oven rack, sans pizza pan. Don't try moving the pizza, though, until it's had a chance to crisp up.

I know, you didn't expect something ice cold from a firefighter, did you?

If the weather forecast looks good, or even if it doesn't—I mean, how often is it accurate, anyway?—why not try the **Coffee Can Pizza** barbecue method (page 112)?

BELLA MARSALA

Here's a quick and easy gourmet Italian chicken dish. The secret is in the sweetness of the Marsala wine. I sure thought I was in trouble when I asked the liquor store guy where they keep the Marsala and he directed me to the fine wines section. To my surprise, it's actually quite moderately priced.

THE SHORT LIST

- 4 boneless, skinless chicken breasts
- A few shots of Fired-Up Spice (page 4)
- All-purpose flour
- 6 tablespoons butter, divided
- ⅔ cup shallots (or red onions), finely diced
- 3 cups mushrooms, sliced into Ts
- 1 cup Marsala wine
- 1¼ cups chicken broth–a 10-ounce can
- 1 tablespoon Dijon mustard
- Chopped parsley, for garnish

THE SIMPLE LIST

Dust each side of the chicken breasts with Fired-Up Spice.

Dredge the breasts through the flour to lightly coat. Shake them a bit to remove any excess clingage. *Is that a word?* Spell-check says no. Let's consult the Urban Dictionary. If it's not there, we'll create it in Wikipedia.

Let's heat up a large frying pan over medium to medium-high heat and get 2 tablespoons butter going. Butter + flour = browning.

Toss in the breasts and fry until they tan to a nice golden brown. Oh, about 3 minutes a side should do it. Set aside.

Bring 2 more tablespoons of butter to the pan, and introduce the shallots to the butter to soften. The mushrooms want in on the deal as well, so toss them in and brown. Try to get them to cough up their 'shroom liquid.

It's Marsala time! Pour in the wine and boil the old grape juice until it's reduced to about half—that's half in metric, as well.

Follow that up with the chicken broth and mustard, whisk together and cook for 3 minutes.

Let's turn down the heat down to medium and re-add the chicken breasts to the pan. Cook the breasts for about 5 minutes or until cooked through. You can give them the spring chicken test to see if they're done. If you press on the breast and it's still spongy, a.k.a. it gives a bit, keep going. When it just becomes firm, it should be ready to eat.

Remove the breasts to individual plates. Add 1 tablespoon butter to the sauce, combine and heat through. If it needs thickening, melt another tablespoon butter in a separate small saucepan, mix it with 1 tablespoon flour and add to the sauce.

Give the sauce the standard "salt and pepper, to taste."

Top the breasts with the Marsala sauce and sprinkle parsley over top.

BOURBON CHICKEN

That doesn't sound like an Asian dish, but it is! Yes, sir, it's a Kentucky stir-fry! You know the deal with firewater and me. I rarely drink it, but when it comes to cooking, I'm hooked! To see my stash you'd think I needed a 12-step program, but not to worry, this Irishman has it under control. Here's a great stir-fry sauce that gets a nip from the bottle to push it over the top.

RELAX, IT'S ONLY A HINT OF HOOCH

- 2 tablespoons peanut oil
- 2 pounds boneless, skinless chicken breasts, cut in bite-sized pieces
- ½ cup water
- ⅓ cup each soy sauce and golden brown sugar
- ¼ cup apple juice
- 2 tablespoons ketchup
- 2 tablespoons bourbon (brandy or rye will also do)
- 1 tablespoon each cider vinegar and chopped fresh ginger
- 1–2 teaspoons chili-garlic sauce—I like a fiery double hit
- 2 tablespoons each melted butter and flour—what, no cornstarch?

THE WOK IS READY TO ROCK . . . HIC!

Fire up your wok over high heat. When it starts smokin', you know what to do—no, don't stretch a hose line and put it out; get the peanut oil in there, followed up by the chicken.

Stir-fry the chicken until just lightly browned. Unless you have a mega wok, you'll likely need to do this in two batches.

Whisk the rest of the ingredients together—except the butter and flour—until totally dissolved. Hit the chicken with the sauce . . . nicely, now!

When the sauce starts to boil, turn it down to a simmer for about 5 minutes, to ensure that the chicken is cooked through and to reduce the sauce and blend and build the wonderful flavours together.

Combine the melted butter and flour into a roux—if roux don't know what I'm talking about, just whisk the two together in a bowl.

Get that flour/butter mixture into the fray, and allow it a minute or so to both thicken and tame—albeit slightly—our sauce.

Serve the chicken and sauce over rice, or go for broke and make up a batch of stir-fried veggies to round out your meal. Sugar snap peas and bell pepper strips work well for this operation. You can even toss the veggies in with the sauce and chicken, as there's plenty of sauce to go around. Around your chin, around your shirt, around your pants . . .

BREADED
PORK CHOPS ITALIANO

Aren't we supposed to be eating more cooked tomatoes, for reasons best known to the tomato producers' marketing board? Something like 7 to 8 servings a day? Well, here's another way to get that it-must-be-goodness into our diets. While we're at it, we'll tune into a great way to cook pork chops to tender, juicy perfection. It's a simple three-step program: bread the chops, fry them to seal in the juices and finish them off in the oven.

PIGS IN A VERY THIN BLANKET

- 4 XXL bone-in centre-cut pork chops, about 1¼ inches thick
- Fired-Up Spice (page 4)
- All-purpose flour
- 1 egg, whisked together with 1 tablespoon water
- Italian bread crumbs, as required
- Extra-virgin olive oil
- 1 zucchini, sliced
- About ¼ pound mushrooms, T'd up
- 2 tablespoons butter
- Salt, pepper and Italian seasoning
- 1 medium tomato or 2 Roma tomatoes, chunked up
- 1 cup of your favourite prepared pasta sauce—choose one with zip!
- Red chili flakes (optional)

NOT TO WORRY, THEY'LL HAVE PLENTY OF HEAT

Get your oven fired up to 350°F.

Give the chops the humane breading treatment, as outlined in section 7:11 of the *Geneva Convention*. Here's a quick refresher for you, in the unlikely event that it's not top of mind.

Season the chops with the Fired-Up Spice, dredge them through the flour to lightly coat, then dip them in the egg wash and finally coat the little piglets with the Italian bread crumbs—yes, the Italians are our allies. If you have the time, send them off to the fridge for an hour or so to set up.

Get a large frying pan rockin' over medium heat and add a light coating of olive oil. Fry the chops for about 4 minutes a side or until nicely browned.

Remove the chops to a baking pan lined with a rack. This will help keep the breading crisp while it bakes.

Off to the oven the porkers go for about 20 minutes, or until cooked through. A hint of pink is certainly acceptable here in the 21st century.

These tender, juicy chops are good to go with a squeeze of lemon juice, but why stop there? Fire up the flavour quotient by frying the zucchini and mushrooms in the butter plus a touch of salt, pepper and Italian seasoning. Add the tomatoes to the mix and pour in the pasta sauce.

Tune up the pasta sauce seasoning, if you like—red chili flakes will fire it up—and you've got a quick and easy topping that will satisfy the masses.

I'm thinking a Caesar salad would sure look good on the side.

CHIMICHURRI
FLANK STEAK

Our culinary world tour continues with a visit to Argentina, where cows are far from sacred. Argentineans love their beef and consume it in mass quantities. Hmmmmm, sounds like the fire house, doesn't it? Our South American friends like to grill their beef and serve it with a tangy herb Chimichurri Sauce, but I tend to break with tradition here and marinate the steaks in the Chimichurri first, reserving some of the Chimichurri to serve as a dipping sauce for a rock 'em, sock 'em, one, two, south-of-the-equator flavour-combo double play!

WHAT'S THAT HERB?

- 1 cup parsley
- 1 cup cilantro—gives the chimi a little funk
- ¼ cup fresh basil leaves—or more parsley
- 2 tablespoons red wine vinegar
- 1 tablespoon each lemon juice and lime juice
- 6 garlic cloves—minced
- 1 teaspoon dried red chili flakes—this can be adjusted to suit your taste
- 1 teaspoon kosher salt
- 1 teaspoon ground cumin—nicely complements the cilantro
- ½ cup extra-virgin olive oil
- 1½- to 2-pound flank or skirt steak
- Freshly ground black pepper
- Fried onions, peppers and mushrooms

PULSE THE PROCESSOR, CUE THE Q!

Get all of the ingredients up to but not including the olive oil together in a food processor. Pulse away until blended. It sounds like we're making pesto, doesn't it? Not too far off, actually, but this is a tangier, vinegarized version without the Italiano cheese and pine nuts.

With the machine running, pour a slow, steady stream of the olive oil into the Chimichurri until it all comes together as one.

Place the steak in a zip-top freezer bag with about ⅔ of the Chimichurri.

Off to the fridge it goes for about 4 hours to overnight, to infuse flavours. The remaining sauce can be placed in an airtight container and set aside.

Get the flank out of the fridge about ½ to 1 hour before grilling.

Fire up your grill to medium-high.

Season the steak with a hit of pepper, then sear both sides on the grill for about 2 minutes each.

Turn the barbecue down to medium and grill the flank to medium-rare.

Let the steak rest for 5 to 10 minutes before slicing, and when you do take a knife to it, you absolutely *must* slice it thinly and against the grain. Slicing a medium-rare flank steak against the grain will take what could have been a tough steak and make it temptingly tender.

Top each serving of steak strips with fried onions, peppers and mushrooms and, of course, a whack of that tangy reserved Chimichurri.

CURRIED CHICKEN DIVAN

Here's an old fire hall favourite that was recently reinvented. Changes to the original include marinating and barbecuing the chicken first, adding cauliflower to the broccoli and roasting the veggies before baking them in the casserole, plus a curry count enhancement. The result is a thicker sauce and a major boost in the all-important flavour department.

SO, WHATCHA FIRING UP IN THAT COOL CURRY CASSEROLE?

- 16 boneless, skinless chicken thighs
- Lemon-Garlic Marinade (page 6)
- Large bunch broccoli, cut into bite-sized trees
- Extra-virgin olive oil
- Kosher salt and freshly ground black pepper
- ½ head cauliflower, also cut into wee trees
- Ground cumin
- 2 10-ounce cans cream of chicken soup
- 1 cup whipped salad dressing or mayonnaise
- 1 to 1½ tablespoons mild curry paste—start at 1
- 2 teaspoons lemon juice
- Just shy of 1 pound grated marble or nacho blended cheese
- Ritz crackers and butter (optional)

CURRY ON, MY WAYWARD SON

Get the chicken in the marinade—zip-top freezer bags work great—and into the fridge for at least 4 hours.

Fire up the barbecue and grill the thighs until just done. Err on the side of salmonella—in other words, don't worry if they're slightly underdone, as they will finish cooking in the casserole, and we don't want to dry them out.

Fire up that oven to 425°F.

Toss the broccoli in a bowl with just enough olive oil to lightly coat, and add a light dusting of salt and pepper.

Ditto for the cauliflower, but add a little cumin to the spice mix as well.

Roast the veggies until *just* tender-crisp. Again, the wee trees will continue to cook in the casserole, so underdone is okay.

Blend the soup, whipped salad dressing, curry paste and lemon juice together. Taste the sauce and decide if you want to add more curry paste.

Scatter the broc and cauli on the bottom of a 9 x 13-inch lasagna dish.

Cut the thighs in half and distribute over the veggies, top with the curry sauce and finish off your creation with a blanket of cheese.

Here's an optional topping. Crumble Ritz crackers on top of the cheese, melt 2 tablespoons of margarine or butter, and sprinkle it over the crackers for a crunchy topping. Decadence has no bounds.

Turn the oven down to 375°F and bake the casserole, uncovered, for 30 minutes, or until all participants are content and cooked through.

Let it stand for 10 minutes before serving, to allow the cheese to set up.

CURRYOUS GEORGE AND
THE SPICY PASTA DISH

Imagine linguine tossed with Cuban-lime-marinated barbecued chicken thighs, a selection of stir-fried vegetables and—due to popular demand—bananas in a curry cream sauce. It's a fired-up blend of heat + sweet = tasty treat. Curry on George, show us the way, you little monkey!

ALL THE MAJOR FOOD GROUPS ARE HERE

- 12 chicken thighs
- Cuban Lime Marinade (page 6)
- ¼ cup butter—being 2 hits of 2 tablespoons each
- 3 tablespoons curry paste—I like mild, but if you like the heat . . .
- 2 tablespoons finely chopped fresh ginger
- Half a head of garlic, minced or pressed
- 1 cup each finely chopped onions, celery and carrots
- 4 cups chicken broth
- ½–¾ cup coconut cream—you can buy coconut cream, or use the thick stuff floating at the top of a can of coconut milk (or even use half-and-half cream)
- 1 red onion, cut into strips
- 2 red peppers, stripped down, too
- 1 zucchini, sliced fairly thin
- Bunch asparagus or broccoli, stalks cut into 3 pieces, woody ends discarded
- Kosher salt and freshly ground black pepper
- Juice of 1 lime, plus additional limes for garnish
- 1 bunch cilantro, chopped—get garnishing; presentation's important
- ¾ pound whole-wheat linguine
- 2 reasonably ripe bananas—they'll sure make George happy!

CURRYOUS GEORGE IS GOING BANANAS!

Get those chicken thighs into a zip-top freezer bag, pour in the marinade and send them off to the fridge from 4 hours to overnight. Bring on the flavour!

Get 2 tablespoons of butter going in a large saucepan over medium heat.

Toss in the curry paste, stir it around a bit and add the ginger, garlic, onions, celery and carrots. Fry until everyone is nicely tenderized.

Pour in the chicken broth and simmer the lot until the liquid is reduced by about half. If the saucepan has a wide opening—meaning maximum evaporation—it should take 30 to 45 minutes. "What's that smell?" the curryous ask. Better run the range fan, to share it with the neighbours.

Get the pot off the heat, let it cool if you have time, then carefully purée it in a blender in batches until velvety smooth.

Return the purée to the pot and add the coconut cream to taste.

How's the time management going here? Somehow you have to find time to barbecue or broil the chicken. Can you work this into your schedule?

Where were we? Oh yeah, you know the other 2 tablespoons of butter up there in the ingredient list? Let's get them into a large saucepan and introduce the red onion. Sauté for a bit, then add the quick-cooking peppers, zucchini and asparagus. Dust the lot with a teaspoon of salt and a healthy helping of pepper.

Chop the cooked chicken into bite-sized pieces, depending on yap size—your yap and their yaps.

When the veggies are tender-crisp, toss them along with the chicken into the Curryous George Sauce and bring to a low boil. Let's get the fresh lime juice and half of the chopped cilantro in there, as well.

Meanwhile, boil the pasta as per the directions on the box—or show the pasta who's boss and do it your own way, Mr. Sinatra.

Drain the pasta well and add it to the sauce. Get George's bananas into the fray and stir through. Let your colourful creation sit for a few minutes, so the pasta can suck up all those awesome eclectic flavours.

Get each serving onto a plate and top it with the remaining cilantro and garnish with lime quarters for drizzling.

By George, I think we've done it! The Man with the Yellow Hat is so proud!

PASS THE PESTO!

Homemade pesto is so good and so easy to make. Just pull out the food processor, load up the ingredients and in seconds a delicious pasta sauce is yours. There's no waiting for a sauce to stew, and nothing to cook beyond the pasta. Pesto is ready to rock right out of the food whacker at room temperature.

You don't need to spend $300+ on a fancy Cuisinart. I have a basic food processor that cost me about $35 several years ago, and it works great. Hey, you can even make pesto in a blender, if you have to.

Pesto can be used in so many different ways. The obvious use is to toss it with pasta, but it also works great as a flavour kicker in tomato-based pasta sauces, scrambled eggs, omelettes, mashed potatoes, salad dressings and marinades. My friend Tara even uses it as a sandwich spread!

Since pesto has a million and one uses, I always try to keep a batch made up in the fridge—stored in a sealed container with a thin layer of olive oil on top, so it doesn't turn brown.

Oh, you can buy store-bought pesto, but it can be pricey, and to me you just can't beat that fresh, homemade taste.

So now that you've heard the pep talk, let's get out there into that big, bad cooking world and get pesto'd!

EVERYBODY GOES PESTO

"Everybody goes!" That's the floor man's cry, heard over the PA at the fire house when every truck in the fire hall is dispatched to the same call. In the case of this pesto, it means all of the ingredients I use in my favourite pestos go into one all-star, deluxe pesto special. Parsley, basil, cilantro and sun-dried tomatoes are all geared up to attend this emergency call for over-the-top flavour, so open the fridge doors, rev up the food processor and spin out!

LISTEN UP FOR YOUR APPARATUS NUMBERS

- 1 cup fresh parsley—exact herb measurement not required
- ½ cup fresh basil—yes, you can rough out the amount of each herb
- ½ cup fresh cilantro—for a little earthiness
- 3 tablespoons sun-dried tomatoes—the ones packed in oil in small glass jars (be sure to drain off the oil before adding)
- 6 garlic cloves
- 2 tablespoons lemon or lime juice (or a blend of both)
- 2 tablespoons slivered almonds or pine nuts—or even both
- 1½ teaspoons kosher salt
- Give that pepper mill about 6 good grinds
- ½ cup extra-virgin olive oil
- ⅓ cup Parmesan cheese

EVERYBODY INTO THE FOOD PROCESSOR, WE'VE GOTTA RUN!

Before you make the pesto, you may want to ask yourself what you're going to use it for. If it'll be working with an Italian or Greek dish, you may choose to use the lemon juice, up the basil count and drop the cilantro. If you're going Tex-Mexican, however, then you'll maybe want to use lime juice, up the cilantro and drop the basil. This is a great all-purpose pesto, but it can be fine tuned to suit the use.

Bring out the food processor and stuff it with parsley, basil, cilantro, sun-dried tomatoes, garlic, lemon or lime juice, almonds or pine nuts, salt, and pepper.

Pulse away on the chopper until the goodies are all ground up.

While the processor is running, slowly pour in the olive oil until combined.

Keep it running and follow up by pouring in the Parmesan cheese.

Give the pesto the taste test. Be forewarned, it will be highly seasoned and quite salty. Not to worry; that's the way we want it.

Toss the pesto with your favourite pasta. Hey, and why not make up a batch of grilled chicken marinated in the **Lemon-Garlic** or **Cuban Lime Marinades** (pages 6) or the **Lemon Lime Lickin' Chicken** (page 144) along with the **Barbecued Veggies in a Basket** (page 185) and some **Great Garlic Cheese Toast** (page 189). You know what that combo would be, don't you? A culinary grand slam!

EVERYBODY GOES
PESTO PIZZA

Here's an eclectic pizza show. Cuban Lime Marinated Chicken shares top billing with a tasty Everybody Goes Pesto, with feature performances from Caramelized Onions, Bell Peppers, Button Mushrooms, Tex-Mex Cheese and Grape Tomatoes. Are you salivating yet, Pavlov? Roll 'em . . .

WHERE'S THE TOMATO SAUCE AND PEPPERONI?

- Cuban Lime Marinade (page 6)
- 4 boneless, skinless chicken breasts (or 10 boneless, skinless thighs)
- A batch of Beer 'n' Pizza Dough (page 136) or purchased shells
- 2 tablespoons butter
- 1 small red onion, cut into strips
- ½ teaspoon each kosher salt and freshly ground black pepper
- 1 orange and 1 yellow pepper, in strips
- About ¼ pound mushrooms, sliced into Ts
- 1 batch Everybody Goes Pesto (page 144) or store-bought basil pesto
- Extra-virgin olive oil
- Tex-Mex or nacho cheese, grated (unless you know of a Cuban cheese)
- 2 tomatoes, sliced (or grape tomatoes, halved)
- Chopped cilantro

LET'S KICK THAT "GOURMET" FROZEN PIZZA'S BUTT

Get the Cuban Lime Marinade mixed together and pour it into one of those handy zip-top freezer bags with the chicken. Feel free to squeeze out all the air in the bag, and toss it in the fridge for 4 hours.

Meanwhile, get the bread maker going on the dough.

Fire up a frying pan over medium-low heat, add the butter and bring on the onions. Dust the tear makers with the salt and pepper and cook 'em until lightly browned, say about 10 minutes.

While that's happening, barbecue or broil the chicken until cooked through. Set it aside to cool and then slice into bite-sized pieces.

Fire up your oven to 425°F.

Intro the peppers and mushrooms to the onions, and fry them up for a couple of minutes. Drain off any liquid the mushrooms kick out.

Depending on the consistency of the pesto you've created, you'll likely want to add just a wee bit of olive oil, to make it easier to spread.

Get your dough rolled out on 2 pizza pans and top with the pesto, those bite-sized bits of chicken, the onions, peppers and 'shrooms and cheese.

Next up it's the tomatoes, and finally a bit of cilantro to finish.

Bake for 15 to 20 minutes or until the dough and cheese look to be goldenly pizzonified. What's that? Well, *of course* pizzonified is a word. Look it up in the Don King version of the English dictionary.

FETTUCCINE JAMBALAYA

It's hybrid time once again in the fire hall kitchen as we take fettuccine noodles down to Bayou country for a fiery pasta makeover. Chicken, spicy sausage and shrimp are the feature players in this abundant gathering of diverse flavours. If the weather is in your favour, our star performers demand to be grilled on the Q. It's in their rider, so any attempt to negotiate this demand will be futile.

WHAT, NO RICE?

- Cuban Lime marinade (page 6)
- 1 pound boneless, skinless chicken thighs
- 1 pound chorizo, hot Italian or andouille sausage
- 1 pound large shrimp, peeled (tails on)
- 3 tablespoons butter, divided
- ¾ cup each finely chopped yellow onion, celery and carrots
- 6 large garlic cloves, minced
- 2 teaspoons Fired-Up Santa Fe Spice (page 5)
- Lots of freshly ground black pepper
- 1½ cups spaghetti sauce
- 10-ounce can chicken broth
- 1 cup half-and-half cream (or 2% milk)
- Chili flakes (optional)
- ½ cup more diced onions
- 1 yellow, orange or red pepper, in strips
- ¾–1 pound spinach fettuccine, cooked
- Green onions, chopped
- Cherry or grape tomatoes
- Jalapeno Monterey Jack cheese, grated

WHAT'S CUBA DOING HERE?

I know, Cuban Lime Marinade is neither Cajun nor Italian, but it works, so quit bugging me! Just mix up a batch and get the chicken with the Fidel Castro influence soaking in a zip-top freezer bag in the fridge for 4 hours or even overnight. Barbecue or broil until cooked through.

Meanwhile, prick the sausages a few times each and get them off to a pot of boiling water for about 5 minutes or so, to de-fat. Drain and allow them to cool. Then either barbecue, broil or fry to finish. Slice them on a 45° angle. Let them cool first, unless you possess asbestos hands.

The third member of our protein team is the shrimp. If you're Q'ing them, try the technique in **Q the Sizzling Shrimp** (page 120).

Let's get 2 tablespoons of the butter melted in a large frying pan over medium heat and add the onion, celery, carrots and garlic. Season with the Fired-Up Santa Fe Spice and pepper.

When the veggies are soft, add the spag sauce and chicken broth. Bring the mix to a light boil and let it bubble away for at least 15 minutes.

Get out the oven mitts and carefully pour the sauce into a blender in a couple of batches and purée. We're counting on the veggies to thicken the sauce, so be sure to leave them in.

While the blender runs at a low

speed, pour in the cream. Taste and adjust the seasoning. Add chili flakes if you like it spicier. Set the sauce aside.

Clean out the frying pan, because it's time for Round 2. Heat up that pan and add the remaining tablespoon of butter plus the second batch of onions.

When they start to caramelize, bring on the peppers for a minute or so.

If you didn't Q the shrimp, then invite them into the pan party. Stir 'em until they just turn pink. Toss in the Q'd or broiled chicken and sausages.

Pour the sauce from the blender into the pan and bring your awe-inspiring creation back to operating temperature. Full steam ahead!

I trust that you've timed the pasta perfectly, so get it into a large roaster and pour the jambalaya sauce over top. Toss it through, adding the chopped green onions and cherry or grape tomatoes, and let it sit for a few minutes so the pasta can absorb those funky flavours.

Plate the servings and top with grated jalapeno Monterey Jack cheese.

FIGHTING THE FIRE BELOW

Bo brought a mason jar full of his famous Scotch bonnet peppers for all to share at No. 1 station. The label on the container dated three years back, a fine vintage, I'm sure. As my coworkers discovered, Scotch bonnet peppers—made famous by Jamaicans in their jerk recipes—pack a scorching wallop. Eaten raw, these peppers are also known to cause dizziness, numbness of hands and cheeks and severe heartburn. We were curious about trying them, but after taking the tiniest of bites we each ran for water—or the better choice, milk—to cool the burn.

As eating contests can be commonplace at the fire house, such as eating seven soda crackers in one minute with no water, or chasing the Cinnamon Dragon by swallowing a tablespoon of cinnamon without a liquid accompaniment, the Scotch bonnets led to a bet to see who'd be willing to drink the nitro pickling liquid they were packed in. The bet was set at three ounces, a collection was taken and our rookie, Darin, took the $50 dare. Dean carefully measured out three ounces and Darin bravely shot the quality-aged juice back. Everyone howled and grimaced, expecting his innards to revolt and the juice to shoot back out, but amazingly, Darin kept the blazing goo down—as was the wager. Fire in the hole, fire in the hole! How's that for a tough firefighter? Not only does he fight fires, he swallows them, too!

ADOBO O'DERRAUGH

O'Derraugh was our surname back in Ireland, and according to folklore the "O" was dropped for religious reasons. Adobo isn't exactly Irish soul food—you'd have to go halfway around the globe to find this dish's origin in the Philippines. There are numerous variations of adobo chicken (or pork) out there, and here's mine. To me, this sauce strikes a nice balance between the tang of the rice vinegar and the sweetness of the Indonesian soy sauce. I know, again, not exactly Filipino, but a lot closer geographically. Give this hybrid version a try. I have a sneaking suspicion you'll like it.

WHAT DOES AN IRISHMAN KNOW ABOUT FILIPINO FARE?

- 12 chicken legs, thighs or both, skin on, bone in, trimmed of excess fat
- 2 tablespoons peanut oil
- 1 large onion, diced into 1-inch squares
- 1 cup sweet soy sauce (in Fire Hall Essentials, page 4)
- 1 cup seasoned rice wine vinegar
- 10 garlic cloves, run through the garlic press
- 3–4 bay leaves
- One tablespoon whole peppercorns, or lots of freshly ground black pepper
- 1 tablespoon cornstarch mixed with 1 tablespoon water

LESS THAN A FILIPINO KNOWS ABOUT STEW

Get a pot of water boiling, add the chicken pieces and turn the range down so it's rolling along at a low boil. See the scum rising to the surface? That's why we're here. The chicken will need only about 5 minutes to rid itself of that fat. Don't try this on yourself. Not only will it be difficult to find a pot big enough, but the pain isn't worth the fat loss.

Meanwhile, get a tablespoon or two of peanut oil going in a wide frying pan and stir-fry the onions for a couple of minutes, to caramelize.

Follow up by adding the sweet soy sauce combined with the rice vinegar, garlic, bay leaves and peppercorns. Bring that adobo sauce to a light boil.

Drain that svelte-looking chicken and add it to that simmering sauce.

Cover the pot and maintain that light simmer for about 10 to 15 minutes, making sure to turn the chicken once with tongs—not thongs—during the cooking time, to keep it balanced, as in nicely coloured and happy.

Remove the lid, keep on keepin' on with the light boil, and turn the chick pieces occasionally. We want the sauce to reduce and the flavours to intensify while glazing the chicken. Cook for another 10 to 15 minutes or so, until the chicken pieces are cooked through.

To thicken the sauce, bring it to a boil. Slowly add the cornstarch mix until the sauce thickens up a bit. Toss the chicken with the sauce and serve over a bed of rice with **Asian Orange Asparagus** (page 183).

FIREBALLS

When Italian is on the menu, show your meatballs the Italian way. Get the cheese, herbs, garlic and seasonings in there, and for full flavour—which is what a wee bit of fat offers—throw in some ground pork. Yeah, I know, ground veal also makes its way into Italian meatballs, but come on, this is a fire hall and every penny counts. If you insist on tradition, why not go for equal parts beef, veal and pork?

ROME ON OVER TO YOUR LOCAL MARKET FOR . . .

- ½ cup Italian-seasoned bread crumbs
- ¼ cup Parmesan cheese
- ½ cup milk
- 2 garlic cloves, minced or pressed
- 1 egg, beaten
- 1½ teaspoons Fired-Up Spice (page 4)
- Freshly ground black pepper–just grind away on the mill for a bit
- ¼ teaspoon cayenne (or ½+ teaspoon if you like it spicy)
- 1 pound lean ground beef
- 1 pound ground pork

GOODNESS GRACIOUS, GREAT BALLS OF FIRE!

Get the bread crumbs, Parmesan, milk, garlic, egg and spices together in a mixing bowl. Bring on the whisk and combine the lot.

Drop the ground meat into the mix in small bits, trying to keep the beef and pork evenly distributed. Combine all of the ingredients together with those manly (or womanly) hands of yours, but don't over-handle as we don't want to serve up density meatballs here.

To cook the meatballs, you have a number of options. You can fry them in a pan or on a griddle over medium heat. This is the traditional method.

But you know me, I rarely stick with tradition, so here are a couple of other options you can try, depending on the local weather forecast.

Being that I like my Fireballs as grease-free as possible, in the winter I usually place them on a broiler pan—you know the ones with the slits to let the grease drip down into the pan below—and bake them in the oven at 400°F until cooked through. You'll want to turn them once during the bake cycle, to brown them evenly.

But if the weather is right, my favourite method is to fire up the Fireballs on the barbecue. Just make sure to carefully oil the hot grill with a brush first, and let the Fireballs set up a crust on the bottom before you attempt to move them with a metal spatula or tongs. To me a Q'd Fireball is a happy, full-flavoured Fireball! Great with spaghetti and sauce, or on **Fire Hall Heroes** (page 26) or in **Fireball Soup** (page 39).

FIRED-UP
FILIPINO PANCIT

I call it the Folklorama Food Challenge—one I rarely live up to, but one I strive to meet, regardless. When I cook for firefighters or friends, I'll often attempt to cook their native foods, to see if I can somehow manage to get them right. So if, for example, I have Korean friends over for supper, I'll make Korean chicken or bulgogi. At the fire hall I once made Fired-Up Filipino Pancit for a firefighter of Filipino heritage, Jon Causon, who was filling in for one of our guys on holidays. As I fired up the wok I asked Jon, "Does it smell like your Mom's house yet?"

"No."

"How about now?"

"No."

How's this for a response when Jon tasted his first forkful? "Jeff, this is nothing like my Mom's . . . but it's really good!" Thanks for the kind words, Jon. I think. So let's head off to the Philippines to check out their traditional noodle dish. If you love pad Thai, you'll really enjoy pancit à la Jeff.

CHECK OUT ALL THE FOOD GROUPS THAT HAVE GATHERED

- ½ pound vermicelli rice noodles (you'll find them in the Asian food section)
- 1½ pounds pork tenderloin, in bite-sized pieces (you can use chicken thighs instead)
- 1 pound large shrimp, deveined and peeled, tail on, please
- Kosher salt and freshly ground black pepper
- Peanut or canola oil
- 4 garlic cloves, pressed or minced
- 2 tablespoons finely minced ginger
- 1 medium onion, diced
- 2 stalks celery, also diced
- 1 yellow or red pepper, sliced into thin strips
- 4 cups napa cabbage or bok choy, cut into coarse squares
- 1 or 2 carrots (depending on size), grated
- Or instead of carrots and cabbage, try a 12-ounce bag broccoli slaw
- ½ cup chicken broth
- 6 tablespoons premium oyster sauce
- 3 tablespoons sweet soy sauce (in Fire Hall essentials, page 4)
- 4+ teaspoons chili-garlic sauce
- Chopped green onions, as a garnish
- Chopped cilantro, same deal as above
- Lemon quarters, for squeezing

PANCIT IS ONLY A SHORT STIR-FRY AWAY

Let's boil some water. No, we're not performing obstetrics; we need the boiling water to soak the noodles. That's how we cook them.

Get the noodles in the bath, following package instructions for time.

Season the pork and shrimp with salt and pepper.

Get your wok rocking till it's smoking. Toss in a couple of tablespoons of peanut oil, carefully swish it around the bowl and add half of the garlic and ginger.

Hey Porky, your bath is drawn, so get in there, Bud! Stir-fry the pork until just about cooked, and add the shrimp.

When the shrimp just turns pink, get the pork 'n' shrimp out of there. Sorry if that sounds in any way offensive to you.

Let's add another dose of peanut oil, and the remaining garlic and ginger.

The onion and celery need to feel the heat, so get them in there, too.

Once they're tender-crisp, bring on the pepper, along with the cabbage and carrots (or the broccoli slaw).

Veggies don't come preseasoned, so give them a little shot of salt and pepper to wake up the taste buds.

Mix the chicken broth, oyster sauce, sweet soy sauce, and chili-garlic sauce together to form your ready-to-rock Fired-Up Pancit sauce.

Tender-crisp veggies, you say? If your produce has reached that stage, then return the pork 'n' shrimp to the wok.

Introduce the sauce and bring it to a boil. Toss, toss, stir, stir.

Follow up with the drained noodles—you may want to cut them down in length, for ease of serving and slurping—unless, of course, you're hoping to act out the *Lady and the Tramp* noodle scene. Not at the fire hall, please!

If your sauce decided to thin out on you, slowly and a bit at a time add about ½ tablespoon cornstarch mixed with 1 tablespoon water to thicken.

Once all is warm, plate the pancit. Top each serving with green onions and cilantro, and place lemon wedges on the side for a tangy squeeze over top. That's it, let's eat!

THE DAY THE STEW BLEW

If you're thinking my cooking abilities were passed down to me paternally, think again. One day my mom called Dad from work and asked him to pick her up. "And take the stew out of the fridge and put it on low, before you go."

When Dad picked her up, Mom said, "I hope you put that pot on low."

Dad didn't answer—in fact, he didn't say a word. He didn't have to. His silence plus the steadily increasing driving speed said it all.

When they got home, Dad scrambled out of the car, sprinted up the stairs two at a time and frantically opened the door. It was a scene routinely witnessed by firefighters round the globe. The house was full of smoke, and food was everywhere—the stove, fridge, walls and floor. Supper had exploded. Somehow there was still some stew bubbling away on the red-hot element, just enough to support the glass lid, but sinking slowly. Melting, melting, melting . . .

Dad's lone words of apology: "I've got to be at rehearsal in half an hour. Can you make me some eggs?"

FIRE HOUSE JAMBALAYA

Let's take a road trip to New Orleans for a mess of that Cajun stew called jambalaya. There are a number of distinct varieties of jambalaya out there, and various carnivorous choices you can make, including the option to use super-spicy sausages. I made this once at the hall and picked up some fire-breathing sausage to fire it up. When we woke in the morning, after a rare night of uninterrupted slumber, my captain glared at me. "I cursed you a million times last night, Jeff! My stomach churned all night. I didn't sleep a wink!"

SO, WHO WANTS IN ON THIS BORN-ON-THE-BAYOU STEW?

- Cuban Lime Marinade (page 6)
- 12–16 chicken thighs, bone in or out
- 1 pound hot Italian, chorizo, or andouille sausage
- A couple tablespoons each butter and extra-virgin olive oil
- 1 jumbo onion, diced
- 2 celery stalks, coarsely diced
- 2 sweet peppers, different colours for presentation, coarsely chopped
- 5 or 6 garlic cloves, pressed or minced
- At least 1 teaspoon Fired-Up Santa Fe Spice (page 5)
- Freshly ground black pepper
- About ½ pound ham (optional)
- 2 cups white basmati rice (see note at bottom of recipe)
- 2½+ cups chicken broth (or more)
- 28-ounce can diced tomatoes
- 1 tablespoon tomato paste—try the garlic or Italian
- 1 teaspoon dried thyme
- 2 teaspoons hot sauce—you can always add more later
- 1 pound large shrimp, peeled, tails on
- Chopped green onions

WE'LL GET THIS DOWN TO ONE POT . . . EVENTUALLY

Blend the Cuban Lime Marinade together. Toss it in a zip-top freezer bag with the chicken and allow it to sit for about 4 hours in the fridge.

No time to marinate? Why, you procrastinator, you. Better get out the **Fired-Up Santa Fe Spice** (page 5) and give the chicken a good dusting.

Barbecue the chicken until just about cooked. Not to worry, it will finish cooking in the stew. A little underdone is just fine.

Prick the sausages and toss them in boiling water for about 5 minutes, to get them to release their fat. They can afford to lose a few ounces.

Drain and plunge the sausages into cold water. Finish cooking them by tossing them on the Q, or by slicing up and frying—directions to follow.

Heat a couple of tablespoons each of olive oil and butter in a Dutch oven. Get the onion and celery in there before the butter burns.

Once the onion and celery start to just soften, toss in the peppers and garlic, a teaspoon or so of Fired-Up Santa Fe

Spice and about a teaspoon of pepper. Stir through. Remove from the pot.

In the remaining cooking liquid (if it's dry, don't worry, just add a little olive oil), brown the sausages (if you didn't Q them) and/or the ham.

Get your oven going at 375°F.

Bring the veggies back into the fray and get the rice in there, tossing it through the cooking liquid just long enough to coat.

The chicken broth, diced tomatoes, tomato paste, thyme and hot sauce want in, so add them to the pot. Bring the contents to a boil.

The chicken and sausages—if you chose to barbecue them—demand to be in on the meld as well, so cradle them in there with the rest.

Cover the pot and bake for about 35 to 45 minutes.

If you are using shrimp, lightly salt and pepper the little fellas and stir-fry or barbecue them until they just turn pink. Get them in the jambalaya for the final 5 minutes or so of cooking time, to meld with the stew.

The rice is the determining factor. If it's plump and soft to the bite, we're ready to rip. However, if it's being stubborn, and there's still some liquid in the pot, simply stir, cover and place it back in the oven. If the liquid is absorbed but the rice isn't happily softened yet, add about ⅓ cup or more chicken broth, cover and back in the oven you go! Add a little more broth at a time until the rice is happily cooked.

Once the jambalaya's rice is softened, take the pot out of the oven and let it sit for that dreaded 5-minute set-up time.

A final taste test is in order. Perhaps a little salt and another shot of Louisiana hot sauce to boost the flavour quotient? Top the jambalaya with green onions

Note: If you use a variety of rice other than basmati, it will likely need more moisture. Basmati's ratio is 1 part rice to 1.5 parts liquid, while most other kinds of rice are 1 part rice to 2 parts liquid. Adjust the amount of chicken broth accordingly.

HIS BARK IS WORSE THAN HIS BITE

Many years ago our fire department conducted in-home inspections, visiting homeowners during the day to check and see if their homes were safe from the hazards of fire. A firefighter who only days earlier had been bitten by a dog while performing this duty was casually walking down the sidewalk, while one of my comrades—and I use that term loosely—hid behind a hedge. As the once-bitten, twice-shy firefighter passed by, the prankster jumped up behind him and barked wildly. The understandably startled dupe clutched his chest with one hand, flinging his clipboard and pen into the air with the other.

FIRE-TRUCK-RED
RUSSIAN CHICKEN

I somehow doubt that this culinary treat originated behind the Iron Curtain, but given our "around the world" theme, I say close enough. One thing's for sure, this is a Winnipeg Fire Department recipe classic. I don't know who introduced this recipe to the ranks, but it's certainly made the rounds, and that means it's tried, true and obviously successful. The big attraction for would-be fire chefs is that it's easy and the ingredients are few, yet it tastes bang-on decadent. I've fired up the basic recipe a bit for my own version, but I've also given options on how to go with the super-simple original version.

THE "FORMERLY KNOWN AS USSR CHICKEN" FIXINGS

- 12 skinless, bone-in chicken thighs (or 4–6 chicken breasts)
- Fired-Up Santa Fe Spice (page 5)
- All-purpose flour
- 2 eggs beaten with 2 tablespoons water
- 1 row of Breton or saltine crackers, crushed up fine (no, don't sit on them!)
- 2 cups Russian salad dressing
- 2 cups apricot jam
- 1 envelope dry onion soup mix

GET THAT CHICKEN TO DON A RED TURNOUT COAT

Fire up your oven to 400°F.

If you haven't done so already, let's rip the skin and trim the fat and cellulite off of those thighs.

Season the chicken with Fired-Up Santa Fe Spice on both sides.

Dip the chicken in flour to lightly coat. Feel free to shake off any excess.

Over to the egg wash station we go. Dip the chicken through the wet stuff and move it along to the crushed-up crackers, to coat it.

Place the chicken in a large roaster or other such baking dish with high sides that will accommodate all that chicken comfortably. Pop the chickies in the oven for about 25 minutes, uncovered, or about 15 minutes if you're using boneless, skinless breasts. This is the browning phase.

Let's mix up that simple-yet-decadent sauce by combining the Russian dressing, apricot jam and onion soup mix in a bowl.

Get the hot chicks out of the oven and pour the sauce over top.

Back in the oven the chicken goes for another 15 to 20 minutes, or until cooked through.

RUSHIN' RUSSIAN CHICKEN

If you want to cut to the chase, you can choose to eliminate the coating. Simply mix up the sauce and pour it over the chicken. Bake the chicks uncovered at 400°F for about 45 minutes, depending on the cut.

The sauce is excellent over rice, so make up a bonus batch to go with it.

This Red Russian Chicken is delicious, and I'm not Putin you on!

HALF A ROASTED
CURRIED CHICKEN
WITH MANGO

The night I created this dish, I removed the chicken from the oven with a single oven-gloved hand, lost control and, rather than have the hot chicken and grease fall on me, stepped back and let it fall to the floor. The CorningWare dish smashed into pieces, denting the hardwood like a hailstorm. Luckily the 10-second rule was in effect, and I managed to save the chicken. During the course of eating, however, the hot chick fought back, springing hot curry sauce all over my favourite shirt, demoting it to painter grade. But don't be dismayed by my incompetence. This truly is a delicious, easy recipe that I, in my infinite wisdom, simply made difficult.

GO DIRECTLY TO THE EXPRESS LANE WITH . . .

- 3-pound chicken, cut in half—this serves 2
- 2 tablespoons garlic butter—you can make your own easily enough (page 164)
- Kosher salt
- A few shots curry powder
- 1 tablespoon peanut oil
- 2 tablespoons curry paste
- ½ jumbo onion, coarsely diced
- 1 red pepper, sliced into strips
- 14-ounce can coconut milk
- 1 large mango, diced into 1-inch squares
- Chopped cilantro

EASY . . . CONCENTRATE . . . HANG ON TIGHT!

Fire up your oven to 375°F.

Get out your favourite CorningWare dish and send it to me. I need one.

Pull out your second-favourite Corning-Ware dish or roaster, give it the cooking-spray treatment and nest the chicken halves in there.

Wiggle your finger under the breast and thigh skin, and deposit a heaping teaspoon of garlic butter between the meat and skin. Butter the skin, too.

Season each half chick with a little salt and curry powder, and bake uncovered for 40 minutes.

Meanwhile, heat the peanut oil in a frying pan or wok over medium-high heat. Get the curry paste in there and cook for 30 seconds.

Bring on the onion and fry for a couple of minutes, adding a touch of water or even lime juice to keep the pan from burning. Get the sweet pepper in there and work it through the curry for another minute or so.

Stir in the coconut milk.

If your sauce is a little thin for your liking, then slowly add a combo of 1 tablespoon each water and cornstarch to the boiling sauce until thickened.

Turn off the sauce and toss in the mango—no need to fry the fruit.

Carefully remove the chicken from the oven. *Safely* drain off the grease, top the chicken with the curry sauce and bake, uncovered, till cooked through, about 20 to 30 minutes more. Garnish with cilantro.

HOOKED ON CHILI

It's no wonder this chili is so addictive—beer, coffee and chocolate have joined forces to infuse this batch with all their best-loved qualities. I know it sounds like a strange combination, but believe me, it works. A bit of heat and a bit of sweet—this complex blend of chili ingredients rocks! Best of all, it's easy to make!

I'M SO HAPPY, WARM AND AWAKE

- 2 pounds ground beef
- 1 pound hot Italian sausages, removed from their casings
- 2 tablespoons canola oil
- 1 jumbo onion, diced
- 4 large celery stalks, diced
- 6 garlic cloves, minced or pressed
- 1 tablespoon Fired-Up Santa Fe Spice (page 5)
- 28-ounce can diced tomatoes, with juice
- 12 ounces beer
- 1 cup strong-brewed coffee
- 10-ounce can beef broth
- 13-ounce can tomato paste
- ¼+ cup brown sugar
- 3 tablespoons chili powder
- 1 square semi-sweet chocolate (about 1 ounce)
- ½ tablespoon dried oregano
- 3 teaspoons ground cumin
- 2 teaspoons kosher salt
- 1 teaspoon ground coriander
- 3 19-ounce cans kidney, romano or black beans, drained
- 2 red, yellow, orange or even green peppers—mix 'n' match
- You choose the number of chipotle peppers
- Freshly ground black pepper
- Sour cream or cheddar cheese and chopped cilantro, for serving

LOTS GOING INTO IT, BUT NOT MUCH TO MAKING IT

Fire up a large Dutch oven or stockpot to medium heat and toss in the ground beef and Italian sausage. Fry it up until browned, drain the grease off and set the meat aside with explicit instructions not to go anywhere.

Now that the meat has temporarily vacated, pour the canola oil into the pot and toss in the onion, celery and garlic with the Fired-Up Santa Fe Spice.

Allow the veggies to fry merrily along until they become tender-crisp.

Bring the meat back into the fray and add the rest of the players on the list, up to but not including the beans and peppers. Simmer the lot for an hour, stirring occasionally to make sure your hard work doesn't stick to the bottom.

Get the beans and peppers, including the chipotles, in there and simmer our brew for at least another ½ hour or until nice and thick. Believe me, runny chili just isn't an option at the fire house.

I should mention that the chipotle pepper is our thermostat. If you like it fiery, put in as many alarms as you can handle. I prefer about 1½ tablespoons worth. The adobo sauce the chipotles swim in also packs heat, so use it sparingly. This combo will lend a hint of smokiness—more like barbecue smoky than the familiar house-fire smoky, however.

If you find that you went a little wild with the chipotles, don't start throwing utensils; simply add more brown sugar as an antidote.

Hooked on Chili is best served the following day. This allows the flavours to meld and build. Wait until you reheat it the next day to do your final seasoning adjustments—salt, brown sugar, pepper, that sort of thing.

Serve with a big dollop of sour cream or a mound of cheddar cheese topped with chopped cilantro. Now we're talking maximum flavour plus maximum presentation.

Oh, one more thing. For a tangy twist, try adding the zest and juice of a large lime to every 2 cups of sour cream.

THE MISSING TOOTH

It was bound to happen. After 47 years, I had finally bid farewell to the last of my baby teeth. With the secondary tooth impacted, I was given a false tooth mounted to a retainer to fill the gap. Three weeks later, while working night shift at the fire hall, I lost it. I was sure I'd wrapped it up in a paper towel and put it in my pants pocket. But somehow, somewhere, it disappeared.

I'd certainly seen this movie before, as I had gone through a similar experience with my son when he was only nine. Connor had wrapped up his retainer in a napkin at a shopping mall food court, eaten his lunch and then dumped his retainer in the garbage, along with the waste, never to be seen again—though it is rumoured that a seagull at city dump is sporting a set of perfect chompers, thanks to the Conman.

Believing it to be a like-son-like-father reverse-genetic predisposition affair, I gave the fire hall the CSI treatment, going through the garbage bins with latex gloves in a mad search for the only thing separating me from hillbilly status. Sadly, I left the hall sans tooth, but asked the relieving shift to keep an eye out for it when they cleaned the hall at morning chores.

When I returned for the night shift, the boys of 1 platoon greeted me with the good news. "Hey, Jeff," Keith said, smiling. "We found something of yours. It was on one of the beds in the dorm. It's over there on the microwave."

"That's great!" With a huge sigh of relief I walked across the kitchen and lifted the paper towel on the microwave in anticipation, only to find . . . a Chicklet mounted on a toothpick.

HOT-LIKE-HUNAN
CHICKEN

If you like your stir-fry with lots of zing, then here's a fiery one to try. I'll start you off with a mild-to-moderate version, and then I'll leave it up to you to add more or less chili-garlic sauce, depending on the shade of red you're looking to change your face to. Don't be shy—come on, fire it up, Furnace Face!

CHILI AND GARLIC, THAT'S THE HUNAN PROVINCE WAY!

- ¾ cup chicken broth
- ½ cup brandy (or dry sherry)
- 3 tablespoons soy sauce
- 3 tablespoons brown sugar
- 2+ tablespoons chili-garlic sauce
- 1 tablespoon toasted sesame oil
- 1 heaping tablespoon each ketchup and plum sauce
- 6–8 cups raw vegetables—I like a mix of peppers, broccoli, snap peas and carrots
- Peanut oil
- 2 tablespoons each minced garlic and fresh ginger
- 2 pounds chicken breast or thigh, cut into 1-inch squares
- 1 tablespoon black bean and garlic sauce—we sure love that garlic
- 4–6 green onions, diced
- 1½ tablespoons cornstarch mixed with 2 tablespoons chicken broth
- Honey-roasted peanuts, coarsely chopped

UP THE YANGTZE RIVER WITHOUT A CHOPSTICK

Combine the sauce ingredients, being the broth, brandy, soy sauce, sugar, chili-garlic sauce, sesame oil, ketchup and plum sauce, and set aside.

Cut up your veggies—peppers in bite-sized squares, broccoli in bite-able trees and carrots thinly sliced on a 45° angle. Let's go, chop, chop!

Heat your wok until it's starting to smoke and add a couple of tablespoons of peanut oil. Introduce about half of the garlic/ginger combo plus half the chicken, and stir-fry till cooked through. Repeat with the remaining chicken (but don't add any more of the garlic/ginger), setting the cooked chicken aside on a platter.

Pour another tablespoon or so of the oil into the hot wok and follow up with the rest of the garlic/ginger, plus the black bean and garlic sauce.

Veggies—minus the green onions—are up. Stir-fry them for, let's say, 2 minutes.

Let's get the cooking sauce in there, and throw in the chicken. Cook, tossing constantly, for oh, about 4 minutes, or until the veggies are tender-crisp.

Bring on the green onions and slowly add the cornstarch/chicken broth combo a bit at a time until the sauce reaches the desired consistency. It should cling nicely to the chicken and veggies. Peanuts, if you're here, get in too!

This dish should be enough to feed approximately 4 ravenous firefighters or 6 humans. Or is that Hunans?

JAMAICAN JERK CHICKEN

Just the thought of this spicy treat is enough to give me the munchies. Traditionally, Scotch bonnet peppers are used in this dish—or at least habanero strength—but you pretty much have to wear a level A hazmat suit to chop up those little devils. I find that chipotle peppers are quick and easy out of the can, plus they have a nice smoky flavour that goes great with a barbecue.

GANGA TELL?

- ½ cup fresh lime juice
- ½ cup malt vinegar
- ½ cup packed chopped cilantro
- 1 bunch green onions
- 6 garlic cloves
- 3 or more chipotle peppers, plus some of the adobo sauce they're packed in, to fire it up
- 3 tablespoons dark Jamaican rum
- 2 tablespoons clear Canadian water
- 2 tablespoons canola oil
- 2 tablespoons dried thyme
- 1 tablespoon each ground allspice, ground cinnamon, ground ginger, and one more from the ground, ground nutmeg
- 1 tablespoon kosher salt—since when did Island food have to be kosher?
- 1 tablespoon brown sugar
- 2 teaspoons fresh ground pepper
- 6–8 boneless, skinless chicken breasts or pork chops

MAKE IT HAPPEN, CHEF-MON!

Hang on, hang on, mon! We need to give the chick time to marinate! So, let's get the secret juice together. Toss all of the ingredients—minus the chicken, of course—in a blender. Pulse away until all is incorporated. Not to worry, it doesn't have to be smooth; a rustic rough chop will do.

Get the chicken breasts into a large zip-top freezer bag and pour the marinade over top. Squeeze all of the air out of the bag and get it into the fridge for at least 4 hours, even overnight. The longer it rests, the spicier things will get, and of course jerk is supposed to be spicy!

Grill the chicken on the Q over medium heat until cooked through.

For a topping, make up a batch of **Tropical Salsa** (page 121).

Making **Jerk Sandwiches** with the leftovers? What leftovers, you ask. Well, if there are any, slice 'em and get 'em on a bun topped with sliced mango, lettuce, sautéed red onion and **Jamaican Jerk Mayo** (that's a combination of ½ cup mayo, 2 tablespoons orange juice concentrate and 1 tablespoon finely chopped chipotle peppers). How's that for a hot lunch?

KUNG PAO AND HOW
CHICKEN

Kung Pao literally translates into "flamethrower"—or at least it will when it hits the back of your throat. But since you control the heat with the amount of chili-garlic sauce you add, it's up to you to determine how many alarms to put in for this dish. If you go too far, a little extra sugar will help tame the red devil.

DID CHAIRMAN MAO KUNG PAO?

- ½ cup chicken broth
- 3 tablespoons each hoisin sauce and sweet soy sauce (a.k.a. *kecap manis*)
- 2½ tablespoons chili-garlic sauce—or ++ to taste
- 2 tablespoons brown sugar
- 2 tablespoons seasoned rice vinegar—for a little Mao Tse-tang
- 2 teaspoons black bean and garlic sauce
- ¼ cup peanut oil, for stir-frying
- 2 tablespoons chopped fresh ginger—try chopping in a mini-processor
- 6 garlic cloves, minced or pressed
- 4 boneless, skinless chicken breasts (or 8 thighs), cut into 1-inch squares
- 1 medium onion, cut into strips
- 1 red pepper, cut into strips
- 12-ounce bag broccoli slaw (or 4 cups napa cabbage or bok choy, cut into strips, plus 1 or 2 carrots, grated)
- Say ½ pound spaghettini or rice noodles, cooked and drained
- 2 navel oranges, in segments, each segment cut in half
- 2 tablespoons orange juice combined with 1 tablespoon cornstarch
- Chopped cilantro
- ¼ cup crushed honey-roasted peanuts (regular peanuts will do, too)

WHAT ABOUT GENERAL TSO, DID HE KUNG PAO?

Let's get the broth, hoisin, sweet soy, chili-garlic, sugar, vinegar and black bean and garlic sauce combined.

Ensure that you have the remaining ingredients level 1 staged before you begin fire ground operations.

Get that wok smokin' over high heat, roll in a couple tablespoons of peanut oil and add half of the ginger and garlic, followed right away by the chunked-up chicken. Stir-fry till cooked through, and set the chicks aside.

Déjà vu the peanut oil/ginger/garlic routine. Send in the onion and fry briefly, then follow with the red pepper, broccoli slaw (or alternatives) and carrots. This will only take a minute.

That fiery mixed-up sauce is ready to hit the hot zone, and so is the chicken you fried up earlier. Oh yeah, and make sure the noodles are ready to go, too.

Keep stirring, and once the sauce comes to a light boil, add the oranges.

Pour in the orange juice and cornstarch mixture a bit at a time, stirring as you go, until the sauce is nicely thickened. Serve immediately.

Top your flaming creation with the chopped cilantro and peanuts.

LAND-OF-THE-PANDA
PORK ROAST

Firefighter Bob Bean suggested I give this one a try after he made it for his crew, to resounding accolades. The marinade is similar to the one you'd find for Chinese barbecued pork, minus the food dye. Somehow red dye No. 40 makes my mouth water about as much as Polysorbate 80, so I made the executive "environmentally friendly" decision to go chemical-free.

HOISIN, CAN YOU SEE

- ¾ cup hoisin sauce
- ¾ cup soy sauce
- ¾ cup rice wine vinegar
- 1½ tablespoons toasted sesame oil
- 3 tablespoons minced ginger (ginger paste is acceptable)
- 10 garlic cloves, minced or pressed
- 1 tablespoon chili-garlic paste
- 4- to 5-pound pork roast

BY THE OVEN'S LITTLE LIGHT

Combine all of the ingredients, minus the pork roast, in a bowl. Give the funky bunch a good stir—with chopsticks if you insist on being a traditionalist. Personally, I'm all thumbs when it comes to chopsticks.

Get out the mandatory large zip-top freezer bag, carefully toss the pork roast in there and add the marinade. Be sure to squeeze out all the air from the bag before sealing it up tight.

Off to the fridge this little piggy goes for 24 hours. The longer, the better, I say. Rotate when possible for even marination. What's that, spell-check? Marination isn't a word?

Fire up your oven to 375°F. Set the roast on a rack in a roasting pan and bake, uncovered, for about 20 minutes. Then cover loosely with foil and turn the oven down to 350 for 1½ to 2 hours (make that 150° on the meat thermometer, though some prefer 160°), occasionally basting the piglet with the marinade as it roasts.

Hang onto the remaining marinade and boil it for a few minutes in a saucepan to create a delicious serving sauce. The sauce can be thickened into gravy, if you wish, by slowly adding a tablespoon of cornstarch mixed with a tablespoon of water a bit at a time until the sauce is just the way you like it.

By the way, this marinade also works great on pork tenderloin. You could even finish it up on the grill for a Land-of-the-Panda barbecue.

Serve with **Jawsman Rice** (page 191) and **A Side of Stir-Fried Veggies** (page 184).

MY PAD THAI

Let's say company is coming over, time is tight and you don't know what to serve. Well, get off your wallet, you tightwad, and order in some exotic sushi. Or . . . you could make this thrifty, traditional, delicious Thai dish in a matter of minutes and blow them away with both presentation and flavour.

MAKING THAT LIST AND CHECKING IT TWICE

- 3 tablespoons fish sauce—whatever you do, do not smell the fish sauce, as this will only sour your taste buds (relax, the results will be incredible)
- 3 tablespoons white sugar
- 3 tablespoons ketchup
- 1½ tablespoons Worcestershire sauce (great, anchovies—more fish!)
- 3 teaspoons chili-garlic sauce—or more if you need additional fire
- ½ pound thick rice noodles (over there in the Asian food section)
- 2 tablespoons peanut oil
- 6 garlic cloves, minced or pressed
- 8 boneless, skinless chicken thighs, cut into bite-sized pieces
- 1 pound peeled uncooked shrimp, cut into bite-sized pieces
- 1 red, yellow or orange pepper, cut into thin strips
- 3 eggs—beat 'em like they owe you money
- 2 cups bean sprouts, washed and ready to roll
- 1 bunch green onions, green parts only, sliced
- About 1 cup coarsely chopped cilantro
- ¼ cup coarsely chopped dry-roasted peanuts
- 2 limes, cut into wedges

SURE IT SOUNDS INVOLVED, BUT IT'S QUICK AND EASY, HONEST!

Let's get all the chopping done, and arrange all our ingredients into a series of highly organized bowls—you know, like they do on TV.

Oh, and let's put the sauce together in a bowl as well. Combine the fish sauce, sugar, ketchup, Worcestershire sauce and chili-garlic sauce.

Hey! I thought I told you not to smell the fish sauce! If you think for one second that I'm not looking over your shoulder, well, buster, you are so wrong! All right then, go ahead. Put a dab of fish sauce behind your ears. You'll have lots of elbow room at the dinner table. Rest assured, the smell will burn off, leaving only a wonderful, subtle flavour behind. Well, unless you actually *did* cologne yourself with it.

Get some boiling water happening. Toss the rice noodles in a lasagna dish or other flat roaster or casserole and cover with the hot water. When the noodles are al dente, which is Thai for "busts up your expensive dental work," drain them in a colander and set aside.

What do you say we fire up the wok to high, and when it starts to smoke, toss in a couple of tablespoons of peanut oil?

Get the garlic in there briefly, followed by the chicken and shrimp.

By the way, you can make this recipe with tofu instead of chicken, but why? I mean what is tofu made from, pencil erasers?

Anyway, stir-fry the chick 'n' shrimp until the shrimp are nicely pink and the chicken is pretty much cooked through. Let's add the peppers now.

Bring the sauce into the mix, and stir it through for about 2 minutes. Yes, Holmes, that's why it's called a stir-fry.

Turn down the heat to medium and toss in the eggs for about 1 minute.

Get the noodles in there and toss them until they are well coated.

Bring on the bean sprouts, green onions and half the cilantro. Keep stirring, you're almost there!

When your creation is heated through, top with the rest of the cilantro and the peanuts, and plate it tout de suite.

Garnish each plate with lime wedges and command the diners to squeeze the lime juice over their pad thai and toss it through.

This recipe serves 4 "if I don't get to eat soon someone is going to die" firefighters as a main dish. Better make the **Thai Coleslaw** (page 62) just to be sure they're satisfied. Otherwise they'll make you pay for their take-out pizza.

FIRE SALES

A captain at our hall was retiring. On his final day, a beautiful hot summer day, his crew placed peanut butter under the door handles of his car, wet his driver's seat, turned all of the accessories on his car on full blast, including the heat and the radio—a nice greeting once he keyed the ignition—and tied about a mile of fire scene tape to the rear bumper.

As a bonus, one of the guys considerately placed an ad in the local newspaper advertising the captain's car, leather couch and a list of other valuable assets, all at give-away prices. Known for his quick temper, the captain received a pile of calls and was forced to press the rewind and play buttons on his brain several times to tell the callers that he was sorry but he was the victim of a prank.

Another kind soul advertised a garage sale at a firefighter's house the night after his booze-infested retirement stag. "Sale starts at 8, lots of free stuff."

It's our way of showing just how much we care.

MOJO ADOBO CHICKEN

This dish may share the name adobo chicken with its Filipino friend, but that's where the similarities end, as we are going south, not east, for this gem. It's Cuba meets the Southwest in a funky, spicy chicken sauce. You can marinate chicken or pork in the sauce, or thicken it up a bit and brush it on chicken pieces to finish in the oven as this recipe suggests, or even serve it as a side sauce. Don't be shy, go for gold and try all three.

THE MOJO ADOBO STUFFO

- ¼ cup soft butter or margarine
- 12 garlic cloves—that's pretty much a head
- 4–6 chicken legs with thighs detached (8–12 pieces total)
- Fired-Up Santa Fe Spice (page 5)
- Spice combo of 1 teaspoon each ground cumin, coriander, paprika and kosher salt (Fidel Castro insists on his food being kosher, doesn't he?)
- 1 tablespoon grated orange zest—that's the rind of about 1 medium orange
- 3 tablespoons extra-virgin olive oil
- 1 cup lime juice
- ½ cup orange juice
- 2 tablespoons brown sugar
- 2 canned chipotle peppers packed in adobo sauce, chopped
- 1 tablespoon cornstarch combined with 1 tablespoon water

THIS'LL GET YOUR MOJO WORKING

Fire up your oven to 400°F.

Make up a little garlic butter by combining the butter or margarine with 2 mashed cloves of garlic. Work the butter under the skin of the thighs and legs.

Dust the top of the chicken pieces with the Fired-Up Santa Fe Spice.

Place the chicken pieces in a size-large roasting pan and bake them for about ½ hour, uncovered.

Mix the remaining garlic, the spice-rack combo and orange zest (in a bowl if you're using this as a marinade or in a saucepan if you're using as a sauce).

Add the olive oil and combine until you get little flavour clumps forming.

Bring on the lime and orange juices, brown sugar and chopped chipotles.

For the sauce, bring the mixture to a light boil. Thicken with the cornstarch and water as it bubbles.

If you feel that your sauce needs more fire, simply toss in some of that rockin' adobo sauce the chipotles are packed in.

Get the Mexi Chicks out of the oven and baste them with the Mojo Adobo Sauce. Back to the oven they go for 15 minutes more.

Remove them from the oven and repeat the basting procedure as outlined in your fire department's GOGs (General Operating Guidelines).

Cook for another 15 minutes or until juices run clear when you threaten them by wielding an axe in their general direction.

TOMATO SAUCE

I can't believe how many recipe books feature the most basic of tomato sauce recipes for pasta—crushed tomatoes, tomato sauce, tomato paste and maybe two or three spices. You can do better. Here's one that came together one night while I was cleaning out the fridge. I'm of the opinion that the more ingredients that go in, the more complex and interesting the resulting flavour will be. Be creative, throw in what you have on hand and let 'er rip!

PURGE THE FRIDGE, CLEAN OUT THE CUPBOARDS

- Extra-virgin olive oil
- 1 jumbo onion, diced
- 4 celery stalks, diced
- 4 garlic cloves, minced or pressed
- 1 pound each ground beef and Italian sausage, removed from casings
- 1 large red, yellow or orange pepper, diced
- 1 zucchini, sliced in half lengthwise, then sliced thin
- 2½ cups mushrooms, cut into Ts
- 2 teaspoons each kosher salt and freshly ground black pepper
- 2 teaspoons Italian seasoning
- 1 cup red wine
- 1 cup chicken broth
- 4 cups bottled spaghetti sauce—wait a second here, Jeff's a cheater!
- ¼ cup Everybody Goes Pesto (optional, page 144)
- 3 tablespoons tomato paste
- 2 tablespoons brown sugar—sweet to balance the acidity and heat
- 1 tablespoon soy sauce
- Dried chili flakes, added to taste

LET'S BRING IT ALL TOGETHER

Get out the Dutch oven and heat the olive oil over medium heat.

Place the onions in the Mediterranean bathwater and follow up with the celery and garlic. Gotta love that garlic—it's coming out of my pores!

Meanwhile, in a separate frying pan brown the beef and sausage meat. Drain and set aside.

Once the veggies have softened a bit, follow up with the pepper, zucchini and mushrooms. Season the veggies with salt, Italian seasoning and lots of pepper. Let's bring life to the produce!

Pour in the wine and let it reduce on a low boil for about 5 minutes.

It looks like the guys on deck want in on this little party, so bring on the chicken broth, spaghetti sauce, pesto, tomato paste, brown sugar, browned beef and sausages and the soy sauce. Oh look, everyone is happy, happy!

Turn the heat down to simmer and let the sauce cook and thicken. I'm thinking about an hour or so, even longer if you have the time and patience. Give your brew a stir every once in a while.

Do a final taste test. If you're like me, you're going to want to add a couple of teaspoons of the red chili flakes, to fire it up.

PUMPED-UP PAELLA

We're off to Spain to sample their national treasure. Paella is cooked in large paella pans over open wood fires in its home country. Unless you insist on tradition or are planning on cooking this at a house fire, follow me for a range-top/oven-baked version. This dish tastes as great as it looks, but does have some pricey ingredients— namely the saffron and seafood. But if you shop right, or if it's celebration time and you don't care what the bill is (it'll be far cheaper than eating out), then this is an amazing dish to serve.

PUMP UP THE MUTANT FRYING PAN

- 8 boneless, skinless chicken thighs
- Lemon-Garlic Marinade (page 6)
- 2 tablespoons each extra-virgin olive oil and butter
- 1 cup yellow or white onions, diced
- 1 cup orange or red pepper, sliced into thin strips
- 6 garlic cloves, minced or pressed
- 2½ cups superfino arborio rice—I know, it's Italian, but it works!
- ½ teaspoon slightly crushed saffron (try a bulk store for best value)
- 1½ teaspoons sweet Spanish paprika
- 5-ounce can baby clams—don't forget to reserve the juice
- ½ cup white wine
- 4 cups chicken broth
- 1 cup ham (you can sub in fried sausage slices or cooked pork)
- 8 marinated artichoke heart pieces, drained (or 24 grape tomatoes)
- ⅓ cup chopped parsley
- 1 pound large shrimp, peeled, tails on
- 12–15 live mussels (or try frozen from New Zealand for best value)
- Lemon wedges, for garnish

PUMP UP THE FLAVOUR, PUMP UP YOUR PALATE!

Traditionally, the chicken in paella is left bone in and fried to start the dish. However, I don't like the fat residue in the mix, so I marinate boneless, skinless thighs in Lemon-Garlic Marinade for a couple of hours in a zip-top freezer bag in the fridge and either barbecue them or broil them. Go ahead, that means you, too.

You're going to need an extra-large sauté or paella pan, as the ingredients need lots of room. The one I use for this recipe is 12 inches in diameter by 2¼ inches deep. Sorry, the math side of my brain is in a coma, so I can't begin to calculate a volume measurement for you, but think big.

Get the oil and butter into the paella pan and bring up to speed over medium-high heat. Toss in the onions, peppers and garlic and fry them until the veggies are happily tender-crisp.

Get the rice and saffron in there and stir through to get the rice coated with oil and butter and to bring out the saffron's flavour and colour.

Give the paprika a sprinkle over the rice and work it through, too. The above operation should take, let's say, 3 to 4 minutes.

Meanwhile, drain the clams and set the juice aside for a short bit.

Pour the wine into the pan and cook until the rice has absorbed it.

Bring the clam juice and chicken broth to the party and bring it all to a boil.

Turn the pan down and simmer for a few minutes, giving the rice a stir occasionally, and get ready to load up the paella with its buddies.

Fire up the oven to 350°F.

As evenly as possible, add the clam meat, chicken, ham, artichokes or tomatoes and parsley. Come on, work the players into the paella, sink those buried treasures. Uh-oh, was there a flood in the forecast, because the paella is ready to overflow its banks.

Top the paella with the shrimp and, finally, the mussels. If you've chosen to use the frozen mussels, since the lid is already off them, try brushing them with a little garlic butter to keep them moist. You can also cook the shrimp and mussels separately, to ensure that you don't overcook them, then place them over the paella before serving.

Off to the oven for 20 to 25 minutes or until the mussels have opened, if using live, or until they're cooked, if using frozen, and the rice has absorbed the liquid.

Let the paella stand for about 5 minutes before bringing it to the table. That's how they serve it in Spain, placed in the centre of the table so the diners can serve themselves. The dish looks so good that it truly deserves to be the table's centrepiece.

Serve with fresh lemon wedges to squeeze over each paella serving.

ANOTHER SATISFIED CUSTOMER

Each year our department's fire halls welcome the donation of used books to be sold at the Children's Hospital Book Sale. Imagine the delight in the eyes of the firefighters at 15 station when a local resident dropped off a box of used books and among the rejected, tired titles they spotted a copy of my book, *Fire Hall Cooking with Jeff the Chef*. Talk about ammunition—this was a great discovery, as firefighters love finding fodder to bug each other about.

Sadly, the book was but a year old and had already been given the icy-cold shoulder. That poor little book's feelings, put up for adoption at such a young age. I felt terrible for him. We can only hope that his fundraising journey led to a caring, food-loving home.

CHICKEN GLAZED

I was about to make my standard Lemon-Herb Roasted Chicken one day when I spotted a huge bowl of leftover basmati rice in the fridge and thought, "It's time to try something different." Enter the sweet-soy-sauce-enhanced chicken!

IT'S GOING TO BE SOME KIND OF FUNKY CHICKEN

- 3 tablespoons minced fresh ginger
- 2 teaspoons chili-garlic sauce
- 2 tablespoons soft butter or margarine
- 2 3-pound fryer chickens, rinsed and patted dry
- 10 garlic cloves
- 1 medium onion, halved
- 1 medium orange, halved
- 1 cup soy sauce
- 3 tablespoons toasted sesame oil
- Freshly ground black pepper
- 10-ounce can chicken broth
- Sweet soy sauce (a.k.a. *kecap manis*)
- 1 tablespoon cornstarch mixed with 2 tablespoons water

YOU WON'T BE SERVING THIS CHICK WITH POTATOES AND CORN

Add 1 tablespoon of the minced ginger and all of the chili-garlic sauce to the butter to make Asian garlic butter. Work your finger under the breast skin of each bird and tuck a heaping teaspoon of the Asian garlic butter in there.

Toss the remaining ginger, the garlic cloves, onion and orange halves into the cavity of each bird and truss the bird together with butcher's string to keep the stuffing from falling out.

Fire up the oven to 400°F. Get our birds onto a rack, breast sides up, in a large roaster. Combine the soy sauce and sesame oil and pour them over the chicks. Grind a little pepper over the birds while you're at it, but don't worry about adding any salt; the soy sauce will take care of that flavour boost. Pour the chicken broth into the bottom of the roaster and get our bird rocking for ½ hour, uncovered.

Time to flip the bird. With hands clad in ugly old oven mitts or mitts covered with paper towels, grab the birds and flip them so they are breast sides down. This is the full self-basting-with-the-fat-from-the-dark-meat position.

If desired, stick a meat probe into the meatiest part of the thigh.

Turn the roaster down to 375°F and let 'er rip uncovered for, say, an hour, depending on the size of the chickens. Give the birds a basting once or twice during the golden hour.

Get those paper-towel-covered mitts back on and flip the birds back to breast sides up. Bring out the sweet soy sauce and paint it all over the birds. The extra sugar in the sweet soy thickens the sauce for cling-a-bility and gives our birds a nice mahogany colour.

Roast, uncovered, for at least 10 more minutes, or until the birds are cooked. If the legs wiggle easily, the meat probe in the thigh says 170°F and the juices run clear, then you're ready to move the birds over to the carving board to rest for 10 minutes.

Don't take your foot off the gas, there's still stuff to do here! Pour all of the roast drippings through a strainer into a glass measuring cup or other see-through container. The fat should separate from the sauce, rising to the top, as it were. Simply drain it off with a turkey baster, salvage master, scoop shovel or other such firefighting/cooking tool. I care about you, so it's important that you degrease the sauce as much as possible.

Pour the remaining sauce into a saucepan and bring to a boil over high heat. Add the cornstarch mixture a bit at a time, stirring as you go, until you get the consistency you're after. By the way, you can add more sweet soy sauce to the sauce mix if desired—I do. I love the stuff so much I'm getting an intravenous line going.

Serve with **Jawsman Rice** (page 191)—that's where the leftover basmati rice comes in.

LET'S JUST HOPE OUR DINNER DOESN'T RUN AWAY!

One of my favourite coworkers, retired captain Dave Barr, loved to use the term "exotic" to describe his meals. One day Dave said to the boys, 'Well, I've got another exotic meal planned for you guys today."

"What are we having?"

"Exotic chicken."

"What's so exotic about it?"

"It has six legs," Dave replied with a knowing smirk.

"What?"

Sure enough, Dave opened the oven and the chicken indeed had six legs. No, it wasn't a refugee from the nuclear power plant; Dave actually got his wife to sew four extra legs on the bird so each member of the crew would get a drumstick. Hmmmmm, if only we could genetically breed a turkey with a centipede—then there'd be drumsticks for everyone!

PORK TENDERLOIN

This recipe is in high rotation on the home front. It's almost a recipe we default to, as it lends itself to meat and veggie substitutions, meaning that I avoid having to make a special run to the store. It's quick, easy, delicious and nutritious.

USE THIS LIST, OR SEE WHAT'S IN THE CRISPER

- A couple tablespoons peanut oil
- 4 garlic cloves, crushed up by the garlic press
- Say 3 tablespoons chopped fresh ginger
- 1½-pound pork tenderloin, cut into medallions and cut in half again (boneless, skinless chicken thighs or breasts also work well)
- Kosher salt and freshly ground black pepper
- 1 medium onion, coarsely diced—I'm talking 1-inch squares
- 2 celery stalks, given the old Chinese-restaurant 45° mitre cut
- 2 carrots, ditto the above
- 1 bunch broccoli, let's say about 4 cups worth, cut into bite-sizers
- 1 red pepper, sliced into strips
- 1 large apple, diced—Mac, Spartan or Gala
- ½ tablespoon (or dare you add more?) chili-garlic sauce
- About 1½-2 cups plum sauce

CHOP, CHOP, CHOP, FIRE UP THE WOK!

Get the wok smokin' and toss in a big T of peanut oil. Bring on half the garlic and ginger—stir, stir—and before the little devils brown, intro the pork. Season the piggy with kosher—yes, *kosher*—salt and pepper. Stir-fry the pork until no longer pink, and get it out of the pan.

Let's add another tablespoon or so of the peanut oil to the wok and get the rest of the garlic and ginger dancing. Introduce the onion, celery and carrots. Stir-fry for a minute or so, then bring the broccoli into the mix.

Does the wok appear to be dry and burning? Then add a dash of apple juice or water to the wok and work it through. Bring on the liquid as needed, but only enough to keep the wok from burning and the air around your mouth from turning blue. Combat blandness: season veggies with salt and pepper and they'll gain flavour as they fry.

When the veggies reach the tender-crisp stage, introduce the red pepper strips and apple to the others briefly. Toss in the chili-garlic sauce.

Hey, pork tenderloin, get back here! Into the mix you go!

The plum sauce is ready to rock, so in it goes. Use your judgment. I use 1½-2 cups , but you may like more or less sauce. Toss and heat through.

If your bubbling sauce thins out on you, then slowly add a mix of 1 tablespoon each cornstarch and water. When it's thick, then quit!

What a blend of colours! Good show! Serve it over a steamin' bed of rice.

SEÑOR CALZONE

That Mex-alian chef, Señor Calzone, is at it again with an Italian dish infused with Tex-Mex. Think of it as a pizza with a bonus crust on top, like you'd find on a dessert pie. This Calzone fella is bursting with flavour, and as if there was ever any doubt, we're making it firefighter-sized!

BUONGIORNO, SEÑOR
- Beer 'n' Pizza Dough (page 136)
- 1 pound ground beef
- 1 package taco seasoning mix
- Butter for frying and (later) brushing
- 1 medium-sized red onion, in strips
- About ½ pound mushrooms, cut into Ts—not tease, please!
- 1 red, yellow or orange pepper, diced fine
- Fired-Up Santa Fe Spice (page 5)
- Spaghetti sauce—you'll know when you have enough, say about 3 cups
- ½ pound pizza pepperoni
- 1 pound shredded nacho cheese

NO SIESTAS FOR THE WICKED— EH, WHAT A YOU LOOKIN' AT?

Mix up a batch of pizza dough and have it ready to roll.

Brown the ground beef in a frying pan on medium heat. Drain the fat and add the taco seasoning and water as per instructions on the package.

Get a couple of tablespoons of butter heated up in another frying pan over medium heat. Toss in the onion and fry until softened, even caramelized.

Follow up with the mushrooms and red pepper, dust with a hit of Santa Fe Spice and cook until the mushrooms are browned. Drain off any liquid.

Introduce the seasoned meat to the veggies, and add the spaghetti sauce. You'll want your sauce to be tight, basically just enough to bring all of the ingredients together in blissful harmony.

Now let's roll out the dough, just as you would for a pizza. The size is up to you, but I like to go for 4 calzones that are 10 to 12 inches in diameter.

Fire up that oven to 400°F.

Place the dough on a cookie sheet or pizza pan. Lay down the pepperoni over one half of each shell and top with the sauce mixture, making sure you leave about a 1-inch border at the edge. Moisten that border slightly with water for stick-ability.

Spread the cheese over the sauce and bring the other half of the dough over top to cover. Get out a fork and press down on the outside edge to seal the seam. Poke vent holes in the top of the crust to let out the steam.

Brush Señor Calzone's top side lightly with melted butter.

Get those pizza pie pockets into the oven for about 25 to 30 minutes, or until nicely browned, top and bottom.

Let Señor Calzone rest for 10 minutes before serving.

For a calzone dip, simply combine equal parts salsa and ranch dressing.

SWEET-AND-SOUR
POWER RIBS

My good friend firefighter Gale Osterman called me looking for a sweet and sour rib recipe. Well, I had to admit, it was like a hacker exposing vulnerabilities in a software program—I didn't have one to share. But not to worry, Gale and I put our heads together and came up with a patch, our version of this classic dish.

THE SWEET STAYS SWEET

- 5 pounds spareribs—cut for sweet and sour
- Fired-Up Spice (page 4)
- Freshly ground black pepper
- Chicken broth (chicken soup base mixed with water is okay too)
- 2 cups brown sugar
- 1½ cups distilled white vinegar (or rice vinegar for you purists)
- ¾ cup ketchup
- 14-ounce can pineapple tidbits—hang onto the juice, my friend!
- 3 tablespoons ginger paste (or finely chopped fresh ginger)
- 4 large garlic cloves, run through the press
- 1 tablespoon toasted sesame oil
- 1½ cups water
- 6 tablespoons cornstarch

AND THE SOUR STAYS SOUR

Fire up that oven to 275°F.

Season both sides of the ribs with a few hot shots of Fired-Up Spice and grind, grind, grind that pepper on them.

Place the ribs meaty sides up in a roaster large enough so the ribs can lie down side by each. Pour in enough chicken broth (or water mixed with soup base) to make it about halfway up the sides of the ribs, just enough to braise.

Bake the ribs, covered, about 2 to 2½ hours, depending on the rack size and current global warming conditions. You'll know they're done when the ribs are tender, the meat pulls back on the bones a wee bit and Greenland becomes a winter getaway hot spot.

Pour off the fat, as it's totally useless now, unless you need to plug a drain.

While those ribs are baking, let's make up the Sweet-and-Sour Power Sauce. Combine the brown sugar, vinegar, ketchup, pineapple juice, ginger paste, garlic and sesame oil in a medium saucepan.

Turn up the heat and bring it to a light boil. Whisk the water and cornstarch together and pour it into the sauce slowly. Let the sauce bubble, stirring nonstop until it's quite thick, say like a barbecue sauce.

Carefully cut the ribs into individual pieces, toss them back in the roaster and pour the Sweet-and-Sour Power Sauce and pineapples over top.

Bake the wee scallywags, covered, for about 45 minutes longer.

You're going to definitely want to serve these on a bed of rice with **A Side of Stir-Fried Veggies** or **Asian Orange Asparagus** (pages 184 and 183).

SWEET
CHILI CHICKEN
AND PASTA

The hit of the sprawling wedding buffet—the dish that had everyone talking—was the tortellini with Thai Sauce. Gail Johnston, the blushing bride, demanded, "Jeff, find out what's in that sauce!" I asked a server and he gave me a vague explanation, which forced me to retreat to the kitchen to figure it out for myself. Through the process of trial and error, elimination, deregulation and photosynthesis, I managed to come up with my version. As a bonus, I've included a great chicken recipe to go with it.

THAI ONE ON

- Chili-garlic butter—1 part chili-garlic sauce to 4 parts butter
- 12 bone-in chicken thighs, pants off, skin on
- Sweet chili sauce—this is different than chili-garlic sauce (see page 4)
- 1 large onion, diced into 1-inch squares
- 3 large carrots and 3 celery stalks, sliced on the bias
- 1 zucchini, sliced into thin medallions
- 1 large red pepper, sliced into strips
- ½ cup dry white wine
- 1½ cups half-and-half cream
- Kosher salt and freshly ground black pepper
- ¾ pound tortellini, or ravioli

THAT THAI KICKBOXER SURE PACKS A PUNCH!

Start your oven up at 375°F.

Mix up a batch of chili-garlic butter and place about a teaspoon under the skin of each chicken thigh. Brush a bit over the skin, too.

Bake the chicken, uncovered, for ½ hour. Remove from the oven.

Let's top each thigh with a healthy dose of sweet chili sauce. Get it back in the oven for, say, another ½ hour, or until cooked through.

While the chicken bakes, heat the butter in a large frying pan over medium heat. Sauté the onion, carrots and celery until tender-crisp.

The zucchini and sweet pepper are ready to join in, so fry them briefly.

Bring on the wine and cook until the wine is reduced by at least half.

Bring 1½ cups each sweet chili sauce and cream together in holy matrimony. Look, our blended sauce is so embarrassed, it's blushing!

Turn the heat down to medium-low, march the chili/cream sauce down the aisle to the pan and heat it through. Fine-tune the flavours with salt and pepper, or even a little chili-garlic sauce, as required.

Serve over your fave pasta, and top with the Sweet Chili Chicken thighs.

Stir-fry option: Try this as a stir-fry sauce. Use the wine in the veggies to steam them and keep them from burning, then go for equal parts sweet chili sauce and half-and-half cream (1 cup each). If the sauce thins out on you, tighten it up with a little cornstarch and water—say about 1 tablespoon each, a bit at a time, as the sauce bubbles.

THAI A YELLOW
SHRIMP CURRY

This dish is in high rotation at home, as my wife and I love it! The kids, of course, think we're nuts, but that's why God invented chicken fingers.

CURRY IN A HURRY? YOU'RE SO FULL OF . . .

- 14-ounce can coconut milk
- 1½ tablespoons fresh lime juice—plus grated zest of the lime
- 1 tablespoon fish sauce (or oyster sauce, 'cause it smells better)
- ½ tablespoon granulated sugar
- 1 tablespoon peanut oil
- 2 tablespoons curry paste
- 2 tablespoons each chopped fresh ginger and garlic
- ½ jumbo onion, into 1-inch squares
- 4 cups broccoli, cut into florets
- 1 orange or red pepper, cut into strips
- 1 pound large shrimp, peeled, tails on
- 1 large mango, diced
- Cilantro for garnish

THE CLOCK IS TICKING, PEOPLE! TIME IS MONEY!

Let's get that can of coconut milk open. *Wait, don't shake it!* Well, if it's too late, not to worry, the recipe will still work. Ideally though, I'd like you to skim the coconut cream off the top, and reserve the milk for the sauce.

While we're here, let's prep that sauce by taking that watery milk and adding the lime juice, lime zest, fish sauce and sugar to it.

Rock your wok over medium-high heat till it's smoking.

Add the peanut oil and intro the curry paste, working it with the spatula to break it up. Get movin', you only have about 30 seconds.

Bring on the ginger, garlic and onion chunks and work them with the spatula for about a minute or so. If the curry is starting to stick to the wok and needs some mobility, add a bit of the coconut cream.

The broccoli wants in, so bring the wee trees to the dance. You can add the coconut cream a bit at a time to the wok, and stir it around as you go.

After a good minute or so, add the pepper strips.

When the broccoli is just tender-crisp (it just starts to give when you poke it with a fork), add the sauce. Work it; get that spatula tossing to combine the sauce.

Now get the shrimp into that spicy bath. It'll only take about 3 minutes or so to cook the shrimp. You'll know they're done when they turn pink. Don't overcook.

If the sauce has thinned out, simply combine 1 tablespoon water with 1 tablespoon cornstarch and add it slowly to the boiling broth until you get the consistency you're after.

Get the mango and cilantro in there, and serve over a bed of basmati rice.

THAT'S A BUNCH OF
BULGOGI

Being that my daughter Elizabeth is a third-degree tae kwon do–aholic, Korean food is a surefire winner with her at home. Because bulgogi traditionally involves red meat, the carnivores at work are sold on it, too. It's all for good reason, as sweetened soy sauce with a hint of sesame makes for a tasty marinade. Send the tender beef off to the Q and you'll have delicious thin strips of moo that go nicely over stir-fried rice, stir-fried veggies or a **Feelin'-the-Heat Asian Noodle Salad** *(page 53).*

LEVEL I STAGING

- 2 pounds sirloin steak or beef tenderloin—go for a thick cut, as the beef will be cut into thin strips, for easy Q'ing
- 2 tablespoons sesame seeds
- ½ cup soy sauce
- ¼ cup + 2 tablespoons brown sugar
- 4 green onions, minced (or ¼ cup finely diced red onions)
- 4 garlic cloves, minced or pressed
- 2 tablespoons toasted sesame oil
- 1 tablespoon minced fresh ginger
- 1 teaspoon chili-garlic sauce (see page 4)

WE'RE GOING INTO FAST ATTACK MODE

Place the beef in the freezer for about ½ hour, so the meat doesn't freeze, but it becomes easier to cut.

Set up your steak so the grain of meat runs from your left to your right. Cut the beef into ¼-inch strips—we're talking against the grain. Place the beef in a zip-top freezer bag.

Fire up a nonstick frying pan over medium heat and toast the seeds—don't add oil, keep it dry. Move the little guys around until they're light brown.

Get all of the remaining ingredients together in a bowl. Whisk them together, adding the toasted sesame seeds as a final touch.

Pour the marinade into the zip-top bag and marinate the beef for at least 4 hours, or even overnight—the longer, the better, the greater the flavour!

Lay out the beef on the Q and barbecue—or broil, if you must—until the meat firms up a bit and sports those elusive fancy grill marks. Remember, at ¼ inch thick, these strips are going to cook up very quickly. You're shooting for medium-rare here, or at least I am.

This marinade goes like fireworks with Korean-style-beef-ribs—you know, the ultra-thin, flat-sliced beef ribs? Simply get them bones into a zip-top freezer bag and let them laze away in the fridge overnight—or for a couple of days; there's no rush. Then barbecue the ribs just as you would the bulgogi steak—a few short minutes on each side will do it.

THE SHRIMP 'N' CHICKEN

Dear Jeff: I made the Thai Chicken Curry from Fire Hall Cooking *and although my guests liked it, I wanted more of a sweet, creamy curry taste. You let me down! What's wrong with you, anyway? How dare you call yourself a chef.—Deb Manding*

Dear Deb: Well, it's a good thing I have thick skin. Anyway, the Thai Chicken Curry is a low-fat recipe that uses yogurt rather than coconut milk. It's always been a hit for me, but you're right, there is a difference. Give this curry a shot; it may be more what you had in mind. If not, then get a lawyer and sue my sorry butt!

HOW SWEET IT IS—AND AS A BONUS, A LITTLE SPICY

- Peanut oil for frying
- 2 tablespoons curry paste, divided
- 1 pound boneless, skinless chicken thighs, cut into thin strips
- ½ jumbo onion, in 1-inch squares
- 3 cups chopped butternut squash (1-inch squares, please)
- 14-ounce can coconut milk
- ⅓ cup chicken broth
- 2 tablespoons fish or oyster sauce
- 1 tablespoon sugar—or more
- Zest of 1 lemon or lime—as in grated rind
- 1 pound large shrimp, peeled, tails on
- 1 large red pepper, cut into strips
- 1 cup sugar snap peas
- 1 tablespoon cornstarch mixed with 1 tablespoon water
- Say about ⅓ cup finely chopped cilantro
- Lemon wedges for serving

LET'S JUST CALL IT THE SWEET SMELL OF SUCCESS!

Get a wok rockin' over medium-high heat until it's smokin'. Add 1 tablespoon peanut oil, swish it around and drop in 1 tablespoon of the curry paste.

Break the paste up with a spatula till smooth and fragrant.

Oh, it's fragrant all right, Jeff! Where's that range fan button?

Get the chicken in there and stir-fry till cooked. Remove from the wok.

Get another tablespoon of peanut oil plus a big T of curry paste in there, and toss the onion into that rockin' wok and work it through the paste.

The squash is on deck, so get it into the line-up. Stir-fry that butternut for a minute or so, adding water to the wok if it starts to go dry.

Combine the coconut milk, chicken broth, fish sauce, sugar and zest and get that sauce into the mix. Turn the heat to a light boil and wok away— no, not walk away—wok away till the squash is tender-crisp.

Get the shrimp, red pepper and sugar snap peas into the wok, and bring back the chicken. Keep stirrin' and fryin' until the shrimp is pink.

To thicken, add the cornstarch/water combo.

Serve over basmati rice and garnish with cilantro and lemon wedges.

TURKEY SCALOPPINI
SCHNITZEL

Is it German or Italian? I can't make up my mind. Bottom line, it's quick and easy, for those days when you just don't have the time to go the gourmet route . . . or don't you? Got 15 minutes? You can have these on the table in no time, and the taste will amaze you. Feel free to substitute veal, pork or chicken cutlets for the turkey, but be prepared to receive a reprimand from the Turkey Marketing Board if you do. This is another high-rotation meal at home. Easy, fast, tasty and nutritious—this dish has it all!

TURCHIA, DIE TURKEI—WE'RE TALKIN' TURKEY HERE!

- 2 pounds turkey breasts—the ones in your grocer's fridge that have been pounded flat with a meat tenderizer
- Freshly ground black pepper and Fired-Up Spice (page 4)
- All-purpose flour
- 3 or 4 eggs, whisked together with 1 tablespoon water per egg
- Italian-seasoned bread crumbs
- Olive oil for frying
- Lemons, cut into wedges

ACHTUNG, AMICO!

Give both sides of the breasts a light shot of pepper and Fired-Up Spice, then dredge them through the flour and shake off any excess.

Dip those breasts in the egg wash and follow up by running them through the Italian bread crumb station until nicely coated.

Heat a large nonstick frying pan over medium heat and pour in enough olive oil to coat the bottom, with a wee bit to spare. Allow the oil to reach temperature—wait for it!—and get the breasts in there. Fry until lightly browned on both sides. Place on a rack to allow any oil to drip away—better dripping into a rack than into your heart.

Serve with lemon wedges and compel your diners to squeeze the juice over top their Turkey Scallopini Schnitzel.

Yes, you can make it **Turkey Scaloppini Parmesan**. If you want to get off the fence and go the full-blown Italiano route, then top each cooked breast with spaghetti sauce and a couple of slices of mozzarella cheese, and either bake them at 400°F until the cheese is melted or get them under the broiler to finish.

Serve with **Caesar Salad From Scratch** (way back on page 52) and **Great Garlic Cheese Toast** (just ahead on page 189) and wash it all down with a hearty German beer.

Auf Wiedersehen! Bada bing!

TURKEY TETRAZZINI

Cooked up a big turkey or chicken and can't stand the thought of making hot turkey/ chicken sandwiches again with the leftovers? Try the Italian solution, tetrazzini!

I CAN'T BELIEVE THESE ARE LEFTOVERS!

- ½ pound whole-wheat macaroni—it's a healthy choice, just do it!
- ¼ cup butter—not quite as healthy, perhaps, but just do it anyway!
- l medium onion and 1 celery stalk, diced
- 2 garlic cloves, minced
- ½ red pepper, diced (about a cup)
- 1 cup each fresh mushrooms and zucchini— slice 'em both, please
- 1½ teaspoons Italian seasoning
- Kosher salt and freshly ground black pepper
- ¼ cup flour
- ½ cup sherry (or white wine)
- 3 cups chicken broth
- 1 cup 'arf-and-'arf cream
- 1 cup Parmesan cheese, divided
- Cayenne (optional)
- 5 cups diced cooked turkey or chicken
- ½ cup fresh bread crumbs mixed with 2 tablespoons melted butter

LET'S GET THIS ITALIAN CASSE-ROLLIN'

You may as well get the macaroni boiled and ready. Strain it when it's Al Dente—that's a term named after the Italian pasta chef who invented it.

Melt that butter down in a good-sized frying pan. Toss in the onion and garlic and let's shoot for some of that telltale caramelized colour as we fry.

Introduce the celery to the onions and fry until it's softened.

Next up it's the pepper, mushrooms and zucchini. Season with Italian seasoning, salt and pepper.

When the veggies are happy, work the flour through.

Slowly add the sherry or wine, stirring with a wooden spoon to combine.

Do likewise with the chicken broth that's waiting in the on-deck circle.

Follow up with the cream and, finally, ½ cup of the Parmesan cheese. You should have a fairly thick pasta sauce— think Alfredo-like consistency.

To thicken—if necessary—simply combine equal parts melted butter and flour, and add a small amount at a time to the bubbling brew.

Give the sauce the mandatory taste test and adjust with salt, pepper and, if you like fire like I like fire, a wee shot of cayenne.

And speaking of fire, fire the oven up to 325°F. Grease a 4-quart casserole.

Toss the macaroni and turkey in with the sauce, work it with the wooden spoon and pour into the casserole.

Top with the bread crumb/butter mix and the remaining Parmesan.

Bake for ½ hour or until browned on top and bubbling.

WHAM, BAM, THANK YOU,
BAMI GORENG

Our culinary expedition continues with a trip to . . . no, not Suffragette City, as the title suggests. Sorry, not Louisiana either, the bam isn't courtesy of Emeril. Rather, we're off to Indonesia. Or is that Holland? Confused? Well, you see, bami goreng's a big hit in both Indonesia and Holland, thanks to Dutch colonists who brought this noodle sensation back with them from the Dutch East Indies.

SO, PLUG THE HOLE IN YOUR TUMMY WITH . . .

- 4 tablespoons peanut or canola oil
- 4 garlic cloves, run through the press
- 2 tablespoons finely chopped fresh ginger
- 2 big boneless, skinless chicken breasts (or 4 thighs), cut into bite-sized squares
- Chicken broth as needed, likely not more than about ½ cup
- 1 small red onion, cut into bite-sized squares or strips
- 1 large carrot, sliced nice and thin so it'll cook quickly
- 2 coloured peppers, cut into strips (a red and a yellow would go well)
- Kosher salt and freshly ground black pepper
- 2 teaspoons ground coriander
- 1 pound medium or large shrimp, tails on, shells off
- ½ pound diced ham—'cause it rhymes with wham, bam
- ½ cup Indonesian sweet soy sauce (a.k.a. *kecap manis*—see page 4)
- 1 or 2 tablespoons chili-garlic sauce (or *sambal oelek*, if you dare!)
- ¾ pound large Chinese egg noodles or regular egg noodles, boiled as per package directions, rinsed and set aside
- 3 eggs, beaten, then fried omelette style and cut into small squares
- Bunch green onions, chopped fairly fine

IT'S INDO-DUTCH-ONESIAN?

Rock your wok on high and add 2 tablespoons of peanut oil when it smokes.

Get the garlic, ginger and chicken breasts in there and stir-fry until the chicken's cooked. You can add some chicken broth if the wok gets dry. Remove the chicken.

Add 2 more tablespoons of oil to the wok and get the onion and carrot in there, followed up about a minute later by the peppers.

Dust the bunch with a little salt, some pepper and the coriander. Oh, and add just enough chicken broth to keep our team from burning up. When the veggies are tender-crisp . . .

Shrimp, wake up, that's your cue! I know you're desperate to join in, so go! Yes, ham, you can jump in too. When the shrimp turns pink . . .

Airdrop the sweet soy and chili-garlic sauce in and mix through. Then introduce our featured guest, the egg noodles. Stir them through the sauce, adding a little more sweet soy if you think it needs it.

Hey, chopped eggs and green onions, get on stage for the grand finale!

Heat through, and this Indie-Dutchie is ready to hit the table.

YELTSIN'S SHRIMP PASTA

Here's a recipe that would make old Boris happy. It's been said that Russians drink vodka like Italians drink wine, so let's bring the influence of both countries together tonight for a tasty culinary clash. I know, with the price of booze it may be hard to justify parting with a cup of the good stuff, but you know, there are times when we just have to say, you're special, I'm special, and for crying out loud, we're worth it! So just say nyet *to Communist budgetary limitations.*

VISIT YOUR RUSSIAN GROCER

- 3 shallots
- 10 garlic cloves—4 for the sauce, 6 for the shrimp
- Extra-virgin olive oil and butter
- 1 cup vodka
- 10-ounce can chicken broth
- 28-ounce can crushed tomatoes—yes, they must be crushed
- 6 tablespoons Everybody Goes Pesto (page 144), or store-bought basil pesto
- 2 fittingly red peppers—in strips
- About ¾ pound mushrooms, cut into Ts
- 1 zucchini, halved lengthwise then sliced into thin half-moons
- Kosher salt, freshly ground black pepper and Italian seasoning
- ½ cup half-and-half cream
- Chili peppers, cayenne or chili-garlic sauce (optional)
- 2 pounds peeled, deveined and ready-to-rock shrimp, tails on
- ¾ pound of your fave pasta
- Chopped fresh basil or parsley, for garnish

SAUCECRAFTERS—GREAT-TASTING SAUCE IN AN HOUR!

Coarsely chop the shallots and 4 cloves of the garlic, and get them into a mini food processor to mulch fine. No processor? Then knife-dice 'em fine.

Bring out your big-butt skillet and introduce it to the range over medium heat. Toss in a tablespoon each of olive oil and butter.

That shallot/garlic mix needs to visit the heat for a few short minutes. Smells good already!

Pour the vodka—*steering clear of the orange juice*—into the pan and start reducing. The goal here is to burn off about half of the vodka. I know, it's a shameful waste, but a necessary evil to concentrate flavours.

The chicken broth and crushed tomatoes are on deck, so get them into the Bloody Mary—I mean, the developing pasta sauce.

A flavour boost is required, so add the pesto a bit at a time to incorporate it into the sauce. Turn the sauce down to a simmer, and cook for about ½ hour. That should tighten it up nicely!

Meanwhile, sauté the peppers, mushrooms and zucchini in a separate pan over medium-high heat with a little butter for lube, and a wee shot of salt, pepper and dried Italian seasoning.

When they're ready, add the veggies to the blushing brew. Pour the cream into the sauce, and stir it through.

Taste test. I'll generally add about a tablespoon of brown sugar, 1 teaspoon of salt, and fresh ground pepper. If you like it spicy—like I do—fire it up with crushed chili peppers, cayenne or even chili-garlic sauce, to taste.

Heat the sauté pan again, toss in 3 tablespoons each of butter and olive oil, and infuse with a whack of garlic—yes, those 6 remaining cloves, minced.

Shrimp overboard! Into the scampi garlic sauce the little fellas go until they just turn pink—don't overcook 'em!

Drain the shrimp and set aside. Get them into the rosé sauce and let it stand for 5 or 10 minutes.

Meanwhile, cook up your pasta al dente. Serve your sumptuous sauce over top, garnished with fresh basil or parsley.

Is your liquor cabinet a little low? Not to worry. I've made this recipe with ½ cup vodka with good results, as well. Simply use the booze you peruse and choose, and you can't lose.

THE NEW TECHNOLOGY

We received a new photocopier at No. 1 station, one that the crew on No. 1 platoon decided to have some fun with. Behind the photocopier—centrally located on the floor watch/foyer area of the hall—is a closet faced by a set of bifold doors. The captain hid in the closet armed with the plug to the copier and an extension cord plugged into an electrical socket. When one of the acting district chiefs dropped by for his routine visit, one of the guys said to him, "Hey, did you check out the new photocopier we got? It's voice activated."

"Really?" said the chief.

"Yeah, I'll show you. Watch," the firefighter said as he walked over to the machine. "Photocopier on!"

That was the captain's cue to plug in the machine, and on it turned.

"Photocopier off!" and off it went.

"Here, give it a try."

"Photocopier on," the district chief commanded.

Nothing.

"Try it again," the firefighter instructed. "Just stand a little closer."

"Photocopier on!" the chief repeated, leaning forward. Nothing.

"Try saying it a little louder."

"Photocopier on!"

The machine again failed to light up.

"Slow down a bit, it doesn't recognize your voice yet."

"P-H-O-T-O-C-O-P-I-E-R . . . O-N!"

As with many gags, the pranksters couldn't contain themselves any longer. The captain in the closet started giggling and the LOL hilarity began.

FIRE SIDES

FOOD AND WINE PAIRINGS BY SIR JEFFREY OF THE FIRE HALL

When serving salmon, considered a somewhat fatty fish, one should strive to pair the fish with a wine highlighted by robust characteristics. Come again? I may be totally wrong here, but how many people would know the difference between a professionally paired wine and whatever happened to be on special? Not me, and likely not many of my firefighter buddies.

When entertaining, what wine would one pair with braised short ribs? Whatever wine your company happened to bring, and be grateful they brought any wine at all, you pompous wine snob!

Ummmm, sorry, I got a little carried away there. I didn't mean to offend.

As an aperitif, one would serve a dry wine to cleanse the palate, preparing it for the meal. A full-bodied wine would accompany the main course, and for dessert, a sweet, fruity dessert wine would be the ideal complement. Hello? Was that three different bottles of wine for the same meal? I think someone's in need of either a 12-step program or a lesson in budgeting.

The way I see it, if you like white wine but you're having beef, by all means drink the white. If you like red and you're having poultry or fish, chugalug the red wine. Or play it safe by purchasing rosé in bulk and pairing it with absolutely everything. You can't lose.

I have to admit, I haven't got a clue when it comes to wine. I don't pretend to know, don't really pay enough attention to know and wouldn't know a $500 bottle of French wine from a mid- to low-priced Canadian model anyway. Hey, in a blind taste test I'd probably pick the cheapie, as it's familiar to me.

Bottom line number one: we can't drink while on duty at the fire hall anyway, so let's just put this whole argument to rest as a moot point. Bottom line number two: good food + plus good friends = good times, and, you know, a little wine wouldn't hurt the equation.

Simple wines with complex foods, complex wines with simple foods. That's good advice. So crack that bottle of Dom Romane Conti 1997 with the tube steaks, and serve Ripple with the Primo Rib Roast. Live it up!

So, as you're now painfully aware, I'm definitely not the guy to talk to when it comes to recommending wine with your meal. However, I may not be a bad choice when it comes to suggestions for a side dish. Whether it's veggies, rice, potatoes, stuffing or even couscous, I have a few ideas for you. Come with me. I'll show you what I'm talking about.

ASIAN ORANGE
ASPARAGUS

*No, not Agent Orange, I said Asian Orange, as in a sauce blend of Asian and orange flavours tossed with tender-crisp stir-fried asparagus. Goes great with the **Land-of-the-Panda Pork Roast** (page 161), the **Roast Chicken Glazed with Sweet Soy Sauce** (page 168) or just about any dish that's influenced by the amazing cuisine of the Far East.*

ORANGE YOU GLAD I DIDN'T SAY AGENT?

- 1 pound asparagus
- Zest of 1 orange—grind that rind with a grater
- ½ cup orange juice
- ¼ cup sweet chili sauce (see page 4 if unfamiliar)
- 2 teaspoons soy sauce
- 1 teaspoon toasted sesame oil
- 1 teaspoon chili-garlic sauce—you can omit this for a tamer version
- 1 teaspoon cornstarch
- 1 tablespoon peanut oil
- 1 tablespoon butter
- 1 tablespoon minced fresh ginger
- Kosher salt and freshly ground black pepper
- 1 large orange, peeled into segments, each segment halved

I LOVE THE SMELL OF ASIAN ORANGE IN THE EVENING!

Snap the woody ends off the asparagus and, thinking Asian vegetables here, cut each spear on the bias—a nice angle cut—into 3 pieces.

Head to the MASH tent if you've somehow managed to injure yourself with the knife. Hawkeye can apply a tourniquet. Be sure to note the time the tourniquet was applied by having Hot Lips write it with a felt tip marker on your forehead.

Combine the orange zest, orange juice, sweet chili sauce, soy sauce, sesame oil, chili-garlic sauce and cornstarch in a bowl. Set it aside.

Bring a wok or large nonstick frying pan to medium heat.

Get the peanut oil and butter in there, swish it around so it takes a full trip around the pan, and toss in the asparagus and ginger. Sprinkle a little salt and pepper over the spears.

Incoming! Hit the deck, enemy planes at three o'clock!

Keep those green spears stirred up and fry until they're tender-crisp. I like to use a fork to test them. When it just pierces the skin, it is time, my son.

Pour in the sauce and stir constantly to coat the asparagus. Bring on the orange segments and heat through. Look at those colours!

So, Asian Orange Asparagus doesn't sound that crazy now, does it? Well, so much for your Section 8; your tour of duty has been extended. Consider yourself a permanent member of the mess crew now, soldier.

For **Asian Orange Sugar Snap Peas,** sub in snap peas for the asparagus.

A SIDE OF
STIR-FRIED VEGGIES

It's a side dish, a vegetarian main dish, or you can make a dramatic entrée by simply adding your favourite meat to the fray. Stir-fries are a snap to make, and when it comes to your choice of veggies, almost anything goes.

MAY I SUGGEST THE FOLLOWING?

- 4–6 garlic cloves, minced or pressed
- 2 tablespoons minced fresh ginger
- 1 jumbo onion, coarsely chopped
- 3 carrots and 3 celery stalks, cut on the bias
- 1 good-sized bunch of broccoli, broken into florets
- 1 zucchini, sliced
- 1 red pepper, cut into strips for presentation's sake!
- Let's say about ¼ pound or so mushrooms, T'd up
- Peanut or canola oil, for frying
- Kosher salt and freshly ground black pepper

AND FROM THE SAUCE CELLAR, A FINE VINTAGE OF . . .

- ¼ cup each sweet soy sauce, oyster sauce and hoisin sauce (check out page 4 for a bio on that funky sauce trio)
- ½ cup chicken broth
- 2–4 teaspoons chili-garlic sauce—start at 2 unless you're very brave
- ¼ cup each water and cornstarch—but you may not need all of it

SURE, THERE'S A LITTLE PREP WORK, BUT THE COOK IS QUICK

Start the proceedings by chopping the veggies and placing the individual garden varieties in separate bowls, to maximize your dishwasher load.

While you're at it, combine the sauce ingredients, minus the cornstarch and water—we're saving that for later.

Let's get that wok of yours fired up over high heat. When there's smoke in that thar valley, add a couple of tablespoons of oil and carefully swish it around to coat the wok. Hot wok + cold oil = nonstick.

Toss in the so-called aromatics—the stuff that smells good when it cooks—the garlic, ginger, onions, carrots and celery. Hey, broccoli, you're in too. To hasten the process, you can add a few tablespoons of fruit juice or water to the wok and cover briefly. A little steam heat will surely help.

Uncover and stir the veggies often (hence the term stir-fry), and when they're just about ready (I like to check by piercing them with a fork), in go the quick-cooking zucchini, pepper and mushrooms.

Let's bring out the flavour in the veggies by dusting them with about a teaspoon or so of salt and lots of pepper.

Before the veggies overcook, let's add the sauce, stirring away till bubbling. That's your cue to introduce the cornstarch mix a bit at a time—keep stirring, now—until the sauce reaches the thickness you desire.

BARBECUED VEGGIES

The firefighter that first tagged me "Jeff the Chef" is the perpetrator of this classic dish. By the way, Craig Last has his own nickname, which he traces back to the first day of training, when his nametag read "Reggie." "My first name is Reggie, but I go by my second name, Craig." Not anymore! Yes, we firefighters are a cruel lot. Hey, if you can spare a square—about a square foot on your raging Q—then get one of those BBQ baskets on there and bring on Reggie's Veggies!

GET THESE VEGGIES INTO A GROCERY BASKET

- 2 medium zucchini
- 2 or 3 coloured peppers—mix up the colours for max presentation
- 1 sweet onion, either red or yellow
- ¼ pound white or brown mushrooms
- ⅓ cup extra-virgin olive oil
- 1 tablespoon balsamic vinegar
- Kosher salt and freshly ground black pepper—work that pepper mill
- Cherry or grape tomatoes

THEN CHOP 'EM AND GET 'EM INTO A BBQ BASKET

Let's prep the veggies. Cut the zucchini, peppers and onion into big, bite-sized chunks. Leave the mushrooms whole, unless you've landed the ginormous mutant variety; if so, then halve or quarter them. You want the veggies sized so they will cook at an equal rate.

Get the veggies into a bowl and toss with the olive oil and balsamic vinegar. I like to let the veggies marinate for about ½ hour. Don't salt them yet, as it will draw moisture out of the veggies as they sit.

Marinating time's up, so let's introduce the kosher salt. A light sprinkling of this coarse salt should do, and work the pepper mill till you feel a near crippling lactic-acid-buildup burn in your shoulder.

Fire up the Q to medium heat, or at least bring the side you'll be using for the veggies up to the mediation level.

Place your basket on the grill and toss in the vegetables. Work them with the spatula every few minutes, to keep them from burning.

Let the veggies go on the grill for about 30 minutes, or until they're cooked through and sport those telltale BBQ marks.

Season the tomatoes with salt and pepper and get them in with the other veggies for a couple, quick minutes on the Q—or simply add them to the mix after you've removed the veggies from the grill.

This recipe also works well in the oven, if the weather happens to turn nasty on you. Simply pour the seasoned combatants onto a rimmed baking sheet and bake at 400°F for 30 to 40 minutes or until cooked through.

CARIBBEAN
COUSCOUS

I know, I know, couscous, that silly-sounding tiny pasta (which some people wrongly believe to be rice) is more of a traditional African dish, but we're giving it a Caribbean twist today with a hit of spicy curry and a balancing blend of sweet fruit. By the way, if you happen to come up with a new name for couscous, let me know. Is it just me, or does couscous sound about as manly as quiche?

IT'S FUSION TIME

- 1½ cups water (or chicken broth)
- 2 tablespoons butter
- 1 cup couscous, uncooked—but not for long
- 2 more tablespoons butter
- 1 medium onion, diced
- 2 garlic cloves, minced or pressed
- 1 sweet red or orange pepper, diced
- 2 Mac or Spartan apples, peeled, cored and diced
- 1 small banana, sliced in half lengthwise, then sliced up
- 2 tablespoons curry paste—I like mild, but you can go hotter
- ¼ cup orange juice
- 1 cup chicken broth
- Chopped cilantro

AND NOW IT'S CONFUSION TIME—I'M KIDDING, IT'S EASY!

Get the water or broth boiling in a medium saucepan and add the butter and the couscous. Hmmmm, no confusion so far.

Get that pot off the heat, put a cover on it and let it stand for at least 5 minutes. Yes, couscous is just that easy to cookcook.

Let's pull out, say, about a 10-inch frying pan and find a place for it on the range over medium heat. Melt one tablespoon of the butter in the pan and add the onion. Sauté our tear-makers until lightly browned.

Toss another tablespoon of butter in the pan and add the garlic, pepper and apples. Fry the lot until the apples start to get tender.

Bring on the banana slices and fry them briefly—bananas don't like to be overcooked, or at least you won't like them overcooked.

Get the curry paste in there and combine it with the fruit and onions.

The orange juice is getting impatient over there in the on-deck circle, so let's pour it into the mix and stir it through. Fry for another 2 minutes.

Here comes the big finish—you're almost there! Toss in the chicken broth and stir it through. Get that cooked couscous in there and blend it in.

When the couscous has sucked up the broth, simply add the chopped cilantro, and you're done! This fired-up funky-fire side dish is ready to rock.

COUSCOUS GOES ITALIANO

*I was making **Breaded Pork Chops Italiano** (page 139) one evening and combing the pantry and fridge for accompaniment ideas. My son Connor was after me to make couscous, but plain old couscous just doesn't cut it for me, so I grabbed what I had on hand and came up with this concoction. Keep in mind that couscous is made from the same grain as pasta (durum wheat), so why not give it the Italian treatment?*

ONE SMALL GRAIN FOR MAN

- 1 tablespoon each olive oil and butter
- 1 cup diced onions
- 2 garlic cloves, minced or mashed
- ½ large or 1 small zucchini, sliced into quarters lengthwise, then sliced up
- ½ red pepper, diced (optional)
- ½ cup marinated (as in bottled) artichoke hearts, drained, please
- 2 Roma tomatoes, diced
- Kosher salt and freshly ground black pepper
- Italian seasoning, to taste
- 1 cup chicken broth
- 1 cup couscous—I like to go whole-wheat
- ⅓ cup white wine
- 2+ tablespoons Parmesan cheese
- Chopped fresh parsley and/or basil, for garnish

ONE GIANT DISH FOR MANKIND

Put out the call for a medium-sized sauté pan. Bring it to temperature over medium heat and get the olive oil and butter heated up.

Introduce the onions and garlic and fry them up until nicely softened.

Toss in the zucchini, red pepper, arti-choke hearts and tomatoes. Bring out the kosher salt, the pepper mill and the Italian seasoning, and give the veggies a light dusting of each. This'll surely get the flavours happening.

Meanwhile, in a small saucepan, bring the chicken broth to a boil and add the couscous. Give it a quick stir to combine, get a cover over it and remove it from the heat. It should be ready to roll in about 5 minutes.

There's no sense in talking Italian unless a bottle of fermented grapes is involved, so pour the white wine in with the veggies and reduce the liquid to, say, about half. No need to measure, I trust your instincts.

Get the couscous in there and combine the lot with a wooden spoon.

Keep the mix going until the liquid is absorbed, stirring every now and again—we're not making potstickers here.

Just before serving, sprinkle the dish with Parmesan cheese and the fresh parsley and/or basil. Go for it, Herb!

Serves 4 as a tasty, bella-fire side.

CURRIED CAULIFLOWER

Cauliflower, like its buddy broccoli, tastes 10 times better roasted than boiled. You'll be surprised how simple it is to cook cauli this way, and once you've tried it you won't go back to boiling all the living flavour out. A great spice for cauliflower is the earthy complement of cumin, so be sure to give the little trees a sprinkle of cumin plus salt and pepper before roasting. Sure, you can stop there if you like, or continue on and go for gold with this Curried Cauliflower casserole. It's not just the alliteration that works for this dish—we're talking flat-out decadence!

GET OUT WHAT YOU NEED

- 4–5 cups chopped cauliflower
- Extra-virgin olive oil
- Kosher salt and freshly ground black pepper
- Ground cumin
- 1 tablespoon milk
- 10-ounce can cream of chicken soup
- ¼ cup light whipped salad dressing or mayo
- ½ cup grated marble cheese
- 2 heaping teaspoons curry paste
- 1 cup crushed up Ritz crackers
- 2 tablespoons melted butter

AND GET THE OVEN REVVED UP AND READY TO ROCK

Fire up your oven to 400°F.

Chop the cauliflower into biteable-sized pieces—big-mouthed-firefighter size, of course. Get them into a big mixing bowl and toss in a light coating of olive oil. This isn't something you need to measure; just add a bit of oil at a time, toss, and add more as required.

Sprinkle cauli with a dash of salt, pepper and cumin.

Move them onto a large baking sheet. Space them out, let them breathe—you know, photosynthesis, or whatever they do there on the pan.

Bake them for about 10 to 15 minutes, or until the little white bushes are just tender-crisp. You can test them with a fork or piercing cellar nozzle. If you can just penetrate 'em, then get 'em out of there!

At this point you can serve them as is, obliterate them with cheese sauce or turn down the oven to 350°F and proceed with the following.

Combine the milk, soup, whipped salad dressing, cheese and curry paste.

Pour the lot over the cauliflower and place it in an ovenproof dish.

Crush up the crackers, add the melted butter to the salty gems, toss together and then spread the crunchy topping over the casserole.

Bake for about 30 minutes, uncovered.

GREAT GARLIC
CHEESE TOAST

If pasta's on the menu, then this is a must-make, must-have, sure-to-enjoy side! Sure, easy for you to say, Jeff. But what are your readers saying about Great Garlic Cheese Toast? *Well, here's a testimonial sent via text messaging: "BTW BFF OMD the GGCT wuz so DLISH. G2G. LOL! ☺"*

THIS BREAD IS ALMOST A MEAL IN ITSELF!

- Loaf of French bread—or your favourite unsliced variety
- ½ cup margarine or soft butter
- 2 tablespoons Everybody Goes Pesto (page 144) or store-bought basil pesto
- 1 cup grated Tex-Mex (or marble cheddar cheese blend)

RESIST THE TEMPTATION TO MULTI-TASK

Prefire your oven to 250 lazy degrees. You call that a blaze?

Slice the bread exactly as you would a hot dog bun, except that (1) this bun's way, way bigger, (2) you're going to cut it all the way through on purpose and (3) wieners, mustard, relish and ketchup aren't going to get anywhere near it. In other words, not exactly as you would a hot dog bun.

Place the bread on a baking sheet, cut side up, and send it to the oven for 10 minutes or so. This will pretoast it—you know, dry the bread out a bit and prepare it for its date with the tasty topping.

Meanwhile, combine the margarine or butter, pesto—there's lots of garlic in pesto, but you can always add more—and cheese. If the spread needs to be thinned, simply add a bit of extra-virgin olive oil to the mix.

Remove the bread from the oven and fire up the oven to broil—low broil, if you happen to have it. Spread the butter/pesto/cheese mix over your bread halves. As a certain retired district chief once told me as I buttered toast one morning at No. 5 station, "To the edges son, all the way to the edges." Of course, this is the same chief who told me to add bacon grease to the hash browns because it makes them taste better. So, maybe not quite to the edges; you can leave a little space around the rim for expansion.

Place the baking pan on the middle rack, and whatever you do, don't forget about it, like I do half the time. If you do, then get out a bread knife quickly and cut the burned stuff off before anyone notices. What's that? The smoke alarm already alerted them? Oh well, never mind!

BABY CARROTS

It seems such a waste, whittling giant one-foot carrots down into wee two-inch babies, but since presentation is the main thing, I guess it's worth the waste, much like whittling down a Douglas fir into a toothpick. Anyway, here's a great way to dress those little fellas up for a dinner party or fire hall dinner. Think of the time saved with no peeling or chopping required.

WHO YOU CALLIN' BABY?

- 2 pounds baby (or regular) carrots, sliced
- 2 tablespoons butter
- 2 tablespoons honey
- 3 tablespoons Dijon mustard
- Fresh dill, chopped (or if you must, use the dried)

GET THOSE SAWED-OFF LITTLE RUNTS INTO THE STEAM BATH

Place the wee ones in a vegetable steamer or boil them until tender-crisp. Steaming is ideal, as nutrients aren't leached out, as they are in boiling. Drain the carrots and set them aside.

Meanwhile, heat a medium-sized saucepan or frying pan over medium heat. Get the butter in there and follow up with the honey and mustard.

Into the pot you go, little orange guys, time for a major flavour infusion! Stir frequently until the carrots are nicely glazed.

Finish up with a shot of finely chopped dill, and serve immediately.

The Honey-Dills go great with just about any meat dish, but especially seafood, and more specifically, and even more especially—how do you like my gooder command of the English language so far?—with salmon.

IT'S MIDNIGHT, TIME TO CRASH!

Here's a prank I've seen work on several occasions with equally satisfying results. The gag is to set a bed frame on six empty pop cans. If removing the wheels allows enough room for the cans, go that route. If the supports for the wheels are a fixture on the bed, then simply remove the wheels and slide the pop cans in between the box spring and the mattress (removing the wheels so the bed remains at an inconspicuous normal height). The cans will easily support the weight of the mattress, but once the victim goes to lie down on the bed, CRASH! The cans give way, and as a bonus, the dupe receives a chiropractic adjustment free of charge.

JAWSMAN RICE

Not to be confused with jasmine rice, Jawsman Rice is named after its creator, Captain Ted Jaworski, a.k.a. Jaws or Jawsman. You wouldn't expect recipes from a firefighter who lives on coffee and cigarettes and doesn't eat lunch because he's "in training," but here's his tasty twist on Asian fried rice.

BACON IN STIR-FRIED RICE? AUTOMATIC!

- 3 cups Minute Rice (or use long grain parboiled or cold leftover rice)
- 1 pound "gotta be lean, Dudie" bacon—as Jaws says, "When I shop for bacon, I mine through the packages until I find the lean stuff. If I find a vein, I pick up 4 packages and freeze 'em." Just like in the nursery rhyme, the Jawsman could eat no fat
- 1 jumbo or 2 medium onions, diced coarse
- ½ pound mushrooms, sliced into Ts
- Soy sauce, to taste
- 6 eggs—beat 'em and add a dash of salt and pepper
- Vegetable oil

"MAINTAIN RAMMING SPEED!" JAWS COMMANDED AS WE DROVE TO AN ALARM

Cook the rice, following package directions, and set it aside to cool.

Dice up the bacon and get it into a wok on medium heat. Fry till browned.

Depending on how fat the bacon is, you may want to pour off some of the drippings. But let's hang onto about 3 tablespoons for the veggies.

Get the onions into the drippings. Now seriously, is there a more inviting, hunger-motivating odour than bacon and onions frying? *Sure smells good in here, what are we having?* Talk about priming the pump!

When the onions get slightly softened, follow up with the mushrooms.

"Hey Jeff," Jawsman called. "Did you hear what happened to [XXXXL firefighter] when they tossed him into the alligator pit?"

"No I didn't. What?"

"He ate 6 before they pulled him out!"

Once the veggies are ready, bring on the rice and stir it through.

Pour in a little soy sauce, a bit at a time, you little tater tot—sorry, that's another Jawsism—taste testing until the flavour is where you want it.

Okay, I'll admit it, I'm deviating from the plot here—the eggs are a personal addition of mine. The Jawsman omits them, but I say where there's bacon, there's got to be eggs!

So, get the rice over to a serving bowl, add a little shot of veggie oil to the wok, and pour in the beaten and seasoned eggs. Fry them just as you would scrambled eggs, and once they're set up, add them to the rice and toss through.

You did it, Dudie! Before he leaves us, Jawsman would like to fire off a parting shot: "Hey, Buddy, how much do you charge to haunt a house?"

LEMON-PESTO
JASMINE RICE

I know, I know, I'm a pesto-holic. I'm always looking for new ways to utilize this fired-up blend of herbs, and I figure, if it works on pasta, it should work on rice. The good news is, it does! In fact, we're talking fireworks!

FIRE AND RICE

- 1 cup jasmine rice
- 1¾ cups water
- 1 tablespoon butter or margarine
- ½ teaspoon salt plus a whack of freshly ground black pepper
- 2 tablespoons butter
- ½ jumbo onion, diced
- 3 celery stalks, diced
- 1 yellow pepper, diced
- ½ cup frozen peas
- ½ cup Everybody Goes Pesto (page 144) or use store-bought basil pesto, at room temperature
- Finely grated zest and juice of 1 large lemon (or, for a Thai twist, sub in 2 limes for the lemon)
- ½ cup cherry or grape tomatoes—they can be halved if they're big

LET'S JAZZ UP JASMINE

To clean the rice and wash off the excess starch, place in a fine strainer and pour water over top. If you're in possession of a rice steamer, get the rice, water, butter and salt in there and fire it up. If not, place it all in a small pot, bring to a boil, cover and reduce to a low boil until the rice is cooked.

While that action is happening, place a couple of tablespoons more butter in a frying pan over medium heat. Toss in the onion, celery and pepper, plus a little salt and pepper to awaken the flavours.

Stir-fry the veggies until tender-crisp. Get the peas in there for a minute, just enough to bring them out of their frozen state.

Fire up your oven to 250°F.

So here we are. The rice is cooked and the veggies are crisped. Toss them both in a bowl and add the pesto, lemon zest and juice. Work it through with a big old spoon, and place it in a casserole. Cover and bake for 20 minutes or so, to allow the rice and its guests some time to party.

Before serving, toss in the tardy— what's that? Oh, sorry, they consider themselves "fashionably late"— tomatoes.

MAPLE-ROASTED
VEGETABLES

Some call this ratatouille. I don't know about you, but anything with rat in the title doesn't sound very appealing. Maple Roasted Vegetables sounds so much better. I'll give you some veggie suggestions, but you don't have to listen to me; simply substitute whatever vegetables happen to be in season, on hand or at the top of your faves list. The only rule is to cut the quick-cooking veggies into the biggest pieces and cut the veggies that take their own sweet time—like root veggies—the smallest, so all the participants arrive ready at the party at the same time.

THE VEGGIE TRAY—THINK COLOUR FOR VALUABLE PRESENTATION POINTS

- 3 cups cubed butternut squash
- 1 large zucchini, cut into chunks
- 1 medium red onion, also chunkified
- 2 bell peppers and 2 large carrots—you know the drill, chunk 'em
- Mushrooms, whole or cut in half, depending on size
- What else do you have in the crisper? Toss it in, don't be shy!
- Cherry tomatoes—leave these fellas whole

THE TASTY RATTING—I MEAN ROASTING—SAUCE

- 3 tablespoons extra-virgin olive oil
- 2 tablespoons real maple syrup—as in, not the pretend pancake syrup
- 1½ tablespoons apple cider vinegar
- 2–3 garlic cloves, crushed
- 1 teaspoon kosher salt
- Grind away on the pepper mill till the veins in your arms resemble fire hoses

SEASON 'EM, TOSS 'EM, ROAST 'EM AND VEG OUT!

Fire up the oven to 400°F.

Cut up the veggies (minus the tomatoes) and place them in a mixing bowl. The veggies like zucchini, onions and peppers should be cut into larger chunks, as they will cook the quickest.

Toss in the roasting sauce, and work it through the veggies. Sprinkle the veggies with kosher salt and pepper. Toss them good, now!

Place them on a large, rimmed baking sheet, and let 'er rip for about 30 to 40 minutes, or until the veggies are tender and the liquid has pretty much been absorbed.

Add the tomatoes for the last few minutes. They won't take long.

By the way, if you have a roast cooking in the oven at a lower temperature, you can sneak the veggies in there on the bottom rack; you'll just need to cook them longer. When you take your roast out, simply crank the oven to 425°F to crisp up the veggies and finish them off.

POTATOES

Can't wait to get through dinner to get at dessert? No need, as this side dish has all you need to satisfy that throbbing sweet tooth of yours. The best way for you to imagine the flavour of this side is to think warm pumpkin pie. How sweeeeeeeeeetttt it is!

SWEET SPUDS ARE A GREAT SOURCE OF CARBOHYDRATE

- 4-5 cups chunked up sweet potatoes or yams
- ½ cup butter
- ⅓ cup brown sugar (you can use as much as ½ cup)
- ⅓ cup half-and-half cream (homo or 2% would also work)
- 2 eggs—beat 'em
- 1 teaspoon vanilla
- 1 teaspoon cinnamon
- ½ teaspoon nutmeg
- ¼ teaspoon ground ginger

OVER THE TOP

- Yet another bunch of brown sugar—this time a cup
- ½ cup all-purpose flour
- ⅓ cup butter
- ½ cup pecans or toasted slivered almonds, candied

AND SINCE CARBS ARE BRAIN FUEL, CONSIDER THIS FOOD FOR THOUGHT

Fire up your oven to 350°F.

Add the sweet spuds or yams to a pot of salted boiling water. Let 'em rock until they're soft, and drain in a strainer.

Get the electric mixer staged, and add the butter, brown sugar, cream, eggs, vanilla, cinnamon, nutmeg and ginger to the drained potatoes.

Combine the lot with that handy power tool until quite smooth.

Pour the spud batter into a greased 2-quart casserole dish.

At this point you could easily take your foot off the gas and simply bake as is. However, if that sweet tooth of yours is still calling (and decadence is job 1), then follow along as I lead you into the land of sweet side dishes.

Going for it? Nice to have you along. In a separate bowl, combine the second batch of brown sugar and the flour. Using the mixer, add the butter in small globs—probably best to clean the blades first—and combine the trio until you notice coarse little crumbs appearing.

Fold in the chopped pecans or toasted slivered almonds.

Top the spuds off with the "show it the sweet before we show it the heat" topping mixture.

Let's get our creation into the oven for, say, about ½ hour or slightly longer, depending on the depth of the casserole you chose for this mission. Once they're warmed through, the sweet spuds are ready to eat.

STUFFING ON THE SIDE

Here's a great stuffing recipe that's meant to be cooked alongside rather than inside the bird. That's a good thing because often by the time the stuffing in a bird reaches the recommended safe temperature, the white meat is overcooked. So let's think outside the bird. I snagged this one from firefighter Chris Blasko, though I believe—truth be known—that it's actually his mother-in-law's recipe.

CARE TO BREAK BREAD WITH ME?

- 8 cups whole-wheat bread (pretty much a loaf), fresh or stale (white, if you must)
- ½ cup butter
- 1 medium onion, diced
- 2 celery stalks, diced
- 2 teaspoons dried sage leaves
- 1 teaspoon Italian seasoning
- 1 teaspoon kosher salt, divided, and some freshly ground black pepper
- 1 red pepper, diced as well, for that festive look
- 4 large eggs
- ¼ cup half-and-half cream (or whole milk)
- ¼ cup hot water combined with 1 tablespoon chicken bouillon

WHY IS IT CALLED STUFFING, IF NOTHING ACTUALLY GETS STUFFED?

Cube up the bread into about 1-inch squares.

Get the butter rolling in a frying pan over medium heat and toss in the onion and celery. Add the sage leaves, Italian seasoning, ½ teaspoon of the salt and a few grinds from the old pepper mill.

Sauté until slightly softened, then bring the peppers to the party. Hang up their coats, get them a drink, introduce them to the other vegetables, and after a couple of minutes of mingling and sauté fun, remove all the veggies from the heat.

Heat that oven to 350°F.

Meanwhile, toss the eggs, cream or milk and remaining salt into a mixing bowl. Get the electric mixer out and blend together, adding the water and bouillon while the mixer is still running.

Intro the veggies to the bread cubes, then toss gently with the egg mix. Your mix should be quite moist, but you can add more H_2O if needed.

Get the stuffing into a greased oven-proof baking dish—a deep 8 x 8-inch should be good—and bake for 40 to 50 minutes, uncovered.

Cut the stuffing into segments—this dish is designed for 6 to 8—and serve alongside your favourite poultry.

SUPER SIMPLE CABBAGE

Here's a quick, cheap and easy side dish that tastes great with but a few ingredients and little effort.

IT'S NOT JUST FOR COLESLAW, YOU KNOW

- Green cabbage, sliced into 1-inch squares
- Butter
- Kosher salt and freshly ground black pepper

OH, I CAN DO THIS

Place the cabbage squares in a steamer basket over a pot of water and steam until tender. No basket? Then simply boil 'em in the drink.

Drain the H$_2$O, toss the cabbage squares with a light coating of butter and toss in a dose of salt and pepper to taste.

By the way, this method also works great with Brussels sprouts (a.k.a. mini-me cabbage).

As an alternate method, try stir-frying the cabbage in a little butter over medium heat. Give it the salt and pepper treatment as you go.

SWEETENED-BY-CHEATIN'
CORN ON THE COB

Here's my fave way to prepare corn on the cob. Not to worry, the grand jury isn't going to call an inquiry into how you made this corn so sweet. Cheatin' may be frowned upon in sports and in the bedroom, but in the kitchen it's fair game!

YES, IT'S JUST THIS EASY!

Bring a big pot of water to a boil—for 4 to 6 cobs use about 16 to 20 cups of water combined with 1 cup of sugar and a tablespoon of kosher salt. Be sure to stir the water to make sure the sugar and salt don't settle.

Add the husked corn and boil it for about 10 minutes The kernels should still be somewhat firm, much like tender-crisp veggies in a stir-fry. Don't overcook, as soggy, mushy corn just doesn't cut it—unless you're fresh out of denture adhesive.

CORN'S HOT AND READY, SO LET'S GET OUT THE BREAD AND BUTTER

Let's do like retired Captain Johnny Webster, and grab a slice of sacrificial bread and lay down a heavy layer of butter, like you're paving a road with asphalt. Now hold the bread—butter side up, of course—with one hand and roll the corn in the butter at approximately 7,000 RPM with the other hand. Dust the cob with salt to taste, affix a napkin and . . . mmmmm, sweeeeeeet buttered corn!

TEX-MEX
SCALLOPED POTATOES

Is it just me, or are many scalloped potato recipes just plain bland? Well, in an attempt to address this very serious condition, I've thrown in a few tasty food items. Fire up the spuds!

HMMMMM, I WONDER WHAT ELSE WE CAN PUT IN THERE?

- ¼ cup butter
- 8 garlic cloves, minced, hacked up or run through the press
- 1+ cup finely diced yellow onion
- 2+ diced fresh jalapenos—really, how many is up to you
- 1 red pepper—dice it up, too
- Fired-Up Santa Fe Spice (page 5)
- 8 medium Yukon Gold potatoes (red or white will also work)
- ½ cup milk—2% or thicker please; thin doesn't win here
- 2 10-ounce cans cream of chicken (or cream of celery soup)
- 1-pound bag grated Tex-Mex cheese blend—if you don't want to make a special trip to the store, good old marble will also do

BAKE THEM TATERS TILL THEY'RE TENDER AND GOLDEN BROWN

Get a small frying pan heated up to medium and toss in the butter followed up by the garlic, onion, jalapenos, red pepper and a sprinkle of that tasty Fired-Up Santa Fe Spice. Cook until the onions are translucent, a.k.a. see-through.

Where the heck is that Popeil Pocket Scalloped Potato Maker when I need it? Sorry, it looks like we're going to have to cut these potatoes by hand—as thinly as possible, please, without making a visit to the emergency room.

Fire up the oven to 400°F.

Whisk together the milk and the soup and put it on standby.

Grease up a 9 x 13-inch lasagna dish. Don't make the mistake I made years back at No. 1 fire hall, when I tried to triple a scalloped potato recipe in a huge roaster. The spuds on the bottom were burnt, while the spuds in the middle hadn't cooked through. So if you need to make more, it's best to get out another dish or two.

Lay down half the potatoes in the bottom of the greased dish, followed by half of the veggie mix and half of the cheese.

Déjà vu the layers and top the second layer with the souped-up mixture.

Bake the spuds for 1 hour, covered. Remove the cover and bake for another 10 minutes or so to brown up the cheese. Pierce the potatoes with a knife to make sure they are cooked through. The lazy ones in the centre will be ready last.

For a one-dish dinner delicacy, try tossing in cubed ham or cooked chorizo sausage. Better leave the refried beans on the side, though.

POTATOES

"Pick us when we're young, keep our skins on, for they are packed with nutrients and flavour, and roast us in the oven with a light coating of extra-virgin olive oil and your favourite seasoning." The potatoes have spoken, giving us the secret to simply delicious gems. How do I know this? Because potatoes talk to me. I am the Spud Whisperer. Seriously, I am. I'll have you know that the Derraugh family was kicked out of Ireland for stealing potatoes during the potato famine—true story—so we know our spuds, personally. Those little baby potatoes are so convenient that I find myself taking advantage of them on a regular basis. They require little prep time, yet look and taste gourmet. For maximum presentation, I especially like the bag of mixed baby potatoes, featuring whites, reds and even purple potatoes. Yes, purple potatoes. Be prepared to hear your crew crying, "What the heck are these?" Relax, they'll love them once they try them. Fingerling potatoes are another gourmet variety you can use. Sliced in half lengthwise, they resemble french fries. I know what you're thinking, "I'll bet the gourmet gems cost more." Yeah, they do, but not to worry, you won't have to resort to stealing them. We're talking potatoes here, so they're still cheap.

GROWTH HORMONE? NOT THESE GEMS

- 2 pounds baby potatoes or fingerlings, peeled if you're a masochist
- About 3 tablespoons extra-virgin olive oil
- 2 teaspoons (+ if you like it fiery) Fired-Up Santa Fe Spice (page 5)

ARE OLIVE OIL AND SPICE PERFORMANCE-ENHANCING?

Place the spuds in a mixing bowl and add the olive oil a bit at a time, tossing as you go. The goal here is to just coat the little fellas with oil, so there should be very little oil left in the bowl. If you're not planning on roasting the spuds right away, leave them as is without spicing.

Just before their date with the heat, sprinkle the Fired-Up Santa Fe Spice over the potatoes, tossing them with a spoon to coat evenly.

Place a baking sheet in the oven for a minute or so and remove. This will help keep the potatoes from sticking to the pan. Works for me!

Spread the potatoes over the baking sheet, being careful not to overcrowd. If your pan resembles Times Square on New Year's Eve, the spuds are going to have a tough time crisping and browning, so give them a little room to breathe. Do up another baking pan if you're making a big batch.

Roast the little suckers for 30 to 40 minutes, flipping them around every 10 minutes or so, until crisped up on the outside and soft in the middle.

By the way, these are also terrific roasted on the Q in a barbecue basket.

FEED ME, I'M DYING OF STARVATION

There's no doubt about it, firefighters' appetites are legendary. The stories of gluttony are many, but one tale strikes me as being particularly amazing. This goes back many years to a fellow firefighter who not only ate his full ration of the typical fire hall supper—one pound of meat, one pound of potatoes, plus bread, fixings, dessert, etc.—but also 18 cobs of corn. Yes, *18 cobs!* If you're thinking this had to be one of the stout-with-a-capital-S guys, you're wrong. This was one of those bone-rack tapeworm guys. Yes, it's the tall, skinny guys you have to watch out for.

Another firefighter, who shall also go nameless, would drop by a fast food joint for a drive-through burger dinner on his way to work at five, eat a humongous lasagna dinner including garlic toast and Caesar salad with his crew at eight, and by ten o'clock was ordering in pizza.

In "Honey! I Shrunk My Gear!" I talk about the proverbial bowl of ice cream being the favourite fire house dessert. Well, you should see some of the skyscraper bowls of scream that firefighters lay into. *Lift with your legs, not your back!*

With some guys it's not only their appetites that cause them to eat so much, it's that they want to get their money's worth. For other firefighters, the grazers, it comes down to boredom. On slow days, they have their heads in the fridge half the day looking for something to eat! I told one crewmate that to do him justice his department ID card should have a picture of him from behind, bent over, browsing the fridge.

Firefighters are survivalists. Check out their lockers and you're bound to find emergency rations like cans of soup and tuna and a box of macaroni and cheese. In most cases the provisions won't leave the locker until they are transferred to their next hall. However, if disaster were to strike, I can't imagine the apocalyptic scene that would erupt if the lockers were bare. I remember saying to an acting lieutenant as he placed a huge brown paper bag in the station fridge, "Didn't anyone tell you that we're eating today?"

"Oh, I know," he of renowned appetite responded. "Let me give you a bit of advice young man: always carry backup."

Yes, it's true: a full firefighter is a happy firefighter, and that's why the fire house chef is considered such an important member of the crew.

HONEY! I SHRUNK MY GEAR!

JUST DESSERTS

It never fails. Before my wife and I go out for dinner—a rarity, given the economic realities of a blue-collar worker under big-family financial constraints—she'll say, "When the dessert menu comes around, please remind me not to have any. I really don't need it, and it just makes me feel bloated."

You know where this is going, don't you?

So, we'll have a great meal, and the server will come around teasing us with the dessert list. I'll pass, but she'll say, "Oh, come on Jeff, why don't you just split one with me?"

"No thanks, I don't want dessert, and you told me earlier to talk you out of having any."

"I'm a big girl. If I want dessert, I'll have dessert. I don't need your permission."

So Lori will have some whopping 4,200-calorie special, and after she insists 37 times that I try some because it's *soooo goooood*, I'll reluctantly try a bite, and naturally agree with her assessment. When I refuse seconds, she'll say, "How can you only have one bite? This is delicious!"

Don't you just hate people like me?

When we get home she'll lie in bed clutching her stomach. "Why did you let me get that dessert? I feel like I'm going to burst. Oh, and by the way, stay on your own side of the bed, because the first thing on your mind is the last thing on mine right now."

So much for having to buy her dinner first.

MEANWHILE, OVER AT the fire house, there's hell to pay if you fail to pick up dessert. Oh, some crews will attempt to agree to no desserts, but there's always a captain or crew member who insists on dessert and, well, if it's there you're probably going to eat it, right? Gotta get your money's worth.

For many fire halls, the post-dinner ritual is the proverbial bowl of ice cream . . . What do you mean, ice cream wasn't mentioned in Proverbs? I have proof—here's one of the passages from the book of Ben & Jerry, 10:34: "And on the seventh day, God gaveth in to temptation, and set forth to create ice cream, topped with decadent chocolate sauce. And all the Heaven's rejoiced, Hallelujah! The Sundae hath been born!"

I know, I'll likely be heading south on D-Day for kidding around with the big guy. But don't worry, I'm used to the heat.

Dessert beyond ice cream may not be something I make every day, but everybody deserves a treat now and again. Coming up in this section are a number of dessert temptations for the sweet of tooth, as well as a big batch of baked goods that are sure to please. So, loosen the belt and put in an order for new gear, 'cause we're going in.

OATMEAL MUFFINS

Whenever I bake these at the fire hall I hear, "Oh man, does that ever smell gooooood!" Yes, the drooling has begun, as the wild pack of dogs begins to circle the kitchen. We firefighters can sniff out good cooking, and apples baking smell amazing! This batch won't last long.

SEE IF YOU CAN SNIFF OUT . . .

- 1½ cups quick oats
- ¾ cup each whole-wheat and all-purpose flour
- 1 teaspoon baking soda
- 1 teaspoon baking powder
- 1 teaspoon salt
- 1 teaspoon cinnamon
- 1 cup raisins (or a combination of raisins and walnuts)
- 1 cup sweetened applesauce
- ½ cup buttermilk
- ½ cup brown sugar
- 2 eggs, beaten
- 1 teaspoon vanilla
- 1 large Mac or Spartan apple, peeled and grated

AND FOR THE OPTIONAL, YET HIGHLY RECOMMENDED, TOPPING MIX

- ¼ cup quick oats
- 1 tablespoon brown sugar
- 1 tablespoon melted butter
- 1/8 teaspoon cinnamon

SNIFF, SNIFF, SNIFF . . . MMM-MMMMM-MMMMMMM!

Grease a muffin tin with 12 parking spots and fire up your oven to 375°F.

Let's get the oats, flour, baking soda, baking powder, salt and cinnamon together in a bowl and stir them up. Oh, sure, the raisins and nuts can join in if they're ready.

In a second bowl, combine the applesauce, buttermilk brown sugar, eggs, vanilla and apple. Give those naughty ingredients a darn good whisking!

Make a well in the centre of the dry ingredients and pour in the wet dudes. Fold the two together until the batter is just combined. Try not to over-mix.

Get the batter into the muffin tin. Place the topping mix over each muffin top—for presentation, of course.

Bake for about 20 minutes. Ah yes, the sweet smell of success!

BUILDING A BETTER
BANANA BREAD

We're talking better as in healthier. I love banana bread, but I have to admit that when I load a big whack of margarine and white sugar into a bowl I wonder if I'm going to live to see pension. Despite the lack of what we firefighters affectionately refer to as "smear" and "white death," this recipe still manages to come through with solid flavour. The verdict is in: tastes good, less filling . . . eat more! You can't lose!

NO SUGARS WERE PROCESSED IN THE MAKING OF THIS RECIPE

- ½ cup applesauce—sweetened, if you need your sugar fix
- ½ cup honey—melt in the microwave, if necessary
- 1 teaspoon vanilla
- 2 eggs—beat 'em
- ½ cup buttermilk—1% buttermilk is nice and skinny
- 3 large bananas—mush 'em up, now
- 1 cup each whole-wheat and unbleached all-purpose flour
- 1 teaspoon each baking soda, baking powder and salt
- ¾ cup raisins or chocolate chips and/or ½ cup crushed walnuts

HAVE A SLICE—COME ON, IT'S NOT GOING TO KILL YA!

Fire up your oven to 350°F and grease a Bundt or loaf pan.

As per the *Muffin and Bread Making Agreement* signed in the late 1600s by Pilgrim settlers, the wet and dry ingredients must remain separate until their final union. So let's do like our forefathers and foremothers, and get the applesauce in a bowl with the honey and whisk them together.

Bring on the vanilla and eggs and give 'em a whisk. The buttermilk, whisk. And, finally, the mush that makes it distinct, the bananas—whisk again!

In another bowl, whisk together the flour, baking soda, baking powder and salt.

Raisins, chocolate chips and or nuts, you're dry, so get in there too.

You may now bake the bread for 45 to 55 minutes. The time depends on what size of pan you use. A Bundt pan will generally take less time, a bread loaf pan a little longer.

Now that we've built a better banana bread, I think we can safely take 2 or 3 slices instead of 1. It only makes sense, don't you think?

CHILI CORN BREAD

Firefighter Renée Vermette made this to go along with the chili I had made at the fire hall for lunch, and since its inception we've saddled it up as chili's regular sidekick. Cooking is all about yin and yang, so as per my typical MO, once again the call is in for some sweet to balance the heat.

OFF TO THE EXPRESS LINE YOU GO WITH . . .

- 1 cup cornmeal (in your grocer's baking section)
- 1 cup all-purpose flour
- ⅓ cup white sugar
- 1 tablespoon baking powder
- ¼ cup margarine or butter, softened
- 1 cup buttermilk
- 1 egg, beaten

A TASTE OF THE SOUTH IS ON ITS WAY, Y'ALL

Fire up your oven to 350°F and grease a baking pan. The batter should be enough to fill an 8 x 8-inch pan, which should satisfy 4 to 6 diners. If you double the recipe you'll have enough to fill a 9 x 13-inch lasagna dish.

Get the cornmeal in a big ol' mixing bowl with the flour, sugar and baking powder. Drop the softened margarine or butter in there in teaspoon-sized bits and beat the mess together until coarse little balls form.

In not nearly as big a bowl, combine the buttermilk and egg.

Make a well in the dry ingredients and pour in the wet. Fold it all together—come on now, fold—until our batter becomes one.

Bake on the centre rack of your oven for about 20 to 25 minutes, or until a toothpick—no, not the one that's currently parked in your mouth—comes out clean.

Serve with a batch of **Hooked on Chili** (page 156).

CAPTAIN JOHN THE MUFFIN MAN

When I was stationed at No. 18, I routinely made muffins for morning coffee. As muffin tins house 12, I always made at least 12 despite only four firefighters' being stationed in the hall. If the district chief and his driver stopped by, that would make six of the muffins spoken for, unless someone, say my captain, for example, went for multiples. Six muffins was not uncommon for Captain John, and on one occasion he set a personal best of seven—bran muffins, that is. Oh, I warned him, but he failed to take heed. Let me put it to you this way: the muffins kicked in during his uncomfortable bus ride home, and only through the grace of God did he make it to his apartment in time.

DOWN-UNDER
PUMPKIN SCONES

The motivation behind this recipe came from fellow firefighters who had visited Australia and were missing the pumpkin scones they'd found so plentiful there. This led me to head up an intense investigation, which included hours of detailed, time-consuming forensic work in the lab, attempting to develop my own version.

A G'DAY STARTS WITH A G'D SCONE, MATE

- 1 cup all-purpose flour
- 1 cup whole-wheat flour
- ⅓ cup brown sugar
- 1 tablespoon baking powder
- ½ teaspoon each ginger, cinnamon and salt
- ½ cup margarine or butter, softened
- ½ cup each walnuts and raisins
- 2 eggs, beaten
- ½ cup pure canned pumpkin—not the pumpkin pie filler mix
- ⅓ cup buttermilk

GET TO WORK IN THE KITCHEN THERE, SHEILA! OR IS THAT BRUCE?

Fire up your oven to 375°F.

Gather the troops. We need a couple of mixing bowls, cooking spray, a baking sheet (those pizza pans with the holes drilled in the bottom work great), a rolling pin and a 3 to 4-inch round cup to cut the scones.

Combine the flour, sugar, baking powder, ginger, cinnamon and salt in the first bowl.

Introduce the margarine or butter and whisk like the Tasmanian devil until the mixture resembles coarse little balls—no, this is not a coarse little double entendre. Get your mind out from down under.

Get the walnuts and raisins in there as well and mix it up.

In the second bowl, combine the eggs, pumpkin and buttermilk.

Give your hands a shot of cooking spray—oh yeah, you're getting down and dirty—and add the dry to the wet, mixing the ingredients with your hands, adding a touch more flour to the mix if the batter is too wet (as in sticky) or a little buttermilk if it's too dry (as in not holding together).

Dust a little flour on the counter and roll out the dough to about ¾ inch thick. Cut out scones with the cup and place on a greased baking pan.

Bake the scones on the centre rack in the oven for 18 to 20 minutes, or until lightly browned top and bottom.

MUFFINS

Here's a great carrot muffin recipe with lots of spice, raisins, nuts and a nice twist of orange. The ingredients look pretty healthy, too. I'm sure Bugs would approve.

SO LET'S GET THE GROCERIES

- 1 cup each unbleached all-purpose and whole-wheat flour
- 1 tablespoon baking powder
- ½ teaspoon salt
- ½ cup brown sugar
- ½ teaspoon cinnamon
- ½ teaspoon nutmeg
- 1 cup grated carrots—no knuckle skin, please!
- Finely grated zest of 1 orange
- 2 eggs
- 1 cup buttermilk
- ¼ cup molasses—add slowly (as if you have a choice)
- ¼ cup butter, melted
- ½ cup raisins
- ½ cup chopped walnuts (or more raisins, if you prefer)

AND MAKE THESE MUFFINS HAPPEN!

Fire up your oven to my number 1 muffin-baking temp of 375°F and grease up a 12-slot muffin tin.

Let's bring the two flours together, with the baking powder for levity, and the all-important bit of salt. Have a sip of coffee for wakening and motivational purposes, then add the brown sugar, cinnamon, nutmeg, carrot and orange zest to the mix.

In a separate bowl, whisk together the eggs, buttermilk, molasses and melted butter until they actually start to get along.

Fold—you thought I was going to say whisk again, didn't you?—no, fold the wet ingredients into the dry until *just* combined.

Pop in the raisins and nuts until just combined again. *Come on, Jeff, get out the thesaurus, mix up the words here!*

Place the batter in the ready-to-rock muffin tin.

Bake for 15 to 20 minutes. Use the finger test to ensure doneness. Tap the muffin top lightly. If your finger sinks, they need more time! If it bounces back, they're done. If they're like hockey pucks, then congratulations! You've completed the necessary requirement for graduation from the Elly May Clampett Cooking School!

Oh yeah, while they're baking, you'd better get a fresh pot of coffee going—pitch the stale stuff sitting on the burner, the 20-minute freshness rule is in full effect—because these tasty muffins are going to want a little company.

WHOLE-WHEAT BREAD

I've certainly been on a bit of a flax binge lately. I guess it's a guilt-trip combo of getting older and needing dietary fibre, plus all the talk we hear about needing more omega-3 oils in our diets. You know what, though? Ground flax adds great taste and texture to bread. It's a health fix that works. Give it a shot and fire up your bread maker today!

MORE THAN "JUST THE FLAX, MA'AM"

- 1¼ cups water
- 2 tablespoons powdered milk
- 1 teaspoon salt
- 3 tablespoons each soft butter and honey
- 2 cups whole-wheat flour
- 1 cup all-purpose or unbleached flour—or another cup of whole-wheat
- ½ cup golden ground flax—brown flax works well, too
- 2 teaspoons bread maker or fast-acting yeast

DOUGH DE DOUGH!

Get the ingredients into the bread maker in the order listed.

Set the contraption for the dough cycle and let 'er rip.

When the cycle is complete, dump out the dough on a kitchen counter lightly dusted with flour. This will absorb any excess moisture and make the dough easier to work with.

Grease up a large bread pan with a shot of cooking spray. Form the dough into a loaf-shaped rectangle and place it in the pan.

Cover the dough with a tea towel and let it rise in a moderately warm spot for about half an hour, or until it rises about an inch above the top of the bread pan.

Fire up the oven to 350°F (or 325 350° for convection). Bake for 28 to 30 minutes.

Before you dig in, a word of advice. You know how you should never grocery shop on an empty stomach? Well, you should never bake bread on an empty stomach, either. If you do, you'll be wolfing back slice after slice dressed with wads of melting butter before the bread has even had a chance to cool.

For a **Flax Multigrain** version, simply substitute 1 cup multigrain bread flour for 1 cup of the whole-wheat flour.

For a **Cracked Wheat, Oat Bran** or **Red River Cereal** version, all you have to do is substitute your favourite grain for the flax. As long as you stick with the basic bread recipe, you should be safe and, above all, well nourished. Read the list of ingredients on a loaf of store-bought bread, and you'll be glad you took the homemade route.

ICELANDIC
BROWN BREAD

About an hour north of Winnipeg is the quaint fishing village of Gimli, home to not only the Gimli Glider and the annual Icelandic Festival—a.k.a. Islendingadagurinn (try saying that even once in a row)—but also great Icelandic brown bread. Although this isn't the exact local recipe, it's as close as I can get, and with the price of gas today, I say, close enough. This is one of the most requested items at the fire hall.

LOAD UP THE BREAD MAKER IN THE FOLLOWING ORDER, LARS

- 1¼ cups water
- 1 teaspoon sea salt—Gimli is a lakefront community, albeit freshwater
- 1½ tablespoons powdered milk
- 2 tablespoons soft butter or margarine
- ¼ cup brown sugar
- ¼ cup molasses—I like "fancy" molasses, but "cooking" will also work
- 2 cups whole-wheat flour
- 1 cup unbleached all-purpose flour—or another cup of whole-wheat
- ½ cup rye bread flour
- 2 teaspoons bread maker or fast-acting yeast

AND SOON THE SMELL OF DELICIOUS BREAD WILL FILL THE AIR

Pile all the ingredients into your bread maker and hit the dough cycle. That should take about 1½ to 2 hours to knead. *Wait a second, I could have just about driven to Gimli and back in that time and picked up the real thing!* True, but think of the gas savings and complete lack of road rage.

Turn the processed dough out onto a lightly dusted counter. Please tell me that the dust is flour and not dust . . . Someone, quick! Put in a Housekeeping 911 call to Martha Stewart!

Spray a large bread pan with an even crop-dusting of cooking spray.

Place the dough in the pan, cover with a tea towel and let it rise in a warm place for approximately 30 minutes. In this time the dough should rise to an inch or so above the lip of the bread pan.

Get the oven roaring at 350°F (325° if you have a convection oven).

Place the bread pan on a rack in the lower third of the oven and bake for 28 to 30 minutes.

Hey, it smells just like an Icelandic bakery in here!

Get carving and buttering—there's nothing better than fresh-baked bread! Well, unless you're celiac. Then there's nothing worse than fresh-baked bread . . . Ouchh! Jeez! I'm sorry! Come on, I was kidding! That was my celiac brother, Murray, smacking me in the head for being so callous. You'd think he'd know me by now.

Anyway, try this bread once and you may become hooked. Consider yourself forewarned!

You're velkomin! That's Englandic for you're welcome!

LONNY'S
BANANA SPLIT CAKE

I'll never forget the look on rookie Justin Kutzak's face as Captain John Webster over-loaded an extra-large soup bowl with about a gallon of chocolate mint ice cream and proceeded to squeeze a bottle of chocolate syrup over top, circling the bowl at least a dozen times. Justin gazed in complete amazement. "Jeff, he can't be serious."

"Oh, he is," I replied. "But remember, he's a seasoned professional with 29 years on the job. Be patient, Justin. Start with a small bowl, and one day, if you work hard enough, you too will be ready to tackle a bowl that size."

That's John, our dessert expert. I'll tell you, he sure raved about this dish after fire-fighter Lonny Sisson made it, giving it two chocolate-covered thumbs up.

LET'S LAY DOWN SOME BASE

- 2 cups graham wafer or Oreo cookie crumbs
- ⅓ cup soft margarine, melted
- 1 tablespoon white sugar

Get a blaze of 350°F going in your oven.

Combine all ingredients and press the mixture into a greased 9 x 13-inch pan to create a solid bottom. Bake for 8 to 10 minutes, to brown. Allow it to cool.

FILL UP THE FILLING— TO EGG OR NOT TO EGG

- 2 eggs (for eggless version, use 8 ounces cream cheese)
- 2 cups icing sugar (use this in the eggless version as well)
- ½ cup soft margarine (not required in the eggless version)
- 1 teaspoon vanilla (plus to thin the eggless, use a bit of the pineapple juice)

Beat all ingredients together with an electric mixer. For the egg filling, beat until light and fluffy. (This could take several minutes.) Spread the filling over the base.

AND TOP WITH THE TOPPING

- 4–6 bananas, sliced lengthwise into 4 pieces each
- 19-ounce can crushed pineapple, completely drained—but you may need the juice
- Whip up 2 cups real whipping cream (or use packaged whipped topping, if you must)
- Chocolate sundae sauce or Brown Cow Drizzle (page 213)
- Strawberries, sliced
- Walnuts, crushed

Lay down the banana slices over the filling and follow with the crushed pineapple. Spread on the whipped cream, then arrange strawberry slices over top. Toss your creation into the fridge for at least an hour. (This is great as a make-ahead dessert.) Serve by drizzling the chocolate sundae sauce or Brown Cow Drizzle over each slice—why not try using an IV bag with tubing for this operation?—and top it off with the walnuts.

MARSHA'S MAGNIFICENT
PUMPKIN TRIFLE

Our friend Marsha Graham brought this to a dinner party, and it was soooooo good that we nabbed her recipe and made it instead of pumpkin pie at Thanksgiving. It was a big hit! By the way, there's twice the cake mix here that you'll need for the trifle, so if you happen to be making this for a crowd, simply double the remaining ingredients to get a mega-trifle happening.

THAT'S IT?

- 1 box store-bought gingerbread or spice cake mix
- 4 cups milk, whole or 2%
- 2 large packages instant butterscotch pudding mix
- 14-ounce can pure pumpkin—not the pie filling
- 1 teaspoon cinnamon
- ½ teaspoon nutmeg
- ¼ teaspoon ground ginger
- 2 cups whipping cream (or if your get-up-and-go got up and left, pick up a carton of lazy man's packaged whipped topping)
- 1 teaspoon vanilla and 2 to 3 tablespoons white sugar, if you're whipping the cream

TIME TO CRACK THE WHIP

We need to get the cake together first, so fire up the oven to 350°F, and while it's heating up follow the directions on the box. Pour the batter into a 9 x 9-inch cake pan. It doesn't have to be pretty, as it's all going to get busted up.

Bake the cake as directed, let it cool and break it into crumbs or chunks.

Meanwhile, in another mixing bowl, combine the milk and pudding mix and give 'er full-throttle power on the electric mixer for 2 minutes. Let the pudding mix stand for another couple of minutes, to set.

Stir the pumpkin and spices into the pudding with your handed-down-from-generation-to-generation, behaviour-insurance wooden spoon. (Or at least that's how I remember that spoon from my childhood.)

Better warn the whipping cream that it's about to get the "Ship High in Transit" kicked out of it. Off to a metal mixing bowl you go, pal. The electric mixer is going to beat you until you're all puffy, or at least until you set.

Introduce the vanilla and a little white sugar to taste, and combine briefly. Omit this step if you're taking the lazy man's way out.

In a trifle bowl or big see-thru salad bowl, layer ¼ of the cake crumbs/chunks, ½ the pumpkin, ¼ of the cake and half of the whipping cream. Repeat the layering saving some cake crumbs for garnish.

Wouldn't a smashed-up Score bar be great in the mix? How about as a topping? Don't hold back, go for it! Decadence hath no bounds!

MOM'S CLASSIC
CHOCOLATE CAKE

At a family birthday party I took my first bite of Mom's chocolate cake, and commented, "Nobody makes better chocolate cake than you, Mom." Suddenly I felt a cold breeze. "Well," I struggled, "except, of course, Lori. Nobody but Lori." Bottom line, my wife eventually conceded defeat and now makes this family staple. It's a simple yet delectable cake that my mom has made since she was 14 years old.

THE BASIC INGREDIENTS

- 1 cup white sugar
- ½ cup butter + 2 tablespoons for the icing
- 2 eggs
- 1½ cups all-purpose flour
- 2 heaping tablespoons cocoa + 1½ tablespoons for the icing
- 1½ teaspoons baking powder
- ½ teaspoon salt
- 1 cup milk + 3 tablespoons for the icing
- ¼ teaspoon vanilla
- ½ teaspoon baking soda
- 2 cups icing sugar—for the icing, of course

TALK ABOUT RECIPES THAT HAVE STOOD THE TEST OF TIME

Grease a 9 x 9-inch baking pan or 2 8-inch round cake pans. The 2-pan trick works nicely, as it allows you to put icing, whipped cream, strawberries—whatever—between layers.

Fire up your oven to 350°F.

Get the sugar, butter and eggs staged together in a large mixing bowl. Incident Command says to cream them together with an electric mixer.

In a separate bowl, mix the flour, cocoa, baking powder and salt. Give them a good whisking, then stir them into the creamed mixture. We're going to refer to this as the creamed mixture.

The milk is staged. *Hang on, don't put it all in!* Here's the plan, and according to Mom, it's essential: to get the cake on course, you need to add ⅓ of the creamed mixture to a bowl. Add half the milk, then another third of the creamed mixture, another half of the milk, and finish up with the remaining creamed mix. Don't ask why, she's been doing it for 60 years and it works. 'Nuff said!

Bring on the vanilla and work it through. Finally, add a dash of water to the baking soda, just enough so it isn't dry, and mix it through the batter as well. Again, don't question her technique or mess with tradition.

Place the cake into the pan(s).

Bake for 20 to 25 minutes if using the round pans, or more like 30 minutes if you're using the square pan.

To create Mom's icing, combine the icing sugar with 1½ tablespoons cocoa and 2 tablespoons soft butter in a bowl. Get out the electric mixer and slowly add about 3 tablespoons milk until the icing is smooth. Once the cake is cool, spread the icing over it evenly with a spatula and use a butter knife for fine tuning—a.k.a. maximum beautification.

NO BAKE, JUST WAIT
STRAWBERRY CHEESECAKE

This is a great, easy-to-make cheesecake, and being that it only calls for one package of cream cheese, it's lighter as well, so you can eat twice as much with nary a hint of guilt. In other words, you'll only have to loosen your belt one notch instead of two or three. A light and easy cheesecake, you say? Show me the way . . .

GO AND PICK, OR PICK UP . . .

- Graham wafer pie crust, prepared (as in by someone else), or you can use the recipe for the base in Lonny's Banana Split Cake (page 210)
- 4 cups fresh strawberries, washed, dried, green stems removed
- 12 ounces white chocolate chips
- 8-ounce package light cream cheese, at room temperature
- ¼ cup sugar
- ¼ cup frozen orange juice concentrate—the thick stuff, no water added
- 1 teaspoon vanilla
- 2 cups whipping cream (or be a cheat and use packaged whipped topping)

OH, AND FOR THE BROWN COW DRIZZLE

- 6 tablespoons milk chocolate chips
- 2 tablespoons corn syrup
- 2 tablespoons Kahlúa

THEN GET BUSY IN THE KITCHEN

Lay out the prepared crust. Cut enough of the strawberries in half lengthwise to make a full lap of strawberries pressed up against the wall of the pan.

Arrange the rest of the whole berries on the crust with their points sticking up. If you have any mega-mutant berries, they might need a trim.

Melt the chocolate chips in a bowl in the microwave. Cool slightly.

Beat the cream cheese in a bowl with an electric mixer until it's smooth.

Next add the sugar, the OJ concentrate and the vanilla to the mix. Beat it again and slowly mix in the chocolate until it all comes together as one.

Whip the cream in a bowl with a mixer until stiff peaks form. Stir about ½ cup into the cream cheese/chocolate mix, to get things rolling. Then fold in the rest of the whipped cream, to incorporate.

It's time to pour the mix over the berries and toss the cheesecake—no, not into the oven—into the fridge for at least 3 hours to set up.

To serve, make the Brown Cow Drizzle by melting the milk chocolate chips in a small saucepan, along with the corn syrup and Kahlúa. Slice up and plate the cheesecake. Do that fancy restaurant deal with the drizzle—you know, back and forth across each piece. Well done!

RICE PUDDING

Landfills overflowing with leftover rice have reached epic proportions, and it's time that we as a society took action on this growing problem. That's why the "Jeff the Chef Green Team" has gone global with its push to get people to serve leftover rice for dessert. Rest assured, this is no dessert to simply settle for. Sure, it's cheap and easy, but it's also a super-tasty treat. So do your part in saving the environment and serve Recycled Rice Pudding tonight. Our children, their children and generations to follow will benefit. Thanks for caring. I'll plant a tree for you.

HEY, I THINK I MIGHT HAVE THESE INGREDIENTS ON HAND

- 2 tablespoons butter
- 3 cups milk—1 or 2% if fat's a concern, or cream it up with half-and-half
- ⅔ cup sugar—white or brown, it's your choice, but keep in mind that the brown will colour your rice a wee bit
- 1 teaspoon vanilla—get someone to pick you up a bottle next time they're in Mexico, or settle on the fake stuff
- ½ teaspoon cinnamon—plus more for sprinkling
- 3 cups cooked rice—long grain, short grain, they all work. I've even made this with a wild and white rice mix
- ¾ cup raisins—how about soaking them in dark rum, for an added bonus?

HEY, IT'S LIKE MAKING RISOTTO, ONLY EASIER

Get a large saucepan going over medium heat. Toss in the butter, and as soon as it melts pour in the milk, sugar, vanilla and cinnamon.

When the bubbling action gets going, toss in the previously owned rice.

The trick here is to get the liquid to the point where it is bubbling at the surface and thereby reducing in volume, but not boiling crazily so the milk burns and the rice sticks to the bottom. Better give it a stir every once in a while, just to be sure.

As the milk reduces, the texture will become creamier. Keep in mind that this rice-to-pudding operation could take ½ hour or so to complete. When the pudding reaches the consistency that turns your fire pump, remove it from the heat.

Stir in the raisins and serve your puddin' in a bowl. Firefighters are no doubt going to top it with ice cream and extra cinnamon.

You can serve Recycled Rice Pudding warm or throw it in the fridge and have it cold. Any leftovers make for a great quick breakfast. There's no reason why we can't reduce, reuse and recycle our rice one more time!

How about **Thai Recycled Rice**? Bring 2 cups of coconut milk to a simmer, dissolve ½ cup white sugar and use the same technique as above, working in 3 cups of cooked basmati or jasmine rice and simmering till creamy. Serve with fresh mango slices.

BANANA CREAM PIE

It's considered common fire hall etiquette to bring a cake into the hall for your birthday and share it with your crew. Some birthday present, when you have to pay for the cake yourself, I know, but it is tradition, and 125+ years of tradition unimpeded by progress is something that should never be messed with. Traditions such as cleaning the tires at shift change (once upon a time it had the purpose of cleaning the horse dung out of the tire treads) and pushing a path of snow a scant three feet in front of the garage doors before shift change in the morning (so the old wooden doors could swing open) live on. Yes, we preserved those traditions through the advent of the motorized fire truck and the overhead door, because we cherish them, even if they make no sense at all.

Oh yeah, getting back on topic, not only do we bring in cakes on our birthdays, but we also on occasion bring in dessert, just because. Over a series of consecutive tours at No. 1, our thoughtful lieutenants brought in homemade desserts. Not to be outdone, our captain kept the streak alive by bringing in homemade banana cream pies. While we were in the midst of tying into the pies, Mike Dowhayko said to our cheap chief, who never failed to take more than his fair share of food, "Hey, Chief, two weeks ago Dennis brought in chocolate cake, a week ago Ray brought us in a trifle and this week the Cap brought in banana cream pies." Mike's sarcastic tone hit high gear as he added, "Do you see a trend developing here?"

Bananas were bailing out through my nostrils as I fought to suppress my laughter. It's often been said that in the kitchen the cook is the highest-ranking crew member. Chef Mike's bold attack on our boss, however, failed to shame the chief into bringing dessert.

Here's the pie Captain Gerry Smit brought in to share. It's his secret recipe—secret because he didn't want anyone to know how easy it is to make.

ALL YOU NEED IS

- 9-inch frozen prepared pie crust
- 5½-ounce box instant banana cream pudding mix
- 1 banana, cut into slices
- Whipped cream (optional)

AND ALL YOU NEED TO DO IS

Follow the directions on the pie crust box. You'll need to brown the crust.

Then follow the directions on the instant banana cream pudding box.

Lay down the banana slices on the cooled pie crust—don't overcrowd them.

Pour the pudding over the bananas and send the pie off to the fridge to set.

Top the cooled pudding with additional banana slices just before serving.

If you feel so inspired, top with whipped cream. Cheat again and buy the stuff in the spray can. Yes, this versatile ozone opponent has its uses in the kitchen, too.

THOSE DINNER BUNS THAT LOOK LIKE
LITTLE LOAVES OF BREAD

Our local bakery has these great dinner buns that look like little loaves of bread. It wasn't until I stumbled upon the right bun tray that I thought, "I can do this." Now I'm in the business of making these mini-buns for dinner. As my budget-conscious, portion-enforcing dad often said as our family of six sat down to eat, "Fill up on bread, boys." Oh, I know, I could just buy these buns at the bakery, but I'm not always that lazy.

I DON'T CONSIDER IT LAZY TO USE A BREAD MAKER

- 1⅔ cups lukewarm water
- 3 tablespoons white sugar
- 2 tablespoons powdered milk
- 2 tablespoons soft butter or margarine
- 2 teaspoons sea salt (or regular table salt)
- 2⅓ cups whole-wheat flour
- 2 cups all-purpose flour
- 2 teaspoons quick-rise or bread maker yeast
- 1 egg, beaten with 1 tablespoon water (optional egg wash)

LOAD IT, LEAVE IT, LOAD 'EM, LET 'EM RISE AND BAKE 'EM

What more can I add to that? Here's the extended dance mix of the above. Simply load up your bread maker with the ingredients, in the order listed. Set your machine for the dough cycle, hit PLAY and leave it alone for its 1½ to 2-hour magic mixing time.

When the machine beeps to sound the completion of its job, get the dough out and roll it out on a kitchen counter lightly dusted with flour.

Knead briefly if you need to, in order to make it easier to work with.

Cut your dough in half, then in half again, and in half again, or whatever mathematically works out to splitting the loaf into 16 equal segments.

Stage the 2 bun trays, the kind that feature 8 openings each, and spray with cooking spray. Get the little dough loaves into their bun-tray nests.

Cover each tray with a clean dish cloth, and allow the dough to rise until about doubled in size—say about arf an hour or so.

Fire up the oven to 350°F (that's 325°, if you have a convection oven).

Care to give the buns a glaze? Simply mix up the egg wash and brush over each of the mini-loaves before they hit the oven. Speaking of which . . .

Bake the wee loaves for 20 to 25 minutes, switching the trays around at the halfway mark. Bake until the buns are nicely browned and cooked through.

THE INFAMOUS WHITESIDE/DERRAUGH
SCONES

It's a family tradition. Scones are a given at Derraugh family get-togethers, or serious questions are asked. It started with my Irish grandmother, Mary Whiteside, who tutored my mom, who, once she trusted my wife, let her in on this essential recipe, too. I believe it's called being accepted into the family. Oh, and by the way, do you happen to have one of those flat grills—as in a breakfast griddle? You're gonna need one.

SOON YOU, TOO, WILL BE A SCONE ADDICT!

- 2 eggs
- 3 tablespoons canola oil
- ¼ cup white sugar
- 3⅓ cups all-purpose flour—plus more for the counter
- 2 teaspoons baking powder
- 1 teaspoon baking soda
- 1 teaspoon salt
- 1 cup Thompson or sultana raisins—give them a wash and dry, please
- 1½ cups buttermilk—the stuff my grandpa used to drink straight up

TRY TO EAT JUST ONE—I DARE YA!

Let's get a mixing bowl out and place the eggs, canola oil and sugar in there. Fire up the electric mixer and beat the trio together well.

I hope you took out more than 1 mixing bowl, because we're going to need another one. Get the flour, baking powder, baking soda and salt in the bonus bowl and give them a whisking to combine.

Pull out the wooden spoon! Well, it worked for my Grandma Mary when she took care of my 3 brothers and me. Of course, we were model children who never fought, argued or required

discipline. Weren't we?

Put that spoon to work. Add the egg mix to the dry and beat them together.

Bring on the raisins and mix them through, then follow up with the buttermilk. Mix it, mix it up good—beat some air into that batter, that's the secret of a great scone! Grandma may have only been 98 pounds, but she had a pair of massive, ripped pythons like Barney Fife from beating her batter. Add additional flour or buttermilk to get a workable dough.

Set the griddle temperature to 300°F. Don't grease it, though, leave it dry.

Place the batter on a well-floured counter. Roll it out to a thickness of ½ inch. Not to worry, the wee scones will grow when the heat hits them.

Cut out the scones with a small juice glass, about 2½ inches in diameter.

Get the wee scallywags on the grill for approximately 10 minutes per side—you're looking for a nice golden-brown hue on the outside and cooked-through delicious goodness on the inside.

You can serve the scones at room temperature, but the ideal way is still warm off the griddle, cut in half, with butter melting as it hits the scones.

CINNAMON BUNS

What a ridiculous saying. Come on, let's be positive and celebrate life as we tie into a batch of these incredibly soft, moist and delicious sweet buns. You know, these are sooooo good that I could have easily named this recipe Death by Cinnamon Buns.

LEADOFF HITTERS

- 1 cup buttermilk
- 1 egg, beaten
- ¼ cup melted butter or margarine
- ¼ cup water
- 1 tablespoon white sugar
- ½ teaspoon salt
- ½ package instant vanilla pudding mix
- 2 cups each whole-wheat and unbleached white flour
- 2½ teaspoons quick-rise or bread maker yeast

MIDDLE OF THE ORDER

- ½ cup butter or margarine, softened
- 1 cup packed brown sugar
- 2 teaspoons ground cinnamon
- ½ cup raisins

AND . . . BATTING CLEANUP

- 1½ cups icing sugar
- ¼ cup soft butter or margarine
- 1 teaspoon vanilla—the fake stuff will do in a pinch
- A little dab'll do ya of buttermilk, say 2 tablespoons to start

YOU'RE TEMPTING FATE HERE, BUT PROCEED IF YOU MUST

Place the leadoff hitters in a bread maker in the order listed. Select the dough cycle, and send it on a mission of extreme indulgence.

When the mission is completed, remove the dough and knead it with your hands for 3 or 4 minutes. This would be a good time for company to show up, so you can fool them into believing you actually made the bread sans machine. Dust yourself with flour for added authenticity. You're the best!

Flour your counter and get out that rolling pin. Hard as it is to believe, it's not just used for settling domestic disputes. Get this, we're actually going to use it to roll out the dough into a 12 x 16-inch rectangle.

Combine the middle-of-the-order dudes—excluding the raisins—in a bowl. Spread the magic mix over the dough as evenly as possible, leaving a ½-inch dry border around the outside edge, like the frame of a picture. Wet the border slightly with a damp finger. Well, of course you'd wash your finger first!

Apparently the raisins are feeling left out, so let's make them feel welcome by sprinkling them over top.

Take hold of the bottom of the 16-inch (wide) side and start rolling, jellyroll style. When you reach the end, give the seam a pinch, to seal it up.

Cut the roll into 1-inch segments, yielding about 16 buns in all.

Get out a 9 x 13-inch lasagna dish, grease it up with cooking spray and place the buns, flat sides down, obviously, in rows of 4. The pan will be fairly jammed, but don't commit *hari kari*, it'll all work out just fine.

Cover the buns with a dishcloth, and place them in a safe spot to rise for, say, about 30 to 40 minutes.

Preheat your oven to 350°F.

When the buns have doubled in size, bake them on the middle rack of your oven for about 20 minutes, or until lightly browned.

Remove dem buns from de oven to cool.

It's true, you could call it a day at this point, but what fun is that? We've made it this far; let's go for deathly decadence here. Get out the electric mixer. Place the icing sugar, ¼ cup butter, vanilla and 2 tablespoons buttermilk in a bowl. Mix, adding a wee touch of bonus buttermilk, until the topping reaches a spreadable consistency.

Drizzle the topping over the buns while they are still warm. If you have the patience, let the buns cool, thereby allowing the topping to set up. Wait. *What do you mean, I have to wait? Come on, Jeff, they look and smell so good! Outta my way, I'm going in!*

WHERE TIM HORTON GOT HIS BUSINESS IDEA

Firefighter pranks don't just take place at the fire house, as evidenced by the annual Canadian firefighters' hockey tournament. One year, teams couldn't stop talking about what good sports the boys from Trail, BC, were. Win or lose, after every game, Team Trail took two dozen doughnuts to the opposing team's dressing room and distributed them to the players. Everyone thought this was a great gesture and thanked the boys for their generosity.

When the tournament wrapped up, the teams united for a banquet to share a few drinks and a million laughs. Team Trail took the opportunity to proudly share Polaroid pictures of their players, sans clothes, with the free doughnuts hung with care, if you catch my drift, from their (ahem) equipment.

METRIC CONVERSION CHART

Volume

¼ teaspoon	1 mL
½ teaspoon	2 mL
1 teaspoon	5 mL
2 teaspoons	10 mL
1 tablespoon	15 mL
¹/₈ cup	30 mL
¼ cup	50 mL
¹/₃ cup	75 mL
½ cup	125 mL
²/₃ cup	150 mL
¾ cup	175 mL
1 cup	250 mL
1½ cups	375 mL
2 cups (1 pint)	500 mL
3 cups	750 mL
4 cups (1 quart)	1 L

Weight

1 ounce	25 g
4 ounces (¼ pound)	125 g
¹/₃ pound	170 g
8 ounces (½ pound)	250 g
²/₃ pound	340 g
12 ounces (¾ pound)	375 g
16 ounces (1 pound)	500 g

RECIPE GPS
THE EASY WAY TO SEARCH AND RESCUE RECIPES

About the
AUTHOR

Talk about a guy who's worn a lot of hats over the years. The author of the bestselling cookbook *Fire Hall Cooking with Jeff the Chef* (2007), Jeff Derraugh is a veteran firefighter who has enjoyed a wide variety of writing experiences. He has held down gigs as a morning radio announcer on Winnipeg's 92 CITI-FM, and was a writer and host of the nationally syndicated radio program, *The Comedy Show*. Jeff is an award-winning advertising writer, and producer, and he has appeared in numerous radio and TV commercials as a voiceover performer and actor. Jeff also volunteered his talents as the co-creator, writer, and voice for the children's fire safety video game, *Mrs. About-Fire's Great Escape* and the website, www.stayingalive.ca. He is currently a columnist for *Fire Hall Magazine*.

Although his University of Manitoba degree is in the liberal, not the culinary arts, Jeff acquired and honed his cooking skills over a 20-year career, working alongside some of the most amazing, yet, unsung chefs out there, firefighters. You can visit Jeff online at his website, www.jeffthechef.ca.